"Yes, one may even say that these jokes are the continuation of the ancient Wisdom literature of Judaism. This is not only because the expressions 'wit' and 'wisdom' derive from the same word root, but also because true and wise things are often spoken in jest."

THEODOR REIK

JEWISH WIT

THEODOR REIK

JEWISH WIT

GAMUT PRESS

NEW YORK

TO MY GRANDCHILDREN
ALEXANDER, LORETTA AND DANIELA

Contents

Chapter I—THE PSYCHOLOGICAL INTEREST IN
THE SUBJECT   11

Introduction; This Book; Collection and Selection; The
Psychological Interest

Chapter II—THE SCOPE   21

Preliminary Remarks; The Scope; Speaking Many Lan-
guages; Comment on Freud's Remark; Shlemihl with
a Difference; Self-Centeredness; Jewish Jokes and the
Gentile; The Wandering Jew; Punishment for Hitler;
The Eternal Fugitive; Note on the Origin of Jewish
Wit; Israelites and Other Anti-Semites; Destruction of
the Hero-Ideal; The Here and the Hereafter; Money;
The Sacred Duty of Charity; The Haves and the Have-
Nots; Sideglance; The Rabbi as a Pathetic and Comic
Figure; Misbehavior Patterns; Jewish Mothers; Family-
ritis; Currents of Judaism; Difficult to Baptize; The
Messiah; Zionism; Love; Some Remarks on Sarcasm;
The Spirit of Scepticism; The Wide Net of Doubt; A
Shocking Thing to Say; The Faces of Truth; Reduced
to Logic; Paradoxical; The Belief in the Omnipotence
of Thought; Comic Curses; His Own Physician; Rever-
ence for Life; Meschugge; Gestures; Two Contemporary Men of Genius; Culinary; The Faint Resonance;

Back to the Roots; Leavened and Unleavened; The Old
Covenant and the New Covenant; Violence; By Any
Other Name; The Echo of the Proverb; The Voices of
Others in You

Chapter III—IN SEARCH OF CHARACTERISTICS   187

Introductory Remark; The Intimacy of Jewish Wit;
Thinking in Antitheses; Bursting Into Laughter But
Not Merry; Moment of Explosive Truth

Chapter IV—PSYCHOLOGY AND PSYCHO-
    PATHOLOGY OF JEWISH WIT   217

Literature on the Subject; The Aspect of Self-Degradation; The Inside Story of the Jewish Stories; Unconscious Claims; Motives for Telling Jewish Jokes;
Features of the Future; In Retrospect

NOTES   243

JEWISH WIT

The Psychological Interest in the Subject

INTRODUCTION

A few sentences Freud had written on two different occasions often returned to me, they must have worked as catalysts. They were in the preface to the Hebrew translation of *Totem and Taboo,* and were originally written in December 1920(1). They affected me especially because I felt about Judaism the same way he did. Freud stated that he did not understand Hebrew, that he was utterly alienated from the religion of his forefathers —as from any religion—and that he was unable to share the belief in national ideals. Yet he had never disavowed being Jewish and did not wish to be different. But what, he continued, would he answer, if someone asked him, "What is still Jewish in you after you abandoned all those things common to your people?" He would reply, "Still very much, perhaps the main part of my personality." He admitted that he would be unable to put this essential thing into clear words, and added: "It will certainly some day become accessible to scientific insight."

That last sentence intrigued me especially. It was like a personal appeal to me and reminded me of some conversations I had had with Freud about Jewish questions.

Another, perhaps even stronger impression I received was from the speech Freud wrote for the B'nai Brith Lodge(2) on the occasion of his seventieth birthday in 1926. Only three of us Viennese psychoanalysts were brothers of the B'nai Brith: Freud,

Dr. Eduard Hitschmann, and I. In that speech Freud asserted
that neither religious faith nor national pride had tied him to
Judaism. He had always been an atheist and, if he ever was
inclined to national superiority feelings at all, he had suppressed
them "as disastrous and unjustified," warned by the example of
the people amongst whom we Jews were living. Yet, he continued, there remained enough other things that "made the
attraction of Judaism and Jews irresistible, many dark emotional
powers, the more powerful, the less they could be put into
words, as well as the clear awareness of an inner identity, the
secret of the same inner construction."

What struck me especially were the words, "the clear awareness of an inner identity, the secret of the same inner construction," and again the admission that those dark emotional powers
eluded verbal definition and description.

In my youth I had published a book *"Das Ritual"*(3) whose
main part had dealt with problems of early Hebrew religion and
social organization. Then came a pause of almost forty years
during which I was occupied with other problems of psychoanalytic psychology, and with writing books dealing with them.
Freud, who had written a preface to my book and had bestowed
upon me the prize for the best paper on applied psychoanalysis
for one of those early essays, had often encouraged me to continue my research work on Hebrew origins.

Only after having reached the age of seventy years did I
return to the interests that had occupied me as a young psychoanalyst. I approached the problems of Hebrew prehistory from a
strictly scientific viewpoint, comparable to that of an archae-
ologist who tries to reconstruct the unknown past of a people
from remnants surviving radical changes. By tracing the most
significant myths of the Hebrews back to their original shape
and meaning, I attempted to reconstruct the prehistory of those
Semitic tribes and of a period long before they had formed
themselves into a people. The result of this attempt at reconstruction was presented in a Biblical tetralogy whose parts were
entitled *Myth and Guilt, The Creation of Woman, Mystery On
the Mountain, The Temptation.*

I understood only later that this tetralogy was an attempt to discover the origin of that secret inner construction of which Freud had spoken in the history, or rather, in the prehistory of the Jews in the period of their formative years, comparable to an inquiry into the early childhood of an individual. But where do I go from here?

THIS BOOK

Psychologists and sociologists at present discuss with great zeal the problems of creativity, and study the elusive quality of the "creative person," the characteristic features of the "creative progress," and of the "creative situation." It would be presumptuous on my part to call the circumstances in which this book was conceived a "creative situation."

A group at the University of Michigan's Institute of Social Research recently formulated a hypothesis on the conditions that seem to lead to creative scientific performance. Only a single condition was present in the situation in which the idea of this book emerged. I quote: "Scientists generally speaking are more creative when they are slightly uncomfortable. They need to be forced to an unusual (or creative) response by a condition of intellectual 'uncertainty' or 'dither' "(4).

I was certainly (and not only slightly) uncomfortable and in a condition of intellectual uncertainty, but, as far as I know, no other quality of a "creative situation" was present. I sat at my desk listless and restless. Nothing was further from my thoughts than the psychology of Jewish wit, nothing further from my mood than jokes and jests. I felt rather bad-humored, if not gloomy.

My thoughts circled around the patient who had left me half an hour ago and the first words he had said in his psychoanalytic session mysteriously echoed within me. This highly intelligent man had been silent for a few minutes and had then said, "We pause for station identification." That phrase, well known from radio announcing, was meaningful in his case because he often experienced a feeling of self-alienation, of search for identity.

Only after that sentence had reoccurred to me, did I understand that it concerned my repeated and frustrated attempts to penetrate that secret of the same inner construction of Jews of which Freud had spoken. "We pause for station identification," was thus meaningful for my research work. The pause had lasted a long time, much too long.

The walls of my office are covered with pictures of Freud. I believe there are about fifty photographs, etchings and drawings, pictures of Freud as a child, as a young man and as an old man. The last photograph shows him in London the year before his death. Sitting at my desk I looked up at the pictures above it as if seeking for his help. But the pictures did not "speak" to me. It was in vain. Then came a funny thought—all the photographs and pictures show Freud in a serious mood, sometimes even with a grim expression. There is not a single one in which he is presented smiling.

The memory of some occasions on which I saw him smiling came back then. I even remembered a few times when he laughed. A few times I made him smile myself by some funny observation. He could heartily laugh at Jewish jokes some of our circle told him.

What a pity that none of us psychoanalysts followed up the splendid insights on Jewish wit, contained in Freud's book *Wit and Its Relations to the Unconscious*(5). Freud dealt in this book with witticisms in general and his observations on Jewish jokes were only part of the general subject. One should separate the Jewish stories from the others and explore them from psychological viewpoints. That is to say, one should examine them from the viewpoint of what they reveal about the psychology of the Jewish people. Such a task would amount to a contribution to the comparative psychology of groups or people.

I myself had some ideas on that subject and had jotted down many notes about it. They must be in one of the folders in that drawer over there. But would such an inquiry not mean going astray, away from the road I had followed? To spend many months on such a research project would perhaps amount to a diversion similar to what one calls in sports "time out," and they say time out is time lost. But what does that mean when one is nearly seventy-four years old and lives on borrowed time in any case? I still do not believe that that occasion at which the concept of this book emerged is worthy of being called "a creative situation." Sometimes I thought of it as being funny; yet, as this book shows, I took it *au grand serieux.*

COLLECTION AND SELECTION

A writer who has certain ideas about a subject, as well as notions which can be verified, will have two assignments before he puts his tentative theory to the test. He will collect as many facts as possible from the material at his disposal, and he will then select a certain number of those facts for the purpose of the test.

I read a great number of collections of Jewish jokes in German, Yiddish, French, Dutch, and English, asked friends and acquaintances to tell me Jewish anecdotes and jotted down all stories of this kind I found in my memory.

In doing this task I had some surprising experiences. Nowhere is the saying "The more the merrier" more inappropriate than in hearing such jokes. Everyone is familiar with the man or woman who is ready at the slightest provocation to hurl a whole arsenal of Jewish stories at you, some of which you knew before the storyteller was born. You feel not only as if you were "back to Methuselah," but also that the trigger-happy person is a terrible bore. "Less would be more" in such a case.

There are no principles determining the preparatory work of collecting. There are, however, certain conscious and unconscious factors determining which examples to choose for the purpose of psychological interpretation. One of these potential factors is, for instance, an aesthetic one, namely to make the decision dependent on the value of the joke, in short, to select those that are "good" and to omit those of lesser quality. After all, those jokes belong to literature. That they are rarely printed or published

makes no difference. Many beautiful folksongs and meaningful
fairy tales were also never printed—yet nobody will deny that
they belong to the literature of a people.

Another possible objection, namely, that many Jewish jokes
are thought of on the spur of the moment and are often quickly
forgotten, will not weaken their value. Butterflies also rarely
stay for long in a single place and quickly fly away, but we
would miss their beauty if they were destroyed.

There is another danger, namely, that we might exclude certain stories because they offend our conventional ideas or could
be objectionable to the reader because of sexual or similar
prejudices. There are, for instance, those stories that poke fun
at the lack of physical hygiene and cleanliness, mock the dishonesty of the ghetto, deride certain types of misbehavior of the
Eastern Jews.

Shall we omit those stories because they may seem offensive?
People say that cleanliness is next to godliness, but it is precisely those Jewish stories which show that it is often more
distant from it than we thought, and that being dirty often
comes closer to saintliness. No, no such omission can be allowed.
The area of psychological exploration which we consider our
home does not acknowledge limitations of such a kind. It's a
free country.

But what then are the principles determining the selection?
Should we, for example, prefer new Jewish stories and neglect
those that are old and known to everyone? Certainly not, because we would then exclude a good deal of significant material.
On the other hand, newer jokes must be considered too. A selection, such as we conceive it, should be similar in character to
that of a bridal dress: "Something old, something new, something
borrowed, something blue."

Another limitation necessitated by the space allowed in this
book: I tried to make each long Jewish story short.

The assignments of collection and selection as preparation
for the psychological inquiry are best illustrated by a comparison. When I was in my late teens, women still used folded fans
as protection against sun and insects. They held them in their

hands in ball rooms and occasionally fanned themselves, raising a small current of cool air after or before dinner.

Let us now assume that a researcher makes an inquiry into the use of such fans. He will, of course, trace those now old-fashioned fans historically(6), and find their predecessors in ancient Egypt and Assyria in the form of palm-leaves or peacock-feathers, fans of the Romans, etc., until he arrives at the modern shape of the folding fan. He will discover that the French ladies refreshed themselves with fans, and he will study their decorations and pictures, sometimes painted by famous artists like Ingres and Corot. In 1891 more than seven million fans were still shipped to the United States from Japan, but fans have now been superseded by other methods of ventilation.

Finally, having arrived at the "modern" form of the folded fan, the investigator will collect as many of them as he can and examine the drawings and inscriptions on their folds. Beside the traditional verses stating that roses are red, violets are blue, etc., he will read many original romantic inscriptions, and sometimes even enjoy wise and witty remarks an admirer wrote on those folds. (On the fan of my young sister I found a critical comment of my own, written when I was a boy. In original German:

> Zur Feder greifen und Verse schreiben
> Was sind das für närrische G'schichten!
> Tänzern soll man was pfeifen,
> Aber nicht was dichten.

> To take a pen and to write poems?
> How foolish are these times!
> To dancers one should pipe,
> But not recite rhymes.)

Studying those drawings and inscriptions, as well as reading contemporary novels and treatises dealing with fashions, the investigator will discover many unexpected uses of the fan besides those of providing comfort in the heat of the summer, or in the hot atmosphere of the ballroom. Stories, heard and read, pictures of old times, as well as the study of those inscriptions, will make him realize that fans were used by the ladies to attract men as well as to keep them away; they were used to indicate certain emotions as well as to hide them.

The comparison of Jewish wit with those fans is perhaps also determined by the fact that both produce only a momentary comfort. Also, the change in the pressure of air produced by a fan is small. Also Jewish jokes have certain social functions which we would at first not have assumed.

THE PSYCHOLOGICAL INTEREST

From where I sat, namely, before the pictures of Freud, the idea of a book on Jewish wit was first conceived as a contribution to the literature of a people.

There was no doubt in my mind that the body of Jewish jokes and ancedotes belong to the area of literature in the same sense as folksongs and fairy tales which never appeared in print. Recently an American writer defined literature as "the way a society talks to itself about itself"(7). If this definition (or characterization) is correct, who will deny that in Jewish jokes "a society talks to itself about itself?" And how it talks! Not only in hundreds of various inflections of the voice, but also in telling gestures and changing facial expressions.

Yes, one may even say that these jokes are the continuation of the ancient Wisdom-literature of Judaism. This not only because the expressions wit and wisdom derive from the same word roots, but also because true and wise things are often spoken in jest.

In respect both to subject and form, jokes are akin to the Hebrew proverbs which were originally transmitted orally and only by degrees came to be treated as a form of literature.

It is true that one will rarely find jokes discussed in books or in articles on Jewish literature, but this should not prevent us from regarding them as part and parcel of belles-lettres, most of which remain unrecorded.

In some respects Jewish jokes hold the same position as *l'esprit* in France. Besides the literary, artistic and scientific achievements of France *l'esprit* is in the words of Sacha Guitry, "a precious and permanent testimony of her presence in the world"(8).

Jokes and anecdotes were, at best, treated condescendingly by the scholar, because they are expressions of humor. Yet they certainly deserve a higher evaluation. Only recently Mark Van Doren stated that there is nothing more serious in men than his sense of humor(9). It is "the sign that he wants all the truth and sees more sides of it than can be soberly and systematically stated." Jewish jokes often reveal those hidden sides of truth.

I realized, only after I got up from my desk and walked the room, that my interest in Jewish jokes was not of a literary kind, but was primarily psychological. Only then did I understand fully the tie-in with the search for identity and with the meaning which that sentence of the patient, "We pause for station identification," had unconsciously obtained for me. The purpose of the book was now clear. It would be a novel approach to the psychological or rather psychoanalytical study of the Jewish people.

New questions emerged here, for instance the problem eagerly discussed in Israel, "Who is a Jew?" Are we a national, religious or cultural community? But we can put this aside as immaterial. I agree with Irving Feldman(10) who recently wrote that he lives in a "community extending in space and time far beyond my own biographical circumstances . . ." He calls it a "society of imagination."

There is the other question, namely, are these jokes really an appropriate subject for psychological inquiry? The answer to that is, we don't know. There are treatises on the philosophy, sociology, and history of Jewish humor. There are, as far as I know, no books on its psychology. A pilot study such as the one I would like to present is comparable to an exploration of an unknown sphere.

The last question: Is it likely that the body of Jewish jokes is a source rich enough to lead to new psychological insights? Those witticisms are a natural product of the imagination and of the intellectual activity of the people, respecting their joys and their sadnesses, revealing what they enjoy and what they dislike. One may expect that an investigation of these witticisms would bring forth significant psychological insights. The scholars who pay attention only to the conscious side of phenomena dealt with the psychology of Jewish wit, but only superficially, and so need not deter the psychoanalysts.

Our work is in another area, that is the recesses of the netherworld. It does not disturb us that jokes and anecdotes do not form the center of Jewish intellectual activity, and that they are relegated to its fringes. Did not Freud turn his attention to the by-products of human behavior such as dreams, slips of the tongue and of the pen? Psychoanalysis is, as he once wrote, "accustomed to divide secret and concealed things from uncon- sidered and unnoticed details, from the rubbish heap, as it were, of our observation"(11). Jewish jokes, too, belong to the region of "rubbish heap" in which strange things are often to be found. The French have a proverb: *"Le Bon Dieu est dans les détails."*

Whether I succeed or fail in my research, I am convinced that an inquiry into the character of Jewish wit will add a new dimension to the psychological understanding of its people. Be- sides bringing a short-lived comfort to its tellers and listeners, these jokes, like the folding fans, want to reveal certain thoughts and emotions and conceal others; they too want to attract and to keep away people. Perhaps they hide certain things even from the Jews themselves.

The jokes we shall quote are comparable to the inscriptions and drawings found on the folds of the fans. They are selected with the sole purpose of studying the psychology of Jewish wit. What follows is therefore a survey of the various groups of Jewish jokes similar to an examination of the inscriptions on the folds of those fans.

CHAPTER II

The Scope

PRELIMINARY REMARKS

The following pieces are grouped together according to the subjects they deal with. They present a survey of the main themes of Jewish jokes, dealing with some of them in the form of essays, while others are casually treated in a few paragraphs, amounting in some cases to not more than extended notes. This unequal way of dealing with them has several reasons: Certain groups of these jokes—the Schadchen and Schnorrer anecdotes, for example—have been discussed so often that they need not be treated in detail. Other kinds of jokes have not been viewed psychologically, as they would deserve. I dealt in this survey with the more neglected aspects of Jewish jokes.

Another determining factor in emphasizing certain witticisms and putting others in the background was the question of their psychological significance. Some jokes are a rich source of insights into the emotional and mental life of the people who produce them, while others yield less fruitful results. It should not be denied that a personal factor operates in this choice. I had more to say about some groups of jokes than about others, and also I had more to say than had been said before. To see and to analyze new sides of Jewish wit was my first consideration.

This grouped survey of Jewish witticisms will also differ from many previous extracts of this kind in other ways. It will not be a synopsis of these anecdotes, but a study of them. This means that the presentation of the various groups of stories will be followed by psychological comments and conclusions. In discussing these problems it was sometimes unavoidable to refer again to examples previously mentioned. Such reappearance in another context will perhaps sometimes make the impression of repetition, but can be excused if in retrospect a new light is thrown upon them.

In this search for and research into the psychological properties of Jewish wit, I am not concerned with the differences of time and place, but am determined to go from one end of the earth to the other, and from the dawn of history to the present. Stories from the Russian or Polish ghetto are here treated the same way as are witticisms from Vienna, Paris and New York, anonymous anecdotes the same way as witty remarks of famous modern writers. My main endeavor was to prime the continuity or at least similarity of the psychological characteristics of Jewish jokes.

If I had known a joke about Adam and Eve made by one of the Yahwist editors of the saga at about 850 B.C., I would not have hesitated to put it side by side with the jest George Jessel made the other day at the Israel Bond dinner in London. Jessel, who was guest of honor on this occasion, attentively listened to the chairman who described and enthusiastically praised Israel's accomplishments in cultivating arid areas. For the first time, said the chairman, since the creation apples were growing in certain territories of the country. In his ensuing speech, irrepressible George Jessel, in dissent, asked: "Who says they never had apples? What did Adam bite into—a pickle?"

THE SCOPE

I

In preparing this book I had, of course, to do some research-work, part of which was to peruse a few collections of Jewish jokes. Reading the typical anecdotes ("Two Jews meet on the street and . . .") I suddenly had the impression that they were monotonous and wearisome. (A story tells that Cain slaughtered Abel because the brother told him such an anecdote which he had known since childhood.) Immediately afterwards I mysteriously remembered a play I had seen in Reinhardt's theatre in Berlin more than forty years ago. I also found a half-forgotten article I had written about that play many years later, and reading it the faded impressions of the performance were revived.

The three-act play was called *The Jews* and was written by a Russian author I did not know, Eugen Tschirikow. It depicts the life of a Jewish settlement in northern Russia around the turn of this century. I only vaguely remember the plot and the characters, who have very few personal qualities. There is the apartment and workshop of the watchmaker Leiser Fränkel. The old man will soon be lonely. His son had joined the socialist party and will leave him, while his daughter had become the mistress of a Christian student. The struggle between the generations is the more bitter because the family feeling within the ghetto is so much deeper and more tenacious, the attachment of the family members so close.

My memory, always more auditory than visual, can revive only a single clear image: the picture of the moment when news arrives that a pogrom has broken out in the neighboring villages. The violent impression of the final scenes: the screaming of the fanatical mob, the swelling noise that becomes the roar of beasts; the growing fear of the Jewish people in the shop of the old watchmaker. The mob burst in like a torrent destroying and killing. The young daughter is assaulted and dies, and the men are murdered. Finally, when everything is utterly annihilated, the cossacks ride up and disperse the murderous mob.

Only the impression of the last scenes of the play have remained for a longer time. Its figures are hardly living human beings. They now appear rather as types, as stereotype dramatis personae. There is the gentle but strong-willed young girl. She loves her father, but must inflict grief and sorrow on him. There is the son who dedicated himself to the revolutionary cause and was expelled from the university. There is a liberal physician who remained religious; there is a weary and ill schoolteacher

who clings to Zionism which he defends with as much ardor as
the son and his friends defend the socialist program. Nothing of
the passionate arguments and of the debates in which all these
people are engaged is preserved in my memory. If the speeches
of these Jewish figures conveyed a message, it was lost to me as
though it were immaterial and irrelevant. The discussions in the
three acts seem in retrospect as shadowy as the characters of the
play. This would not have been the case if the drama had been
more than an effective and crudely constructed theatrical piece.
The drama is the second-rate work of a playwright who knows
how to build up some strong dramatic effects.

What remains in my memory besides the outline of the plot?
What emerges from the dark, what words still resound when I
recall the performance? Only a few sentences and the silences
following them; nothing else. But unlike so much talk in the play,
those sentences are not written by a hack playwright. They are
based on experience; they were heard not only with the ear, but
with the heart.

There is a scene in which the brother of the watchmaker,
Aaron Fränkel, who has come on a visit from a neighboring
village, is in conversation with the young girl. She tells the
uncle that she and her brother have been expelled from the
university because they had taken part in socialist riots. "Ai-ai-ai,"
Aaron cries, "you were always such a quiet girlie!" The pretty
young niece assures him that she is still a quiet girl, but the
uncle says: "You'd do better to marry. Then you will have
children and your own rebels on your hands."

In the same scene the uncle tells her what went on in his
settlement. Every city and every village has a ghetto. The Jews
may live only within its bounds. They vegetate in this small
district. The Jews there are poverty-stricken, to be sure, "but,
thank God, they have many children."

Their quarters became too small because of the many children. The Jewish cemetery stretched out into the city. They had
hoped to buy property for a new cemetery outside the city. But
the authorities had not permitted that because this new property
would extend the ghetto area prescribed for Jewish people. The

authorities decided that a dead Jew is also considered to be part of the population. The Jews exerted desperate efforts until the ministry finally yielded and consented to the purchase of property for the burial of their dead. Then a new obstacle arose. A cemetery must have a watchman. But the watchman must be a Jew, of course. No Jew may live outside the ghetto. Somebody who listens to Aaron's report interjects: "There is only one way out, take a dead Jew as watchman."

There are, however, other difficulties arising from the situation. The authorities will not permit a Jewish watchman on the grounds of the new cemetery. On the other hand, they no longer allow the Jews to bury their dead in the old cemetery. Sanitary reasons forbid this. The next sentence spoken by Aaron Fränkel and its Yiddish intonation still rings in my ears: "But the Jews couldn't wait any longer and one of them took the liberty of dying."

I remember only one other scene at the close of this first act and then only the curtain line. The scene is the shop of the watchmaker, a basement room with a low ceiling. The walls are covered with clocks and watches of all kinds, big and small, old and new. Throughout the scene the incessant tick-tock of the pendulum is heard when there is a moment of silence. A debate is going on in the room. Leiser Fränkel's son and his Gentile friend are passionately arguing that only the teachings of Karl Marx can provide a solution to the Jewish problem. The neurotic little schoolteacher, on the other hand, insists that Zionism is the only way into the open for the Jews. Intelligent and foolish arguments are introduced into the debate which becomes a heated quarrel of those hot-headed and hot-tempered people. It leads from allusions to fiery attacks, from subtle sarcasms to irascible and crude insults. The fanatical teacher turns from laughter to neurotic sobbings. Suddenly all the clocks in the shop, one after the other, begin to strike twelve. The silence that follows is broken by the tranquil voice of the old watchmaker, Reb Leiser. He stands in the middle of the room and looks, with his long white beard and bushy eyebrows, like a biblical patriarch. "For ten years," he says, "I've wanted that all my clocks should chime out at once, at the same moment. Yet it never would work. They are like human beings—they can't get together."

The fact that the play is a mediocre work, a kind of sensational nine-day wonder of a drama without any great human or artistic values, is responsible for the fact that it did not survive and is now half-forgotten. The sensation is not there any longer and the play has lost its force in a time that saw the tortures and the murder of six million Jews. Why did not this drama of the destruction of the Jews, related to me by blood and fate, have a more profound effect on me? Why did the immediate effect of the performance fade so soon? Where is the delayed reaction that outlasts the excitement of the few hours spent in the theatre?

I believe it is there, preserved in the memory of these few jokes. The emotions stirred up by the drama were no longer associated with the plot of the play, but unconsciously transferred to those sentences my memory has retained as if they contained the most valuable of what the playwright had to say. The personal appeal, the *"tua res agitur"* became disconnected from the tragic events presented on the stage and was displaced to the humorous sidelight of the experience. All the profound emotion aroused in us became concentrated upon some fleeting sentences in the dialogues of that first act. It cannot be accidental that the emotional charge is transferred from the tragic to the comic. It means that the center of the emotions is changed, but it does not mean a loss of their power.

The characters speak to me more poignantly in their jests than in their accusations and complaints. As long as we see them behave in a certain way, they appear as marionettes, dangled here and there by the all-powerful hand of destiny, and finally struck down. But when they joke, the puppets are transformed into human beings. Yehovah has forbidden the Jew of our time to express his tragic experiences in a way appealing to a world that is hostile or, at best, indifferent. But by conferring upon him the gift of wit, his God has given him the power to speak of what he suffers.

It seems to me that the emotional transference is not restricted to this particular case, but has general significance and can be traced to a familiar pattern. This affective transference molds Jewish wit and gives it a quality which has remained almost entirely unnoticed and therefore the more notable. Life is often tragic, but its pathos reflects itself most distinctly in jokes. No, it is not accidental that instead of the terrifying pogrom scenes of the play a few comic sentences flashed through my mind for it is those sentences which contain the quintessence of the drama.

These few phrases, which are spoken out of the depths of a destiny unique among the people, give us some clue to a psychological insight into the nature of the Jewish joke. In the best examples of this kind of humor there is behind the comic façade not only something serious, which is present in the wit of other nations too, but sheer horror. The unconscious emotional transference which created Jewish wit and remained one of its definite and distinguishing characteristics, is repeated in the listener and determines its profound emotional effect.

The examples taken from Tschirikov's play are not selected for their type significance nor for their aesthetic value. Yet they may represent large groups of the Jewish joke and perhaps mark its scope. The uncle's advice to the young girl that she marry instead of taking part in university riots is in its meaningful allusion ("Then you'll have children and your own rebels on your hands") is a charming example of the family wit of the Jews. In East Europe this people formed before the Second World War a unified cultural and social group with strong and enduring family solidarity. Jokes and witty remarks like those of Aaron Fränkel sprang up in everyday life and vanished with the day.

In the atmosphere of the family, this kind of friendly and teasing remark flourishes best and was often extended beyond the boundaries of family life because Jews of all countries form a single large family. Allusion, joke and witty remark easily merge into one another and are often indistinguishable. The familiarity in these jokes testifies to the mutual confidence and the good will of each to the other. This kind of Jewish joke is worldly-wise and illustrative of the ways of human nature. Familiarity in this case does not breed contempt, but human sympathy and kindliness. Long after we have smiled at a joke of this kind, we become aware of its profoundity. It is also not accidental that witticisms of this kind concern life within the family.

There is Aaron Fränkel's tale of the cemetery incident in the ghetto of his village. We hear of the magisterial decision that the dead may not be buried beyond the ghetto nor within its old cemetery. Then follows the bitter remark that a poor Jew unable to wait for the end of the lawsuit was bold enough to die. Here is an example of another kind, of the sarcastic genre of Jewish wit. The pathos, in the original Greek sense of suffering, is inverted here and finds expression in a grimace of mockery and revolt. Here Ahasuerus, the eternal, wandering Jew, speaks and is silent. He knows there is no peace for him on earth and in this case not even below it. There is no rest for him, not even on the spot that is euphemistically called "the good place" in Jewish tradition. Aaron Fränkel casually murmurs a jesting remark and shrugs his shoulders. He does not scream aloud in indignation and does not strike out in rage and despair. Yet his ironic wit strikes with the keenness of a sword and is wielded with the mighty hand of hatred. It is the same irony that strikes in the words by the biblical prophets and is felt in Heinrich Heine's prose and verse and in the books of Jewish writers down to our own day.

There is that scene of the first act of the play: a moment of silence after the fierce, passionate arguments of the fanatics and after the shrillness of the zealots. The clocks begin to strike and old Reb Leiser stands up and pointing to them utters those remarkable sentences in a quiet voice. This is no longer the force of hate that speaks, but the power of love. When the silence is broken and the old watchmaker says that for years he has tried to harmonize all the clocks, but in vain, for like men they cannot get together, it is not only he that speaks. In

this man in the *caftan* priests and prophets, sages of many centuries who hearkened to the laws of human destiny, seem to be
resurrected. His three simple sentences, his analogy showing a
comic face, bridge the gap of two thousand years to the proverb
of the Fathers and to the words of Isaiah. While we still smile,
we feel awe mounting. From an everyday jest we are conducted
into the realm of the immortal. A banal snatch of tune resounds
in an eternal melody. In words, lightly and casually spoken,
words which sound like a joke and possibly are intended as a
joke, the ultimate longing and sorrow of man are voiced. There
is something in this kind of Jewish wit which makes us bow
our heads.

It is wit in wisdom and wisdom in wit, the same which,
generation after generation, the Jews have salvaged out of the
experience of their own lives and that of others. Here is the
voice that sounded in many passages of the Talmud and of rabbinical commentators, in the similes, legends and parables of
the Halacha and in the analogies of the Hasidim. There is no
essential difference there between witty comparisons of the
kind Leiser Fränkel utters and the profound thoughts of the
Jewish sages which spring from the deep fund of ancient experiences. A boy had asked Rabbi Mendel Kozker, 'Where does
God live?" The rabbi answered, "Wherever He is admitted."
The same spirit that speaks out of the remarks of the old watchmaker Reb Leiser dwells in epigrams of this kind.

Looking back upon those examples of the charming family
joke, examples of the bitterly sarcastic and the profound, worldly-
wise groups of Jewish wit, the scope of this kind of humor becomes transparent. At the same time the emotional dynamics of
unconscious transference becomes understandable. What do
these jokes subtly say but the very things which the play on
the stage vainly tried to present with brutal effects? When at
the end of the drama a storm of pillage, murder and destruction
sweeps away all that these poor Jews called their own, we are,
of course, carried away. But the tragedy is more emphatic in
its overtones of wit. The news that so-and-so many people have

been murdered in a pogrom fills us with rage, disgust and despair. What is said in these jokes shakes us to the roots and will not be forgotten.

Aaron Leiser tells the story of the cemetery, the tragicomical tale of a poor persecuted minority, packed into a tiny corner in life and deprived of six feet of land in death. The tragedy is clearer to us in this grotesque incident than in the blood-and-thunder scene of the pogrom at the end. A tale like that of the cemetery echoes longer and more distinctly than the tumultuous roaring of the wild mob breaking into the houses of the ghetto.

The wise uncle advises the young girl to bear children and thus, with rebels in her own house, to be distracted from the urge to revolt against the state. His remarks, so human and so humorous, express the ephemeral character of political movements more clearly than the fiery debates in the following scenes of the play. His advice voices an inkling of the real values of our personal life and of the significance of the trends governing the fate of all generations. Is it so important to revolt against the order and form of government, against the insolence of office? Is it so important to overthrow this regime, to change it into another, when after all is said, our lives must describe the same tiny circle of joy and sorrow?

Reb Leiser's comparison of the clocks with people certainly had no lofty purpose, but it soars and gains a solemn beat. In it is an implied reference to the shortness of our span on earth, and it tells us of the folly of our little quarrels over what in our imagination are irreconcilable matters. Each of those clocks which the old man has vainly tried to harmonize is, perhaps, convinced of the infallibility of its time and proudly looks down upon the others. Yet it will not be long before the works of each runs down. For the clocks as well as for men, the rest is silence.

In these examples of Jewish wit a heavy shadow falls across the brightness of the words. Jest usurps the kingdom of tragedy. The realm of the comic is as wide as that of the tragic, and in Jewish wit it is wider since it encompasses the hopeless and the catastrophic. Where once was lament, there is now laughter.

SPEAKING MANY LANGUAGES

I

Until a few years ago Jewish wit did not belong to the mass communication media. It was restricted to the Jewish group and could almost be called a kind of tribal communication. Jokes were told by one Jew to another. Gentiles as listeners were not taken into consideration. Besides certain psychological reasons which forbade telling such stories to Gentiles and which we will not dwell upon here, there was the almost insuperable obstacle of the language barrier. Most Jewish jokes are expressed in jargon, in Yiddish, neither spoken nor understood by most Gentiles. (There are, of course, exceptions. A Gentile Viennese journalist spoke such excellent Yiddish that he was often considered a Jew. When one of his colleagues once teased him about his facility in speaking Yiddish, he said: "I can, you must.")

Since so many Jewish jokes are now heard on radio, television, and stage the audience, especially in America, has been quickly enlarged, while certain jargon-expressions have been absorbed into American everyday language and colloquialism. Words like "meschugge," "schmock," etc., are now freely used by Gentiles.

Moreover, such words have found their way into the language of journals and newspapers and even into literary works. When I came to America in 1938, I found a review of an operetta which said that the melodies have "schmalz." Now the German word "Schmalz" means fat. You will not find this word used to characterize a touching, languishing or sweet melody. It would be as though you were speaking of a dripping tune. In German you use the adjective "schmelzend" (melting) to describe the nature of such a melody. The word "Schmalz," in this sense is certainly not taken from the German, but from the American-Yiddish jargon.

The distortion of the German language was sometimes made

the subject of mockery by Jewish-German writers. Thus the Viennese satirist, Karl Kraus, once made fun of an early Zionistic convention that took place in Bad Ischl near Salzburg. Thinking of the Jews taking part in the convention and conversing at the riverside of the Ischl, he changed the beginning of a Schubert song "Ich hört ein Bächlein rauschen" ("I heard a brook murmur") into "Ich hört ein Bächlein mauscheln," indicating that the conversations were conducted in Yiddish(1).

Jewish and Yiddish phrases are, of course, prevalent in Jewish wit and comical stories, but they occasionally infiltrate the casual conversations and informal letters of great German-Jewish writers. I will mention here only two representative examples, Heinrich Heine and Sigmund Freud. No one whose native tongue is German and who has made a literary study of the works of these two men will deny that they were master stylists.

In Heine's case literary critics have remarked that even certain passages of his prose have a characteristic Yiddish intonation. In his early writings one can even discover traces of old linguistic uses, and a confusion of cases as well as false syntax which is to be found in Yiddish. Especially when the writer speaks *en pantoufles,* there is, as a literary historian recently observed, a "strong coloring" of his colloquial language by Hebrew and Judeo-German words(2). "Until the end Heine used such words in letters to his mother, to his brother and sister and to certain Jewish friends with relish." Such occasions must be differentiated from others in which the poet uses Hebrew or Jewish phraseology to attain humorous effects.

I will quote a single example, but a particularly significant one, from the letters of Sigmund Freud. Hereby hangs a tale the understanding of which is necessary for the appreciation of this letter Freud wrote me. Pastor Dr. Oskar Pfister, who was one of the most eager followers of Freud in Switzerland, had published an article on psychoanalysis in the *Theologische Literaturzeitung* in 1914. I wrote a critical review of this article for the *Zentralblatt für Psychoanalyse.* In this review I had made some sarcastic remarks about Pfister who endeavored to explain to his readers that psychoanalysis does not deal with aggressive and sexual drives only, but with unconscious moral trends as well. Freud read the manuscript of my review which the editor of the *Zentralblatt,* Sandor Ferenczi, had shown him. Freud's critical remarks in his letter to me concern a French colloquial phrase I had used in my review. Here is the letter Freud wrote me, dated Karlsbad, July 24, 1914(3).

Dear Herr Doctor:

I have satisfied your need for merciless criticism in speaking with Ferenczi and accusing you of various naughtinesses in your review. The *"à qui dites-vous ça"* is a Jewish joke, too good for those Goyim, and makes a bad impression. I am, of course, in agreement with the content of your criticism.

I asked Pfister about his article in the *Theologische Literaturzeitung* and then got the article and the enclosed letter. Please return it. You will perhaps be persuaded by it to show more understanding in your criticism of the poor pastor's soul vacillating between the upperworld and the netherworld.

Cordial regards,
Yours, Freud

Two items in Freud's letter interest us in the context under discussion. The first is the expression "Goyim" which means, of course, non-Jews. Such Hebrew, Yiddish expressions occur in Freud's letters rarely and only in his correspondence with relatives and friends. The other item is the designation of the French phrase *"à qui dites-vous ça"* as a Jewish joke. Is it really a Jewish joke? We will return to this point and prefer to grapple with some other interesting questions which could be raised here.

II

Jewish jokes in print are, properly speaking, incomplete. They should really be heard and seen. Their communication is not only verbal. The gestures and the facial expressions, the

rise and fall of the voice of the story-teller, are essential parts
of the telling. Such anecdotes are not only told, but also acted
and when you speak of their language, those external factors
must be considered. The poet Nonus, who lived at the time of
Theodosius, called the gestures languages and said of the hands
that they are mouths and of the fingers that they are voices.

The factor of language will appear in a different light when
we think of a representative example like the following: A physician who had been summoned to help the Baroness Feilchen-
feld in her confinement declares that the critical moment has
not yet arrived. He suggests to the baron that they play a game
of cards in the adjoining room while they wait. After a while
the doleful cry of the baroness reaches the men: "*Ah, mon dieu,
comme je suffre!*" The husband jumps up, but the obstetrician
assures him: "That's nothing; let's play on." A little while later
the woman in labor is heard again: "My God, what pains!" The
husband wants to rush in. The physician says: "No, it is not yet
time." At last, there rings from the adjacent room the cry "Ai-
ai-ee-weh mir!" The doctor quickly throws down the cards,
saying: "Now it's time."

Freud, who analyzed this anecdote in his book on wit, remarks that the labor pain causes the original nature of the
woman to break through the strata of education. The successive
changes in her cries provide the clue for this process. The transition from the French to the Yiddish cries interests us here because the return to the mother-tongue or to the jargon once
spoken restores the emotional atmosphere of childhood and
sweeps away all superstructure.

Jewish wit uses the mixture and the confusion of languages
to reach its effect in a different direction also. When the descendant of the last Austrian Kaiser Karl lived in New York, he
hoped that he would be called back as emperor to Austria or
Hungary. A Jewish wit of New York called the pretender the
"Perhapsburg." Thinking of prewar-Austria, a pun comes to
mind in which the German name is transformed by a Jewish
expression. In the period when Vienna was still a cultural center
and the home of an intellectual and artistic elite, the Duchess

Pauline Metternich played a great role in society. In her salon, aristocrats and artists met and formed a glamorous circle which sparkled spectacularly. A lady who was much less equipped to have that stimulating social role, but who tried to compete with the Duchess, was named "Metternebbich" by the Viennese Jews (nebbich = to be pitied).

In some Jewish anecdotes the meaning of German or French words are confused with Yiddish expressions. These mistakes then show parodistically the lack of education or knowledge of the subjects who are the butt of the joke. Such unintentional mistakes or blunders differ considerably from those jokes in which words or names are transformed and distorted in order to expose certain people to mockery. An instance of this: the hero of the play *Der Spiegelmensch* by Franz Werfel, performed in the Vienna Burgtheater, had the Thracian name Thamal. Karl Kraus, reviewing the drama, wrote that he does not like that Unthamal. (Tham is a Hebrew word = charm. Unthamal would thus mean a man without any charm.)

III

Not so long ago I read the interesting book *The Wandering Jew* by Moncure Daniel Conway which follows the legend of the Eternal Jew to its sources(4). In it, it is reported that the Bishop Paulus von Eizen saw the mysterious figure of Ahasuerus in 1547 in Hamburg. "In whatever country he entered he knew the language at once. At that time he spoke the Saxon language as one born there." Other German officials also encountered the Jewish shoemaker who had been present when Christ was crucified and who had restlessly wandered through many countries. They were astonished that they heard him speak good Spanish as well as German. A Turk reports to a friend that he had encountered Ahasuerus in 1644: "One day I had the curiosity to discourse with him in several languages and I found him master of all those I could speak."

By a strange detour my train of associations leads me to a psychoanalytic session I had had the day before. The patient,

a middle-aged, very intelligent Dutch Jew, had said: "How
pleasant it is to jump from one language to another and to be
understood!" Psychoanalysis was conducted in English, but the
patient sometimes quoted French sentences he had read or the
text of Viennese songs. He often inserted Hebrew words or used
Yiddish expressions. In this particular session he had remembered some childhood scenes in Amsterdam and had repeated a
dialogue then heard in his mother-tongue. (He knew that I had
spent several years in Holland. I then spoke Dutch better than
I now speak English, and although I have been out of practice
for a long time I understood what he said very well.)

Following that train of thought I wondered about the fact
that almost all Jews were at least bilingual, spoke Yiddish or a
Spanish jargon besides the language of the country in which
they lived. Yiddish is itself essentially Middle High German,
interspersed with Slav, Hebrew and Aramaic words and phrases.
Yiddish is the ideal language of Jewish wit and it is remarkable
that these jokes are told in an old tongue that was once German,
and that the Jews maintained a strange loyalty to the language
of the country they had once considered their home, although
the German had subjected them to terrible martyrdom in both
the Middle Ages and modern times.

Looking back into the history of the Israelites you will wonder about the fact that those tribes so often adopted a strange
language. Even after the invasion of Palestine they spoke Ca-
naanite rather than their original Hebrew. The Aramaic, akin
to Hebrew, in which a great part of postbiblical literature is
written, was the language which Jesus spoke. It became the
vernacular speech of his people since the Babylonian exile. Since
then the Jews, in their migrations from one country to another
adopted the language of the people among whom they lived.

The fact is that the Jews rarely spent their whole life in one
country, but became refugees again and again. Think only of
the Jewish men of genius in our time: Heinrich Heine, Karl
Marx, Ludwig Börne, Sigmund Freud, and Albert Einstein were
all fugitives from Germany. As a result of their migration the

Jews became well-versed in several languages. Jewish wit often uses that polyglotic facility to achieve a distinguished humorous effect. Like the patient whose words I quoted before, Jewish wit seems to enjoy making that casual transition from one language to another, the change from one linguistic area to another.

The following is an example of such transition and of its strong comical power. The first lines of a poem by Heinrich Heine, perhaps the best representative of Jewish wit, are:

> "Dying spoke to Solomo
> Old King David: "à propos . . ."

> "Sterbend sprach zu Salomo
> König David: à propos . . ."

The witty effect is achieved by the poet in having the biblical king use a modern French phrase.

COMMENT ON FREUD'S REMARK

The passage from Freud's letter quoted before elicits a perhaps trivial, but relevant comment in connection with our subject. Is the phrase, "À qui dites-vous ça," really a Jewish joke as Freud says or is it an everyday common saying? I remember that I wondered about it when I received Freud's letter more than forty-five years ago. Compared with the German "Wem sagen Sie das?" or with the American "You're telling me!", it has still a Jewish flavor.

Shortly after the First World War Freud referred an American patient to me for psychoanalytic treatment. I still remember that the man after I had given him the first psychoanalytic interpretation of a dream remarked: "Tell that to the marines!" Unfamiliar with that slang expression, I was very surprised: What had the subject of my interpretation to do with the navy? What I am driving at is that slang expressions like this do not have the same peculiar Jewish taste.

Anybody who grew up in New York's Brooklyn, London's Jewish quarter, or in Amsterdam's Joodestraat, will remember phrases of that characteristic flavor, often felt by the Gentiles. There are even such sentences of decidedly Jewish modulation that are scarcely translatable into other languages without losing their meaning. Here is an instance. Some years ago I sat near a table on which an old Jewish man played bridge with three young women. It was in a garden-café at Gastein near Salzburg. The old man dealt the cards and one of them fell to the ground. The young lady at his side bent down saying: "Let me help you!" But the man said: "Mir ist nicht mehr zu helfen," which to the ears of any German or Austrian Jew is a distinct Jewish phrase. How does it sound in English? "I can't be helped any longer" is much too serious and positive and has certainly not that slight comical effect as that Viennese-Jewish sentence.

On the other hand, there are certain sentences that are almost unimaginable spoken in Yiddish or Jewish-German. For instance, a saying used by Viennese street-Arabs when I was a little boy: "Ich schlag dich so dass'd in kan' Sarg mehr einipasst" ("I hit you until you cannot be fitted into any coffin"). Something in Jews, perhaps their old reluctance to violence, refuses to translate such a sentence into their jargon.

The point I would like to make is the following: Often, as in the sentence quoted from Freud's letter, not the words spoken determine whether an expression sounds Jewish or not, but the cadence, the voice and the fall of the voice. You have to hear the sentence spoken to form an opinion. When you read it, it sometimes remains mute. It is as if you saw couples dancing far away without hearing the music which moves them; in other words, you see the motions without feeling the emotions. It is not the phraseology, but often the modulation in which the sentence is said which gives it a Jewish taste. The same words, otherwise modulated don't sound Jewish any longer. To return to French: "C'est le ton qui fait la musique."

A sentence may sound nonsensical if it is not spoken with that certain intonation. In the words of an old American hit song "It don't mean a thing, if it ain't got that swing."

SHLEMIHL WITH A DIFFERENCE

I

Among the Hebrew and Jewish words that are used among American and German Gentiles the expression Shlemihl should not be forgotten. More than a century ago a German poet introduced the word even into literature. Adalbert von Chamisso wrote the fantastic story of Peter Schlemihl (5). The hero of the novel is a man who lost his shadow. What is the original meaning of the Hebrew word Shlemihl? According to the definition of an expert(6), it is a person who "handles a situation in the worst possible manner or is dogged by an ill luck that is more or less due to his own ineptness." A Shlemihl is thus the victim of his own stupidity or simplemindedness.

The scholars trace the word back to the name of a man who appears in a biblical story (Numbers 25). It is reported there that the people of Israel at Shittim began to commit whoredom with the daughters of Moab. One of the Israelites brought a Midianite woman unto his brethren. When the priest Phinehas seen it "he rose up from among the congregation, and took a javelin in his hand. And he went after the man of Israel into the tent, and thrust both of them through, the man of Israel, and the woman through her belly . . . Now the name of the Israelite that was slain, even that was slain with the Midianitish woman, was Zimvi, the son of Salu . . ."

According to other sources, the name is derived from that of a man who is the luckless protagonist of a medieval story. This man, Shemuliel, returned home after a year of absence to find his wife had given birth to a child. The rabbi decided that the child was legitimate while the neighbors were very dubious regarding the paternity. The man had to accept the rabbinical decision and became the prototype of the Shlemihl who is involving himself in difficult situations from which he cannot extricate himself.

The great Hebrew-Spanish poet Ibn Ezra (1092-1167) was

exposed to the slings and arrows of a fortune as outrageous as
that of any Shlemihl. Driven from place to place by poverty and
restlessness, he wrote the self-descriptive epigram: "If I should
undertake to sell candles, the sun would never set; if I should
deal with shrouds, no one would ever die . . ." From these lines
of a poet of the twelfth century, a direct line leads to the humorous and pathetic figures that Charlie Chaplin created and
who have their home in the Jewish East End of London.

When he spoke of Ibn Ezra and other Spanish Jewish poets,
Heinrich Heine thought of the Shlemihl, and arrived at a witty
variation of the biblical story. In the *Hebrew Melodies,* the poet
reports that Israel often committed whoredom with daughters
of Canaan and that the priest Phinehas was zealous for the sake
of the Lord. But according to an old oral tradition amongst the
people,

> Twas not Zimri that was really
> Striken by the spear of Pinehas,
> But the latter, blind with fury,
> By ill luck
> Chanced to kill
> A guiltless person
> In the sinner's place,
> Named Schlemihl ben Zuri Schaday.
> He, then, this Schlemihl, the First,
> Was the ancestor of all
> Race Schlemihlian. We are descended
> From Schlemihl ben Zuri Schaday.

Heine thus traced the origin of the word to this Shlemihl, the
First, whose descendants are Ibn Ezra and other contemporary
Spanish-Jewish poets, and finally, Heine himself.

II

Tavye the Dairyman, one of the best figures of Sholom
Aleichem, once remarked, "With God's help I starved to death."

Ill luck is here attributed to the disfavor of God, but the Shlemihl knows somewhere that he himself stands behind the wings
as the stage manager of his own destiny. He knows, with He-
raclitus, that a man's character is his fate. Many Jewish proverbs
accentuate the purposefulness of bad luck as if they recognized
that the Shlemihl is prone to misfortune. Here are a few instances: "When a Schlemihl kills a chicken, it walks; when he
winds a clock, it stops," or "he falls on his back and breaks his
nose."

Psychoanalysis would characterize a Shlemihl as a masochistic character who has the strong unconscious will to fail and
to spoil his chances. The Shlemihl is thus a certain type, easily
defined or characterized psychologically, a type met with not
only among Jews, but also among Gentiles. Yet the fact that
there is that precise Hebrew name for this type seems to point
to a different direction. The expression Shlemihl is not identical
in its meaning with the English "unlucky fellow" or the German
word "Pechvogel," because the Hebrew term includes a connotation of ineptness or simplemindedness. The proverb previously
quoted seems to imply that the Shlemihl has an unconscious
purpose in arranging his bad luck. A German proverb says,
"Jeder ist seines Glückes Schmied" ("Every man is the founder
of his own fortune"). The Shlemihl is the hidden architect of
his misfortune. The ironic phrase "Jewish luck" hints at a more
general connotation beyond the narrow limitations of an ineffec-
tual Jewish type.

III

We did not forget that the aim of this collection and comments on Jewish jokes is to provide us with material for a psychoanalytic exploration of the Jewish group. Are the Jews the
Shlemihls among the nations? Are they, so to speak, the collective type of Shlemihls? When one follows their history through
four thousand years, one would almost be inclined to assume
that. Is it not as though a subterranean compulsion to repeat
can be observed in their fate? They wander from one place to

another, from one nation to another and everywhere their vicissitudes seem to take the same course. They are accepted, work their way up and many of them reach an elevated social position and make distinctive and sometimes superb contributions to the civilization of their guest-nations and to that of the world. Then inevitably expulsion, pogroms and annihilation overtake them. It is as if they were asking for trouble and tribulation, and as if they got it. This is not only valid for the history, but also, to use a phrase of Somerset Maugham, for the "everlasting present" of the Jews.

If the Jews thus seem to be the Shlemihl among the nations, they are that with a decided difference. Are they not the only nation that survived from remote antiquity, not only in name, but also in substance? It is as if there were such an iron will to live and to maintain their existence that like an eternal Jack-in-the-box, they rise again. Their number is decreasing; they can be counted; but they cannot be counted out.

The old theological view spoke of their "mission" in the world. We prefer to say that they had and have a definite function as catalysts within the civilizating process. We considered the Shlemihl a masochistic character and he has indeed all the earmarks of this characterological type, including that tendency I once summed up in the formula, "Victory through defeat"(7), the irresistible will to master a reluctant destiny. Perhaps they are sometimes ruined by success, but they are then rescued by failure. Here is the other side of the valuable coin.

The Jews are the Shlemihls of history with a difference: they cling to the deathless hope that they will not always be vexed victims of a cruel fate, but will be finally vindicated victors.

SELF-CENTEREDNESS

In a Jewish story a physician enters the room of a patient and asks the male attendant how the patient was during the night. The nurse answers: "The patient was very restless, had 103 degree temperature and could not fall asleep. I gave him compress." The next morning the physician asks another nurse, this time a Jewish one, the same question. "Oi, had I a night!!" is the answer.

The story does not simply contrast the objective report with the highly subjective one, but illustrates the comic self-centeredness of the Jewish attendant. The fact that he refers first to his own state does not exclude the fact that he took the best care of the patient. It only shows that he naively pours out his complaints.

This same self-centeredness appears in a much wider frame in other Jewish jokes not dealing with the actual, but with the alleged or imagined anti-Semitism of the surrounding world. Those witticisms seemingly make fun of the habit of many Jews of suspecting anti-Semitism everywhere even when there is not the slightest reason for such mistrust. These witticisms contain a caricature of the attitude of certain Jews, but they do not originate in a void. There is a tragic background against which the jokes stand out. The Jews are frequently accused and attacked in the most absurd context and it is not strange that they occasionally feel themselves subjects of aggression in situations where hostile intentions do not exist.

Here is a telling anecdote of this kind. A Jew runs into his friend Itzig as he is just leaving the building of a radio station and asks him, "What did you do here inside?" Itzig answers: "I just app-p-plied for a p-p-position, for an ap-ap-po-pointment." "You tried for a post?" "Yes," Itzig answers, "for a p-p-p-post as a-a-announcer." "Did you get the job?" Indignant Itzig answers: "Nn-n-no, those-those p-p-people are a-a-all a-a-antisemites."

Such a suspicious attitude to one's surroundings is in exaggerated or pathological form manifested in the paranoid character who everywhere suspects hostile or aggressive behavior of others towards himself. The patients develop certain notions which psychiatry calls "ideas of reference." They imagine that everyone—sometimes even inanimate objects—are constantly focussing their actions and words on the intention to hurt, to degrade and to humiliate them.

There is a certain attitude especially of the older generation which approaches a kind of group-reference idea. Here is an example from American life, again in a joke. A boy, upon coming home, very excitedly tells his father: "The Yankees were defeated by the Dodgers this afternoon." The father asks "Is this good or bad for the Jews?"

JEWISH JOKES AND THE GENTILE

It was mentioned before that Jewish witticisms were essentially of a kind of group communication which became part of mass communication in America during the last decades thanks to the fact that so many Jewish comedians told their jokes over the radio, on television and on the stage. This change is itself remarkable because it indicates a new attitude toward the Jews and their mentality.

In *Wit and Its Relation to the Unconscious,* published in 1905, Freud pointed out that there is a difference between jokes made by Gentiles and those told by Jews. Jokes ridiculing the Jews are, said Freud, "nearly all brutal buffooneries in which the wit is spoiled by the fact that the Jew appears as a comic figure to a stranger." Jewish jokes also make fun of the weaknesses of their people, "but they know their merits as well as their shortcomings."

Only a few instances are known to me of opinions or impressions voiced by Gentile observers about Jewish humor. Yet it would be highly interesting to learn how the Gentiles react to Jewish jokes and what kind of emotional attitude they assume in listening to witticisms of this kind. Robert Graves's lecture, "The Feeling to be a Goi," given in Tel Aviv and published in the magazine *Commentary*(8), is of a general nature and does not refer to Gentile reactions to Jewish jokes. Since we restrict our remarks to this particular question, we have to exclude the interesting article of the English poet from discussion.

Another recent paper by a Gentile psychoanalyst deals specifically with the problem and contains a good deal of psychological insight of the kind we are here interested in. I mean the still unpublished lecture by Martin Grotjahn(9). It is entitled "Psychoanalysis and the Jewish Joke: A Contribution to the

Understanding of Masochism." We will have occasion to discuss its scientific views about the nature of Jewish jokes in another part of this book. The personal attitude of the author comes clearly to expression in the introductory remarks of his lecture. Dr. Grotjahn contends that the Jewish population is at the present time so sensitive and so sensitized against anti-Semitism that the non-Jew talking about Jewish jokes is immediately suspect. He himself does not need to defend himself against the reproach of being anti-Jewish. While he still lived in Germany, he identified with his Jewish friends and emigrated to America. Thus prefacing his psychoanalytic contribution, he develops his theory about the psychological character of Jewish wit. His attitude is objective and scientific, but his basic friendly feelings toward Jews are evident. We will return to the subject of his psychoanalytical lecture.

I would like to refer here to two kinds of reactions to Jewish wit, both voiced by Gentiles. The one by a famous British writer, the other by a well-known German professor of sociology. Their juxtaposition and their contrasting lead to an interesting aspect. The impressions the two authors communicate are so vividly and clearly transmitted that we don't need to spell them out after we have presented them. They also reflect a change in the concept of Jewish jokes determined not only by the individuality of the observer, but also by the difference of their generations.

Somerset Maugham depicts in one of his stories, "The Alien Corn"(10), a Jewish intellectual, Fred Robenstein, who has an inexhaustible fund of Jewish stories, and, being a good mimic, assumes the Yiddish accent and reproduces the Jewish gestures to perfection. The story-teller adds that it was as good as a play because Robenstein was himself a Jew, and insisted on one's laughing without reserve, but that he, the Gentile listener, for his part, could not laugh without an undercurrent of discomfort. "I was not quite sure of a sense of humor that made such cruel fun of his own race."

Let me compare this statement with another reaction of a Gentile to Jewish wit. In his preface to a recent collection of

Jewish jokes(11), Professor Carlo Schmid tells us that he became acquainted with Jewish wit after the first World War. He had the impression that the jokes were made by Gentiles about Jews because they could not possibly be originated by Jews who had still maintained their self-esteem. Later on he was differently affected by this kind of joke because he recognized its wisdom and melancholy. He now thought that one should take those jokes very seriously. Some of them, to be sure, are based on comic situations or express mockery about human stupidity, but in some of them there is something special and specific. They lead into regions before which the jokes of other people stop. Schmid points to the contrast of the law and of life with its demands and necessities, to the insight that life has its own probabilities which need not coincide with its realities nor with the rules we establish. Those jokes acknowledge and simultaneously ridicule the belief in the power of thinking, and assert that a state of affairs can occasionally be turned into its opposite. In some of them, love of mankind or charity conquers the rigidity of the Law. Jewish wit shows again and again that in a world that can be best comprehended with the tools of logic, equations cannot always be solved without remainders.

Whatever you may think of Professor Schmid's formulations, you will admit that they endeavor to gain a true and sympathetic insight into the character of Jewish wit. This striving for understanding differentiates them from other attempts at characterization and goes beyond that "undercurrent of discomfort" experienced by Somerset Maugham.

The Prince of Wales, who became King Edward VII, enjoyed Jewish jokes and roared at them. He shared this passion with his friend Lord Nathaniel Rotschild. A biographer tells us, that the house of Rothschild was at the time not only a great international center of finance, but also a treasury of Jewish jokes(12). A Prussian nobleman, Baron von Eckhardstein, had standing orders to collect and report all good jokes and to dispatch them to the Rotschilds in New Court "whence they would find their way before long to Marlborough House," where the Prince of Wales resided.

If one wants to measure the psychological advance in understanding of Jewish wit by the Gentiles, one will remember that not long ago two very eminent men of science denied that the Jews have any kind of humor. Ernest Renan(13) stated that the Semitic people lack the faculty to laugh, and Carlyle(14) asserted that the Jews did not show the slightest trace of humor at any period of their history. These men, as so many of their generation, did not see that misery has its mirth as well as abundance and happiness. A Jewish proverb claims that "Leid macht auch Lachen" (Suffering creates laughter too). Even a scherzo can move in a minor key.

The Wandering Jew

Jewish history is the story of migrations interrupted by short or prolonged sojournments. Since earliest times the Hebrews were nomadic tribes. This kind of group existence can be traced back to their prehistoric period when they were compelled to leave their home in North Africa because drought and barrenness compelled them to move on. This is, in my view, the traumatic experience of their earliest time, comparable to traumatic events in the infantile phase of an individual, comparable for instance to the forcible separation of a child from his mother, comparable in its nature as well as in its consequences. Since then the Jewish people have been subjected to that unconscious compulsion of repetition, to the inescapable tendency to repeat the experience of migration. These wanderings are mostly forced on the children of Israel by persecution, and frequently amount to expulsion from the country that they considered their home. They are threatened with expulsion everywhere. They are aliens in every country and must resign themselves to their fate, and accept it as their destiny. There is no doubt that it was first the external factors of segregation and persecution that resulted in forced wandering. Their dispersion over the world, the diaspora, is the result of their forced wanderings.

The dark compulsion of repetition has now attained such an irresistible power that migrations are sometimes voluntary. A well-known Zionist leader once declared that it is easier to get the Jews out of Exile than the Exile out of the Jews.

One of the by-products of those forced migrations is that, for a long time, an emotional attachment to the country they have left survives in the emigrants. When we Viennese came to the States as refugees we carried with us vivid memories of the city that was no longer our home but, according to our passports, only our native town. We had suffered too much to speak as did the German refugees who were called in France *"les chez-nous"* because they so often spoke of Germany as "bei uns" but our affection returned again and again to the Vienna of our childhood and manhood. Some of us refugees in the United States said, "We are sad that we have to be here, but happy that we are allowed to be here." Since then we sing with the native Americans their anthem and know that we have found a new home; that here is "our children's country."

The migration of the Jews, especially those forced to emigrate by persecution, has become the subject of many jokes since Hitler. Here is an example from the time when Hitler entered Austria. A Jew asked the advice of the travel-office about where he could immigrate. The clerk and he considered the various countries as possibilities and realized that the entrance into each was beset with difficulties. In one country you needed a certain amount of money for entry, in another a labor permit or a certificate of employment. For another country the passport had no validity; a fourth land did not want any immigrants, and so on. While the two men thus considered the various countries, they whirled the globe near the desk. Finally the desperate Jew asked, "Haven't you got another globe?"

PUNISHMENT FOR HITLER

How did the Jewish joke react to Hitler and the Nazis? Here is an interesting psychological question. The following remarks are restricted to a particular subject, namely to the punishment of that human monster, the arch-criminal Adolf Hitler.

No doubt many Jews imagined all kinds of torture which should be inflicted on the fiend, torments reaching from permanent agony to marooning him on a lonely island. Others considered lifelong solitary confinement or forced labor. But all this was discussed in bitter earnest and not as a matter of jests.

What interests us here is how the possible punishment of Hitler is reflected in Jewish wit. Here are two instances of Jewish jokes from the time of the Great War. The first was told in Vienna, long before Hitler occupied Austria. To appreciate the *vis comica* of the anecdote, one has to remember that at that time customers at the coffee-houses in Vienna took several newspapers to their table and read one after the other. It sometimes happened that a customer had to wait a long time for a newspaper he wanted until another customer had finished reading it. A Jew imagines that Hitler sits in a Vienna coffee-house while a Jewish customer reads all the journals and puts them aside after he has read them. In the Jew's imagination, Hitler then comes to his table and politely asks: "Please, is the *Wiener Journal* free?" The Jew will answer: "Not for you, Herr Hitler!" The point is not that the punishment for the criminal is so harmless, but that the Jew cannot imagine a more cruel and more exquisite torment than the withholding of the desired newspaper and the suffering of agonizing suspense of the loathed enemy.

The other example is perhaps less harmless, although still not brutal in the sense of an appropriate punishment. During the war a soldier's magazine published a prize-question about what would be the appropriate punishment for Hitler after his capture. The prize was won by a Jewish soldier of the American army in Italy. His answer was: "He should live with my in-laws in the Bronx." It seems that to this young married man the tortures of Dante's Inferno were mere child's play compared with an existence of such hellish cruelty. Two factors in these jokes seem to be remarkable: the mildness of the penalty inflicted on the hated murderer of six million Jews, and the local color (Vienna and New York) of the imagination in the anticipated punishment of that arch-criminal.

THE ETERNAL FUGITIVE

The story of the Wandering Jew comes from passages in the Gospels, which have been enlarged, dramatized and often melodramatized. The migrations of the Jews were conceived as consequences of a mysterious curse that Jesus pronounced on the shoemaker who did not allow the Messiah to rest when He carried His cross to Calvary. Byron sang in his *Hebrew Melodies*

"Were my bosom as false as
Thou deemst it to be
It was but abjuring my creed to efface
The curse which thou sayst is the crime of my race."

But it is not the wandering of the Jew which is tragic; it is his homelessness, or rather the paradoxical fact that he is considered a stranger everywhere. It would be more appropriate to talk of the eternal fugitive than of the eternal wanderer. In the joke of the refugee who asked the clerk in the travel office "Haven't you got another globe?" it is not, as it seems superficially, the difficulties of immigration and work permits that give the tragicomic note to that sentence but the acknowledgment of homelessness.

How far can this particular destiny be traced back in Jewish history? The answer is: it cannot be traced back far enough there, because it was already there before recorded history had begun. So early a document as the Pentateuch recommends kindness towards "the stranger within thy gates" and reminds the children of Israel that they had been strangers in Egypt. And before their years in the country of the Pharaoh? They were not at home in Babylon and not in Canaan.

It is this awareness that they were and are strangers everywhere which gives so many Jewish jokes a shadowed edge of sadness. ("I can suck melancholy out of a song as a weasel sucks eggs" says Shakespeare(15). I could, at this point, quote many sentences from the writings of modern authors, from Heinrich Heine to Arthur Schnitzler, sentences which prove that they were aware of that feeling of homelessness, and could put these sentences side by side with some Jewish witticisms.

Instead of these quotations I will refer to some sentences by three Jewish men of genius who expressed that emotional experience in words that sometimes sound witty although they are unmitigatingly sad. I am quoting contemporary creative Jews whose greatness cannot be denied. In all three cases the tragicomic aspect of this "strangeness" was that these men were born and bred in a country which they had to leave, that they shared its civilization and spent the best part of their manhood there, and beyond any doubt felt "at home" there for many years. Let me add that none of the three found full recognition and acknowledgment in their native countries during the best years of their lives.

Gustav Mahler once remarked: "I am a thrice homeless man: as a Bohemian among Austrians, as an Austrian among Germans and as a Jew among the people of the whole world"(16). Sigmund Freud who lived most of his life since early childhood in Vienna until the Nazis drove him out at eighty years of age, remarked in a conversation with a fellow physician that he was neither an Austrian nor a German, but a Jew. Once, when the tax office wrote to him suggesting that perhaps he had not declared enough income, and added that his fame reached far beyond the borders of Austria, Freud answered: "It only begins just there"(17).

Albert Einstein declared: "If my theory is proven correct, Germany will claim me as a German and France will declare that I am a citizen of the world. Should my theory prove untrue, France will say that I am a German and Germany will declare that I am a Jew."

Where are these mysterious people at home? To which nation do they belong? That bitter joke, "Haven't you got another globe?" supplies the answer. They are nowhere at home and they belong to no nation. But in another way they are heralds of a future time when distances between countries and continents will have shrunken even more than now and when national distinctions will have paled to insignificance.

NOTE ON THE ORIGIN OF JEWISH WIT

In her recent book, Dr. Salcia Landman(18) states that the origin of Jewish wit is inextricably connected with certain historic and social situations of modern times; it is born with them and vanishes with them. She asserts that certain circumstances within the European Exile Jewry are responsible for Jewish jokes and adds that there seems to be no connection between this phenomenon and the Bible and Talmud. The typical Jewish joke could have evolved only in the Eastern European and Middle European Jewry after the beginning of emancipation and with the enlightenment, and it died with the annihilation of the Jews in these places.

I do not agree with this author about the geographic and historic places to which she attributes the birth of Jewish witticism. Furthermore, I assert that there are easily recognizable connections with Biblical and Talmudic jokes and I believe that the news of the death of Jewish witticism is, à la Mark Twain, grossly exaggerated. This is not the place to discuss this problem, but it seems to me appropriate to add a note about another question to the preceding remarks on the special characteristics of Jewish jokes.

It has often been stated that many of the stories and anecdotes which are called typical Jewish jokes are also to be found in German and Slavic sources or, in other words, that they were borrowed from these people and, so to speak, translated into Yiddish or into Jewish-German jargon. This is undoubtedly correct in many, though not in all, cases often quoted, where a recognizable resemblance exists.

Another factor that has, as far as I know, never been noticed and properly evaluated, has to be taken into consideration in this context, namely, the assimilation to the culture patterns of the Gentiles among whom the Jews lived for many centuries.

Is it unimaginable that the Jews should assimilate to these people in habits and customs of everyday life and not also in literature, music and in their jokes? The assimilated Jews shared the intellectual and emotional atmosphere of Paris, Vienna and Berlin and the influence of the contemporary humor on the creation of Jewish jokes cannot be overlooked although to my knowledge it has almost never been expressly acknowledged and described.

Is it accidental that the Düsseldorf Jew, Heinrich Heine, wrote the ballad *The Lorelei* which was so typically German that the Nazis denied Heine's authorship and declared it a national song? Is it accidental that the Jew Jacques Offenbach from Cologne on the Rhein, composed, when he was transplanted to Paris, typical French music and created the *"genre canaille"*? Some of the tunes of Gustav Mahler, for instance, the dance tunes from his Fourth Symphony are characteristically Viennese. The waltzes of the Jews Leo Fall, Oscar Straus, Edmund Eysler, Emmerich Kálmán, etc., are genuinely Viennese and a Jew composed one of the most popular Viennese song-hits, the *Fiaker-lied.*

The point I would like to make and to drive home, is the following: many of the Jewish jokes assume the local color and flavor of the countries of their origin to such an extent that they are often called typical of Berlin, Vienna, Paris and New York without, however, entirely losing their Jewish character. The result of such an assimilatory and absorbing process is then a German-Jewish or French-Jewish compound made of two or more substances.

There is, as far as I know, only one remarkable exception to the general lack of consideration of the fact that the wit of the Jews is often a mixture of many substances, and that is the remarkable study on Heine's wit which Erich Eckertz(19) published more than fifty years ago. The author, who was especially interested in the history of literature, investigated the various ingredients that entered into the composition of Heine's wit. Eckertz differentiated the elements of the nervous Semitic, which is akin to the French vivacity of temperament and which is close to it in its antithetic kind of thought and grace of form. There is also the Rhenish-German element brought by the poet from his home in Düsseldorf, and the element of the Parisian to which Heine always felt attracted and which he easily appropriated from the time he came to Paris as a refugee and through the many years while he lived in the beloved city.

Eckertz, who was a historian of literature, not only characterized those three decisive elements, but also gave representative examples for each of them in quoting passages from Heine's poems and prose. He asserted that this racial mixture is the most important condition of Heine's wit, at least its most characteristic one: "The very homelessness underlying the common effect of three races, prevents the formation of a great and unified work of art, and favors the small, concentrated manyfold wit, but the individual elements themselves, the Jewish, the Rhenish and the French are the most advantageous imaginable for wit."

I cannot copy the analysis of those elements and have to refer the reader to Eckertz's interesting study where he will find abundant examples of those components in Heine's witticisms. I prefer to offer contemporary examples of Jewish witticism with distinct local color and restrict myself for reasons of expediency to samples from Berlin and Vienna. Here are a few from the city on the Spree, from the time before the Nazis destroyed the Jews there. The famous seventy-five-year-old painter, Max Lieberman, who was once President of the Prussian Academy of Arts, leads a young, pretty woman through his studio and shows her his pictures. The young lady assures him after a stimulating conversation, "Master, this was the happiest hour of my life." The old man smilingly says, "We would rather not hope *that*." This cheeky remark has certainly some of the genuine Berlin flavor and it is not accidental that it was said in Berlin dialect ("Dat woll'n wer doch nich hoffen"). Equally typical of Berlin is an anecdote to be found in the novel *Die Nacht des Dr. Herzfeld* by the once well-known Jewish writer Georg Herman. In a Berlin coffee house some middle-aged bachelors regularly meet at a certain time. A female officer of the Salvation Army approaches their table and presenting a collection box says: "Please, for fallen women!" One of the middle-aged bachelors answers: "I am giving directly." This is unmistakably of Berlin character, without denying the Jewishness of the speaker.

Let me contrast these examples with others taken from Vienna around the same time, Jewish jokes of typical Viennese coinage. Here are passages from the play *The Far Country* by Arthur Schnitzler. The leading figure, Friedrich Hofreiter, had an affair with Adele Natter, the wife of his banker. The affair—not her first, nor her last—had ended not so very long ago. Adele tells him that she knows that he has been flirting lately with another young woman in a very impudent manner, but he denies any sexual intentions towards that young girl whom he had known so many years and finds Adele's suspicion ridiculous: "A girl whom I have dangled on my knee!" But Adele replies, "It's likely that there are such girls with you in various age groups." During the ensuing dialogue Adele asks Hofreiter not to address her with "Du": "Finished is finished. I am for a clear state of affairs," she adds. Her previous lover remarks: "That they have to be clear too, I did not know."

In her ironic remark, Adele gives Hofreiter a hard hint, but he has his revenge: she is ironic, but he is sarcastic. The atmosphere of the play is unmistakably Viennese and so is the dialogue of the figures. Yet there is a flavor of Jewish phraseology clearly perceptible.

I could add here a great number of common sayings and idiomatic phrases from Vienna, Berlin, New York, Paris and Rome which all bear the marks of genuine local language and which nevertheless are undoubtedly of Jewish origin. The examples that are quoted here are perhaps sufficient not to prove, but to support, my thesis that a great number of Jewish jokes show that Jews also assimilated in this area of transitory literature to the country and the culture pattern within which they lived. The local color leaves no doubt that this assimilation, or even appropriation, of certain features of Gentile mentality has been highly successful. It is often said that certain folksongs and waltzes of Jewish composers are perhaps more Viennese than those of Gentile musicians, born and bred in Vienna. In spite of excellent results in intellectual and emotional assimilation, there remained a essential part that is still Jewish in character. Heinrich Heine is a great German poet and Jacques Offenbach an eminent representative of French comic opera. Yet, as scientific investigation has proved, their work still bears the indelible mark of their Jewish past. Whatever ingredients you add to a dish, you can still judge by the taste whether it is salted or not.

ISRAELITES AND OTHER ANTI-SEMITES

I

The title of this section is borrowed from a small book of satirical poems written by the Viennese Dr. Fritz Loehner and published under the pseudonym Beda more than forty years ago. The poems dealt mostly with contemporary Jewish problems, particularly with those Jews who disavowed or disguised their origin and descent and often acted and spoke as if they were authentic Germans, or rather Teutons. We students at the Vienna University often quoted some of the verses which exposed that considerable part of Austrian Jewry with merciless mockery. We laughed with the writer at that nationalistic and Christian masquerade, and the demasqué that was wittily portrayed in verses at times reminiscent of Heine's poems.

As a matter of fact, one of Beda's poems (the books are, alas, not accessible any longer) calls up the ghost of Heine. At that time it was suggested that a monument for Heine be erected in Hamburg. The Hamburg senate unanimously rejected the suggestion of a monument for the great writer who had so often made fun of the German nationalistic party, the predecessors of the Nazis. In Beda's poem the dead Heine hears the news of that brusque rejection and decides to turn around in his grave and thus to offer his backside to the magistrate. He says he will now "sich ausstrecken" and ends with the line:

> Jetzt kann mich der ganze Hamburger Senat—
> Nie mehr aus dem Schlafe erwecken.

The German verses, no longer remembered verbatim, say that now the Hamburg senate can never again awaken the poet from sleep in his Parisian grave. The German text alludes, however, to another possibility open to the senate. Concealed behind the verse is the colloquialism familiar to any German, "Kann mich in Arsch lecken" ("may kiss my arse").

Other verses of Beda ridicule the behavior of two Jews who run across each other in the Alps. Both are dressed in genuine Tyrolian costume (knee breeches, knapsack, etc.) and behave like native mountain-climbers. They discover during their conversation that they come from the same Moravian city, and when they remind each other of common acquaintances ("Kennen Sie die Familie Cohn?"), there is no doubt about their Jewishness any longer, and the one expresses his astonishment about how one chances upon the other in Jewish jargon: "Wie man sich trefft im Ampezzotal!" ("How one runs across a person in the Ampezzo-valley!")

But we will not discuss here the comic encounters and the various forms of dénouement developed on such occasions, but a question, akin to this one, namely a special kind of social contact in certain layers of Jewish society.

II

Since we already spoke of Vienna, let me preface the following remarks by an anecdote that was told about this city, which now seems to be a ghost-town haunted by the ghosts of relatives killed by the Nazis. Every day, in a coffee house, two Jews sit and play cards. One day they quarrel and Moritz furiously shouts at his friend: "What kind of a guy can you be if you sit down every evening playing cards with a fellow who sits down to play cards with a guy like you!" In turning the aggression against the other the self-degradation of the person is retained. More than this, self-contempt becomes a weapon with which to abuse and degrade the other person since he is connected with such a contemptible and low subject. (A witticism whose comic effect is attained by the same psychic dynamics is told by Heine in his *Letters from Berlin*. The writer gives an account of a fancy-dress ball in the Berlin Opera house. A masked lady there says to a young man: "I know you, handsome mask!" The young man rather ungallantly replies: "If you know me, beautiful, you cannot amount to much.")

We remain in Vienna, although a Vienna of a different social milieu, when we refer to a fragment of a conversation the Jewish writer Heinrich Berman has with his aristocratic friend, George von Werkenthin, in Schnitzler's novel, *The Way To the Open*. Heinrich says that he is fed up with a certain kind of Jew, and tells his friend a story of a Polish Jew who was sitting in a railway compartment with an unknown gentleman and who behaves very shyly and conventionally until he realizes by some remark of the other that he is a Jew too. Whereupon he immediately stretches his legs on the seat opposite with a sigh of relief: "Asoi."

George considers the story "quite good," but Heinrich asserts that it is more than that, it is deep like so many Jewish stories: "It expresses the eternal truth that no Jew has any real respect for his fellow Jew, never. As little as prisoners in a hostile country have any real respect for each other, particularly when they are hopeless. Envy, hate, yes, frequently admiration, even love; all that there can be between them, but never respect, for the play of all their emotional life takes place in an atmosphere of familiarity, so to speak, in which respect cannot helped being stifled."

Freud, who quotes the same story, remarks that it reflects the democratic direction of Jewish mentality which does not acknowledge any difference between master and servant and which regrettably also disturbs discipline. He sees in the anecdote the basic democratic Jewish attitude together with its shady sides. Berman remarks that the essential point of the story is in the "eternal truth" (a *contradictio in adjecto?*) that a Jew cannot have real respect for the other Jew and traces this attitude in the relationship of the Jews back to their common social situation.

There is another facet to that gem of an anecdote. But before we turn our attention to it, we would like to remind the reader that the attitude depicted in it has deeper roots than the contemporary social situation. I would like to make use here of a literary reminiscence. A long time before Freud and Schnitzler, the famous Viennese playwright Johann Nepomuk Nestroy (1801-1862) wrote a travesty on Hebbel's tragedy *Judith and Holofernes*. In one of the scenes of this parodistic comedy, Jewish soldiers are drilled within the walls of ancient Bethulia that is besieged by the Assyrian army. The sergeant orders: "Attention!" One recruit says: "What does he mean 'Attention'? Is he more than we? Is not one Jew equal to the other?"

The Gentile Nestroy, who was a good observer and knew many Viennese Jews of his time, certainly had no notion that this funny bit of dialogue refers to an old biblical view.

DESTRUCTION OF THE HERO-IDEAL

We deemed it important to show that Jewish wit follows certain tendencies in choosing its objects as well as in the mocking manner of dealing with that target. It seems to me to be significant that Jewish witticisms have a certain continuity and constancy, that they have essentially the same character throughout the centuries and that they are not limited by differences of social class or culture level. In other words, those tendencies are pervasive through different times and in different places. They penetrate the surface everywhere and permeate the various layers of Jewish societies. The same spirit in which the prophets of the Old Testament attacked the pagan gods continues to make fun of the Christian trinity in the jokes of the ghetto and in the words of the rabbi in Heine's poem *Disputation*.

Take one of the favorite targets of Jewish jokes: militarism. Here is a representative example. The recruit Isaac Katzenstein is asked by his officer: "Why should a soldier sacrifice his life for the Fatherland?" "You are quite right, Lieutenant! Why should he?" The Jewish soldier's answer is a rhetorical question. He conceives of it as if the officer had expressed the same doubt that prevails in the recruit. Fatherland or native country is a mythical abstraction to him and almost an absurd notion. A straight line leads from here to the Heine poem containing the line, "Lebenbleiben wie das Sterben für das Vaterland is süss" ("To remain alive as well as to die for the Fatherland is sweet.") In jokes of this kind not only the idea of patriotism is exposed in its ridiculousness, but also the notion of dying for such a phantom or illusion. A love of death, which Clemenceau once attributed to German militia, is here contrasted with a reverence of life which is to the Jew the greatest good.

Beside and beyond the questionable notion of patriotism, military discipline and soldiering are alien to Jewish mentality. Martial spirit appears to him as a special kind of madness and anyone who longs to be a soldier as an eccentric. Karl Kraus once remarked that it is meaningful that children play soldiers, but why do soldiers play children? Not only is the military profession alien to the Jew, but also the ideals to which the soldier clings seem ridiculous and chimerical.

More than one hundred years ago Friedrich Hebbel let Kandaules, King of Lydia, in *Gyges and His Ring* speak:

> Ich weiss gewiss, die Zeit wird einmal kommen,
> Wo alles denkt wie ich; was steckt denn auch
> In Schleiern, Kronen, oder rost'gen Schwertern,
> Das ewig wäre?

> I know for certain that the time will come
> When everybody will think as I:
> What's there in veils, crowns or rusty swords,
> That could be eternal?

Jewish jokes belong to that avant garde of thought that professes the same deep conviction.

Jews in general show little appreciation for military training and heroic deeds on the battlefield. This does not mean that these people are cowardly. Wherever and whenever they deem a idea worthy, they sacrifice their lives. Jews have fought with deathly determination not only in ancient times when they dared to battle with the great powers of the Middle East, but also in our time, when they fought the Nazis in the Warsaw Ghetto and the Egyptian Army in Suez. But their ideas or ideals were different from those maintained by modern states. The Jew, the eternal dissenter, is unable to share the belligerent ideals of the Gentiles. In the words of Lewis Carroll's *Lobster Quadrille* he "would not, could not, would not, could not join the dance."

Jewish jokes do not appreciate the honors bestowed upon the military profession, nor the high esteem in which deeds on the battlefield are held. When the German Emperor William I died, one of his generals, the eighty-year-old Marshal W. carried the Kaiser's sword on a cushion as he walked behind the coffin for several miles in the funeral procession. The Berlin Jews called that satisfaction that to officer derived from such honors "Goyim Naches," which means "pleasures of the Gentiles." (The corresponding French phrase: *"Le goy s'amuse."*)

All Jewish jokes of the period asserted that German Jews are equal with the Gentiles before the law, "only, God be thanked, they are not allowed to become officers." A few decades before the period of Jewish witticisms of this kind Heinrich Heine wrote "As in Madagascar only noblemen had the right to become butchers, Hanoverian nobility had previously an anologous privilege, since only noblemen could occupy the position of officer."

To show the pervasive dislike of the military ideas and spirit of the period let me only refer to a man who like Heine was a Jew from Germany and lived and worked like the poet in Paris: Jacques Offenbach. Let me remind the reader of that precious parody of the military spirit in *The Duchess of Gerolstein*. I still

hear the tune of that *"couplet du sabre"* and see the bombastic
General Boum, representing stupidity and valor:

> Voici le sabre de mon pere,
> Tu vas le mettre a ton coté
> Ton bras est fort, ton ame et fiere
> Ce glave sera bien porte. . . .

> Behold the sabre of my father,
> O take and bind it to thy side
> Your arm is strong, your spirit fiery,
> May it to victory soon attend you
> Soon, soon return with you in pride.

Heinrich Heine writing in the *Travel Pictures* (The Town of
Lucca) speaks of the contrast between his view and that of
Cervantes and contends that the "madness and the fixed ideas"
he, Heine, created out of these books are of an opposite kind to
the madness and fixed ideas of La Mancha: "He wished to reestablish the waning knighthood, I, on the contrary, wish wholly
to annihilate what has survived from that to me, and this from
totally different motives. My colleague mistook windmills for
giants. I, on the contrary, see only vociferous windmills in our
modern giants. He mistook a leather wine-skin for a crafty
wizard, and I see only a leather wine-skin in our modern wizards.
He mistook every beggar's inn for a castle, every donkey-driver
for a knight, every stable wench for a court lady. I, on the
contrary, look upon our castles as trumpery inns, our knights as
donkey-drivers, our court ladies as stable wenches. Just as he
mistook a puppet play for a state affair, so do I hold our state
actions to be a pitiful puppet play."

The Jew stands alone against a world of feudalism, of military
systems, and of a nobility born from that system. The Jewish wit
pokes fun at those values which seem to belong to another era.
Here is the anecdote of Rothschild into whose Frankfurt office
the Duc of Gramont comes. "Take a seat, Baron," says Rothschild

who is very busy. "I am the Duc of Gramont," remarks the indignant visitor. "Take another chair," says the banker.

In a passage of his *North Sea* Heine remarks that a love for hunting lies in one's blood. "When ancestors in ages beyond recollection killed stags, the descendant still finds pleasure in this legitimate occupation. But my ancestors did not belong to the hunters as much as to the hunted and the idea of attacking the descendants of those who were our comrades in misery goes against the grain." Here is a reference to dark race-memories as a source of inclinations and disinclinations.

Jewish jokes sometimes transgress the narrow boundaries of social criticism, directed against an arrogant feudal society, and are aiming higher at the "Weltanschauung" behind that system. There is, for instance, the story of the Jew who attends a performance of *Parsifal* at Bayreuth and turns in despair to his neighbor saying: "I cannot laugh!" This sounds like nonsense; no one would expect a viewer of that solemn opera to laugh as he follows the tragic events on the stage. He who can enjoy this joke must unconsciously share the view of the Jewish listener; he must also be tempted to conceive of the significant scenes of the tragedy as comic and to make fun of the heroes of the play as knights of the sorrowful countenance.

This joke will certainly find response not only among Jews. Nietzsche would have laughed out loud at it; perhaps also Emile Zola in spite of all *Souvenirs de Bayreuth.* Not only Jews will consider the Parsifal-mystery funny(20). (I once had a conversation with Freud who called the views of the Saxonian master, Wagner, expressions of typical puberty-idealism. Freud could appreciate only Wagner's *Meistersinger* and the *Siegfried Idyll.*)

Jewish wit considers the hero ideal as funny—in both meanings of the word—and does not appreciate the fame of knighthood. Yet, the Jewish story knows its own kind of glory.

THE HERE AND THE HEREAFTER

Once, many decades ago, when I spent my summer vacations
in Edlach in Austria, near the Semmering, I made the acquaintance of a physician who practiced there and had taken care of
Theodor Herzl in his last illness. The doctor, whose name I no
longer remember, was an excellent internist who had many non-
medical interests. At the time he was occupied with writing a
series of articles in which he tried to prove by a discussion of
textual evidence that Shakespeare must have suffered from
insomnia. I still remember some walks we took together during
which he elaborated his thesis. In one of these conversations he
arrived at a comparison of sleep and death from Hamlet's sol-
liloquy via a detour.

The physician contended that the idea of a hereafter was
alien to the Jews. I contradicted and pointed out that many
significant vestigial features of an ancient belief in life after
death are still to be found in Judaism. Such traces are, for
instance, the Kaddish prayer, the observance of the "Jahrzeit,"
the commemoration of dead relatives, the solemn putting up of
a tomb stone, etc. Some of those remnants can be traced as far
back as the time when the Hebrew tribes lived in ancient Egypt,
others are residual features of a primitive Semitic ancestor-
worship. In our conversation I pointed to the possibility that the
new religion of Yahwism had most ruthlessly suppressed the old
superstitions which were common to the Egyptians and to the
Hebrew tribes living for some centuries in the land of the
Nile(21).

The physician and I agreed that the Jews were of two minds
about the existence of a life beyond death, that an old superstitious belief in the hereafter was in conflict with a newer concept, that there is no continuation of individual life beyond the
grave. At the right moment the doctor remembered a Jewish
anecdote confirming this ambiguity. Old Schloime speaks to his
children who surround him before he dies: "My whole life I

endeavored to live according to the Law and deprived myself of most pleasures and had a poor and miserable existence. I was always hoping that I would be rewarded in the beyond. I would laugh if there were nothing in the beyond." This anecdote is in its wording characteristically Jewish since the content of the sentence should rather shake the person in his depths, and fill him with melancholy. As many Jewish stories it is not comic, but tragicomic in its protest against the great Unknown which always demands self-sacrifices and renunciations and offers only promises whose realization is very doubtful. The story expresses smilingly what a picture of Goya shows in bitter earnest. There is a skeleton coming from his grave. The inscription is a single word: "*Niente.*"

The Jewish joke energetically takes the side of rationality and enlightenment; its refuses to believe in the hereafter. It does not want to listen to the old renouncing song, to the "hush-a-by-baby" with which the poor people are lulled when they suffer on this small planet. Jewish wit does not acknowledge that there is a life beyond the very earthly and short existence here below. Heine often spells out the idea that our kingdom is restricted to this earth and foresees a future without any consolation in the beyond:

> Yes, green peas a-plenty for every man,
> As soon as the crop of them mellows,
> The heavens we shall gladly leave,
> To the angels and the sparrows.

Yet in spite of contrasting life here below, life to come, the poet sadly confesses that he would like to be remembered after death. ("Keine Messe wird man singen, keinen Kaddisch wird man sagen. . . ."). Together with the belief in a life hereafter he dismisses as superstitious the idea of resurrection:

> Doch mir ist bang, ja mir ist bang,
> Das Auferstehen wird nicht so rasch von statten gehen.

For I'm afraid, yes, I'm afraid,
That the Resurrection
Is not soon to be expected.

(The skeptical French have a saying: "*Si on est mort, c'est pour longtemps.*")

Many decades after Heine's death a French writer, Tristan Bernard, Jewish as was Heine, was asked what he thought about a life hereafter and answered, "With regard to the climate I would prefer heaven, but with regard to company I would give preference to hell."

Yet the Jewish composer Gustav Mahler created in that last movement of the Second Symphony a grandiose vision of the hereafter and of the resurrection of the dead.

MONEY

I.

There are very many Jewish jokes about money which refer to the irremediable and extreme poverty of the masses in East Europe. The preoccupation with money reflects itself in the abundance of Schnorrer stories, in witticisms about how the penniless Jews imagine the life of their few rich co-religionists, and their manipulations and tricks practiced to avoid payment of their debts, or the petty frauds they engaged in, of deceptions, swindles, and dishonesties among themselves—a merciless list of malpractices and deceits conditioned by their material misery.

Let me quote two rather mild instances. Lilienblatt waits for his train. There he sees Wendriner who has owed him, for a long time, two hundred marks. He does not want to press the debtor for payment, but wants to remind him of the money due in a delicate manner. He goes over to him, taps him on the shoulder and says amiably: "I'm pleased to see you, Wendriner. How is your wife, what's new with the kids?" Wendriner says: "Thus you speak, Mr. Lilienblatt, but do I get paid by anyone?"

One of the richer Jews shows his friend his new cottage and

orchard and declares: "I have insured all against fire, burglary and hail." The friend is astonished: "Fire and burglary, that I understand—but how do you produce hail?" Jewish wit does not spare those who are successful in escaping from financial worries and could secure for themselves a comfortable and even a luxurious life by a too smooth assimilation and by dubious financial procedures. I heard a man half-admiringly, half-mockingly, say about such Jewish upstarts: "From Poland to Polo in one generation!" All kinds of deception and cunning, of fraud and trickery, devised and committed by Jews, either to get money or to avoid paying money, are exposed and candidly revealed by Jewish jokes.

With such concentration on the theme of money-lender and debtor, on payment and debt, and with so many variations of the theme, one will be astonished to observe that a certain motif seems to be avoided, namely, the joke about the hard-hearted and cruel Jewish money-lender or usurer in his relation to the Gentiles, to the alien world of the West.

If there are Jewish jokes of this kind, they are few and far between. Such a void is the more conspicuous since, as we said before, most Jewish jokes about money matters relentlessly expose the unscrupulousness and lawlessness of many Jews in money dealings with the Gentiles and within their own community. The reason for this absence cannot be that there is a particularly careful treatment of the subject of Gentile borrower and Jewish lender.

There are several other good reasons why we should wonder about the lack of Jewish jokes of this kind. The first concerns the fact that there are many Jewish comical stories and jokes about collisions between Gentiles and Jews, among them some that concern business relations of various kinds. Secondly, there is no doubt that Jews, during the Middle Ages, were historically often occupied with money-lending and money-changing, with loans, promissory notes, actions for the recovery of debts, etc. Bankers and financiers are only the modern continuance of that lower form of profession in which many Jews in medieval times were engaged. No doubt, there were among them some who pitilessly collected money and rigidly enforced payment, by legal proceedings or illegal means.

Furthermore, there must also have been usurers among them, known as such in the ghetto and among their own people. Why, then are there no or almost no Jewish jokes about those lenders with relation to Gentiles, since there are so many witticisms about money-disbehavior among themselves?

When I wrote that usurers must have been known in the ghetto, I almost made a slip of the pen because I wanted to write "on the Rialto." This relates, of course, to Shakespeare's *Merchant of Venice*. Here I am coming to the last, but by no means least conspicuous fact that puzzles us. In literature—and not only in English literature—the figure of the unfeeling and merciless Jewish usurer who shows no human consideration towards the Gentile debtor is a familiar one, is, so to speak, a prototype of the Jew. His extreme callousness and repellent cruelty is exposed not only in the "Jew whom Shakespeare drew" but in many other figures. Why do such types or their continuations in modern time not occur in Jewish wit which is so unsparing and merciless in its criticism of Jewish faults and failings?

I would not even risk a guess about the reasons for that remarkable absence of this motif in Jewish wit, if I, and certainly other psychoanalysts before me, had not arrived at a certain conjecture founded on psychoanalytic insights in our clinical practice(22). In the unconscious imagination of the Gentiles, the Jew plays the part of the castrator since he circumcises his sons. Circumcision is, as we have learned, unconsciously conceived as a milder form of castration. There seems, superficially, a great distance from the figure of the castrating Jew to that of a cruel and relentless usurer who mercilessly enforces payment from his debtor, but this is not the case in the unconscious processes. Shylock's demand to cut a full pound of flesh from Antonio's body is an unconsciously displaced expression of the castration threat that menaces the Gentiles and makes the Jew such a terrible and terrifying figure.

There are certainly other psychological reasons for the

absence of Jewish jokes about the described type but I dare say that the main reason is to be found in this area. For the Jew the notion of himself as a castrator, an idea which plays such a great role in the unconscious imagination of the Gentiles, is not valid and does not affect him. Money may have another unconscious significance for him, but it is not connected with such notions as castration.

"What other significance?" one will ask. The discussion of those motives would lead us too far astray, but at least a hint is implied in a passage I will quote in the following paragraphs.

At this point I will boldly step out from the frame of my subject of Jewish wit and walk across to another, seemingly opposite, area, that of tragedy.

II

The Count of Charolais is a tragedy by Richard Beer-Hofmann, published in 1905, often performed in Austria and Germany, but almost unknown in America and not yet translated into English.

The scene of the play is the capital of Burgundy several centuries ago. The first act takes place in an inn. Preceding the scene from which I am going to quote, old general Charolais was shot on the day peace was made with the enemy's army but there will be no solemn funeral for the great man in the cathedral because he left great debts in order to feed, clothe and pay his soldiers. The council refuses to pay these debts of honor and according to an old law of that time, the creditors seize the body of the general and keep it in the debtors' prison until it is redeemed by prompt payment.

The young count of Charolais, who loved his father dearly and is plunged into desolate mourning, tries to do his utmost to secure last honors for his dead father, but he is penniless and no one helps him. The three creditors, a miller, a decorator and a Jew, are determined to keep the body until the debt is paid and ask the Red Itzig to be their speaker in the negotiations with the young count. The Jew knows that the two want him to speak for

them so that they may still be considered gentlemen and he is
to be the hard and wicked usurer, but he accepts their
suggestion.

The following will be fragments from the dialogue between
young Charolais and Red Itzig(23). The count softly tells the
Jew:

The others have agreed to follow you.
All then depends, on you and though you are
A Jew, you are as much a man as we, Itzig.

Itzig: A man? Like you? I never heard that yet!
All my life long you have never let me feel
That I am human. Must I be today
Because it suits your need? For the five minutes of your
convenience?

Today, I refuse,
I am a Jew! What want you of the Jew ?
For you want something with this courtesy!

Charolais: Give me my father's body—give it to me! My life
Hangs on it! I beseech you! Oh, believe me,
Begging's not easy for me,
Itzig!

Itzig: To command is a count's right; beg—that is my duty.
Well, then, my Lord, give me my money—give it to me!
My life hangs on it. Oh, not as you say
"My life," meaning you have an ache within.
If I am penniless, who will protect me
Against lords, courts and counts? With easy conscience
They'd have me slain. You see, in my case truly
My life depends upon it—yes my life.

Here is thus a historic and sociological reason why the Jew of
the past centuries hung on money with such obstinate and

breathless tenacy. It was not love for luxury and leisure, it was a life-saving expedient.

It will intensify the impression of this dialogue-fragment when we follow the conversation between the nobleman Charolais and the Jewish money-lender because the quoted passage is only a small part of the painting that unfolds itself. The young count asks Red Itzig to consider that he is enduring to see his father's body rot in a prison, the body of a man who made those debts so magnanimously for his country. He asks the Jew to think of that:

> Think not of us. Or, no, think rather this were you
> That pleads—and that the body were your father's.

Itzig says that he has been thinking that all this time. His father

> did not rot in prison, that is true.
> The city in which he was born gave him
> The most expensive of all funerals!
> Even before daybreak they marched forth
> Soldiers, societies, fraternities, in crowds,
> The entire clergy. It was most honorable
> For a mere Jew. His Majesty the king
> Himself was present, on the windy square
> With all his court—and all that for a Jew!
> And all the bells of all the churches peeled
> As the processions with their flags passed by
> My father; and there was great speech-making
> In Latin and Spanish, and all day
> They bore the heat of July in that square
> Just for my father's sake. When dark came on
> And night
>   *(with mock pride)*
>   the king with his own hand at last
> Did light the faggots round about the stake
> By which my father stood. And because that,
> Even that was honoring him not enough,

They did beg to intone their songs, and also,
Because he was a Jew—and to be honored,
They sang to him *our* everlasting psalms,
And in his honor praised the Lord, *our* God!
> *(with a distorted smile)*
I do not know how much of this he knew.
For by this time he had begun to burn,
First from below, and had begun to cry,
And kept on crying loud, terribly loud,
My father—oh, so loud—and my ears heard it:
Schma Jisroel!
> *(he wipes the sweat from his forehead)*
Do you still wish, my Lord,
That I think of my father, so that I
May pity you, because your father's body
Rots in a dungeon?

The young count says that what his father was to him, the Jew
can never understand. But Itzig, close to Charolais, speaks very
gently and confidently:

I can not? It is not so difficult—
And if it were? Do you think I am dull?
That I do understand I'll prove to you!
You mean that you had nothing in the world.
No brother. No one. And you do not look
Like one bent on wildways with wine and wenches
And since you are poor to boot and so have little
That brings delight, and also old enough
To understand. . .
Eh? Two days gone
There was one human being in this world.
Who had no hope or care, but you alone.
You could have done to him whatever you would,
It would not have subtracted from his love.
He would have begged, and gladly, for your sake.
He had one wish, one very modest one,

That you might live to close his eyes in death
And not he yours. Nightly he had one prayer—
That God might let him die ten thousand deaths
Rather than have aught ill befall his child.
And though you wander all the round of earth
And though you live to be a hundred—never
Not that love found again! Gone for all time . . .
Hope not! A friend? We know them. And a woman—
Is just a woman. Children—
    (he laughs bitterly)
Thus are our fathers; thus our mothers feel—
Doubtless it is the same among your people.
Well, have I understood you, my Lord Count?

Charolais: If you can feel all that, where is your feeling
For my deep woe?

Itzig: I feeling? And for you?
That my heart's feeling meet the very fate
Encountered by my money? I give you
My feeling—full weight, lovely, clean and clear—
Even as I gave my money? You will take it,
Even as you did my gold. And when I come
In order to require it back again
Then you will say, even as you did say
About my money: "Jew, I spit on it."

Now the count is frightened by the Jew who looks upon him
with an evil glance. "Go," he yells, "you are an evil, evil man!"

Itzig: "An evil man!" And why
Should I be kind to you? Give me one reason—
A single one! Or do you think I should
Be kind because all human beings should
Be kind unto each other? First, my Lord,
Tear out this heart contracted and convulsed
By the inflictions of a thousand wrongs;

Put out these eyes and give me other eyes
That are not wounded by too much of weeping.
Smooth out my back that's bent to crookedness
With bowing down in enforced humbleness;
And give me other feet unwearied
By the eternal wandering of exile;
Crash through my skull, tear out the brain beneath
So that I may forget and last of all,
Cut me these veins and let my blood run out
That nothing's left that was my father's or
My father's father or his own or his—
No drop of all that blood, of all that woe—
And when you have done all that, my Lord Count,
And I am still among the living—then
I'll speak with you righ humanly—I mean
As a good man should speak unto his brother!
—Till then let me be what to you I am
And should be though I were I know not what:
A Jew, a Jew, a common, vulgar Jew

I can still see the thin figure of Itzig, with red hair and beard, in his kaftan, still hear his raucous voice that rises, falls and becomes silent.

The Jews, that people of martyrs, have voiced very few lamentations and complaints. It is as if their lips, otherwise so articulate, are sealed when they should utter griefs and sorrows with which they have been overwhelmed during two thousand years.

Only once in a long while, as in the pleonastic episode of *The Count of Charolais* does their sadness and bitterness break out and burst in burning words. Only very rarely the pent-up emotions break through a mysterious blockade. The rest is silence.

THE SACRED DUTY OF CHARITY

In Eastern Jewish thinking charity would certainly be considered the highest virtue of that sacred triad. To contribute to general philanthropic causes as well as to the individual poor is conceived of as a religious duty. This care can rarely be connected with the adjective "tender"; it belongs to the public and published task of the rich or privileged.

It has often been said that the Jewish giver does not bestow benefits on the poor in giving him money, and his actions do not deserve the name of goodness or kindness. He simply fulfills his religious duty, and the beneficiary need not, in the strict sense of the word, be grateful to him. On the contrary, the donor owes some gratitude to the receiver because the beneficiary gave him an opportunity to attain high religious merit. This is the meaning of the countless anecdotes of the Schnorrers, of their grasping and insolence and of their claims on the donor of alms. These Schnorrers sometimes treat their benefactors as if the roles were reversed, as if they were doing them a favor in accepting money. There is the old anecdote of the beggar who is advised not to visit the rich man one day because he was in a bad mood. The beggar, full of indignation, says: "What do you mean, should I make him a present of the money? Does he give me anything?" There is yet another story of the Schnorrer who hears that his benefactor has gone on a journey to a health resort and bitterly remarks: "With my money he goes to a spa?"

It is no privilege, but almost a burden to be rich among poor Jews because their claims and demands become so persistent and exacting and are so imperatively and arrogantly presented that the benefactor becomes overwhelmed. Even the shocked pity that is stirred in him may sometimes suddenly turn into cruel refusal. In one of the stories the Schnorrer describes his utter poverty and the misery of his family in vivid colors to the millionaire. The rich man is profoundly shaken. He rings the bell for his butler and says to him, "Jean, throw this man out. He breaks my heart!"

The cynical attitude in these Jewish jokes is not always shown only by the beggar. It sometimes emerges surprisingly in the person who is irritatingly importuned by the Schnorrer. One Schnorrer complains to a rich man that he has not eaten for three days. The millionaire says: "Sometimes one has to force oneself."

THE HAVES AND THE HAVE-NOTS

All has not been said about the Jewish Schnorrer-jokes when one considers them exclusively as manifestations of rigid charity, as it is dictated by the Torah, the religious law. It is certainly true that giving alms to the poor is a sacred duty of the rich people who comply with the command of the Jewish faith, and that the insolence of the Schnorrer distorts it in such a way that it almost appears as if he bestowed a favor on the donor, as a self-evident and justified demand. Yet those Schnorrer-jokes can be looked at from other points of view; they proclaim that social justice must be executed and that its administration means that the division between the haves and the have-nots must be moderated—in the last analysis must be abolished as unjust and unjustifiable.

Jewish wit is on the one hand turned against the exaggerated or preposterous claims made on those who are richer than the beggar, and on the other hand it supports those demands as valid in the name of a better distribution of the good things in life. Echoes of the old ideas and ideals of the prophets reach the ear in those Schnorrer-witticisms. It is only one step from the ridiculous to the sublime.

In some of those jokes the contrast between the rich Jews and the poor is so poignant and accentuated that other concealed tendencies penetrate the surface. The rich banker Veilchenblum shows his friends the rooms of his new house. He opens the door of the large dining-room and says: "In this hall, eighty persons can, God forbid, have dinner." An the surface the anecdote certainly makes fun of the stingy fellow, but, as we look deeper we see reflected the continual, financial insecurity experienced also by rich Jews. I suspect there is a half-conscious or unconscious superstitious feeling in the rich. Perhaps he sees himself and his family in such beggar's state, he is perhaps dimly aware of the thin line of defense between himself and the Schnorrer and thinks: There, but for the Grace of God, go I.

The counterpart of this anecdote is the story of the Schnorrer who stands before the grandiose tombstone of Rothschild and says: "These people know how to live!" When you dig beneath the comical façade, you recognize the melancholy moral of the matter. Of what use is wealth? At the end we all return to the dust from whence we came. The sight of the impressive tombstone of Rothschild awakens not only the thought of the gracious living of rich people—that is merely the humorous façade of the story—but also the idea of the inevitable end of all mortal beings.

The inner obligation that demands that one share one's abundance with the less privileged finds its expression in a letter of the young Heine to his rich uncle Salomon in Hamburg. That banker had made a successful financial coup and generously let his nephew have a certain share of his windfall. Heine, thanking and praising his uncle, reminds him of a proverb: "One should not let a Jewish child watch someone eating a delicacy," which means, of course, one has to give the child a taste of it.

The poet also occasionally traced the not always generous behavior of his uncle Salomon further back than to childhood. He once attributed even the choice of his profession to prenatal influences. Contrasting his own mother with Salomon's, Heine said: "My mother always read poems with pleasure. She got a poet as her son. His mother liked to read tales of robbers; therefore her son became a banker."

A Jewish proverb, sometimes heard when I was a child, had the character of a malediction or imprecation. It said: "You shall be the wealthiest in your family." We children at first did not understand that it was quoted as if it were a curse. Was it not something devoutly to be wished to be the wealthiest of the family? Did it not provide an opportunity to support poor members of the family? We, ourselves children of a poor family, did not understand then that to be the wealthiest of a Jewish family means to be always worried about whether the means at one's disposal would be sufficient to help all poor relatives; and that one will not be permitted to enjoy one's wealth because of the constant awareness that there are poor relatives whom one must help. But that solidarity and that consciousness are not restricted to one's family nor to Jews; they do not permit national nor religious discrimination. In the end they embrace the family of man.

SIDEGLANCE

In old Vienna they told numerous comic anecdotes about Mrs. Pollack who came from the ghetto and whose husband became rich during the first World War. Mrs. Pollack belonged to the group of *nouvelle riches* who were eager to be seen in theatre and concert hall, but who could not conceal their lack of education. During the intermission she was asked if she liked the tragedy whose opening night she attended in the Vienna Burgtheater. She answered: "The play is beautiful, but it is not suitable for a première." A lady-friend of hers complained that she had to go to the *Marriage of Figaro* tomorrow. Mrs. Pollack said, "Can you not send them a telegram?"

The space at our disposal does not allow us to cast more than a sideglance at figures like Mrs. Pollack and at her generation typical of a too quick assimilation to Western civilization. Jewish witticisms also mock those *nouveau rich* in their ridiculous showiness and purse-proud manners. A recent New York story reports that a woman asked her friend where she has her diamonds cleaned when they get dirty. "At Tiffany's," was the answer. "I give them to Cartier's" says the first woman and turns to a third friend asking: "Where do you go with your diamonds for cleaning, Belle?" "Who knows about cleaning diamonds?" replies Belle, "I throw them away when they get dirty."

A separate group of Jewish jokes is founded on intentional or unintentional misunderstandings. Here is a example. A man stops an old Jew on Broadway and asks: "How do I get to Carnegie Hall?" The slow answer the Jew gives is: "You must practice constantly, young man." Another story of this kind. A man runs into a friend on the street and asks: "How are you, Joe? And what about that pain in your neck?" "She is playing bridge tonight." A joke is sometimes born as a slip of the tongue. An example: Mrs. Goldstein is in the lobby of a hotel and asks the man at the desk "Where is that lift goy again?"

THE RABBI AS A PATHETIC AND COMIC FIGURE

A rabbi was once, in the good or bad old days, not only the minister and spiritual leader of the congregation, but also the authority who arbitrated in all important civil affairs and family-crises. All this has changed and his position and function has been reduced. There are numerous examples of that social down-grading, for instance this complaint of a rabbi who is at a very small congregation: "First I was rabbi in Mannheim—there were Jews, but no money. Then I was rabbi in London—there was plenty of money, but no Jews. Now, in this congregation, there is neither money nor Jews." Another joke, also treating the financial question: "How much salary do you get?" a friend asks the rabbi of a small congregation. "Three florins in the week," answers the rabbi, and hastens to qualify his statement: "That means, three florins in that week in which I get anything." The rabbi became a pathetic and funny figure even when he occasionally joked himself. A rabbi tells an amusing anecdote in his sermon. All listeners laugh. Only one Jew remains entirely serious. "What's the matter with you?" asks his neighbor in the synagogue," Are you ill?" "God forbid. No. But I am a stranger in this congregation."

MISBEHAVIOR PATTERNS

Jewish wit pokes fun at a variety of the foibles and failures of the people, but the majority of these jokes concern the bad behavior of the Jews in public places, their lack of cleanliness, an

alleged avoidance of physical hygiene and of bathing. The theme
of lack of bodily cleanliness, often indifference to vermin, bugs
and lice, is added to the favorite subjects of Jewish wit in the
narrower sense.

Looking at this group of Jewish witticism you will seriously
doubt that cleanliness is next to godliness, for the people who
are mocked in them are the most pious, the orthodox Jews. But
this is not the point. Those jokes consider rather the Jews living
in the ghetto of Eastern Europe, in utter poverty, and packed
like sardines in a can. They are depicted not in their own surrounding, but in contrast with the Western civilization and its
demands of bodily cleanliness. In this confrontation which sometimes takes the form of a conflict, the Jews appear as backward
and dirty—"dirty Jew" was almost a colloquialism and contemptible. Often those poor people are portrayed as so uncul-
tured and uncultivated that they don't even know what the
others mean when they speak of bathing. Here are two examples
of such jokes. Teitelbaum asks for a room in a hotel. The man
at the desk says, "With bath?" Teitelbaum answers with indignation, "What do you mean? Am I a trout?" A gentleman asks his
neighbor at the table in a summer resort: "Did you take a bath
this morning?" Cohn is astonished: "Why? Is there one missing?"

Dr. Landman (in her book mentioned before) is inclined
to assume that the bathing jokes are originally not of Jewish
origin, but the product of anti-Semites. They were then taken
over and elaborated by the jeered Jew into self-mockery. (By
the way, why should they do that?—that's the rub or, rather, the
pit of the matter. Here the psychological problem emerges as
the most important aspect. Most writers avoid answering that
question, many don't even raise it, while some authors beg it.)

She points out that a total neglect of the human body was
already prevented by religious precepts which prescribe washing
of hands and baths at certain, frequent occasions. Indifference
to any physical care was introduced by early Christianity in the
rejection of the corporal and of the worldly. The Spanish inquisition considered the possession of a tub by newly baptized Jews

or Moslems as a sign of relapse and heresy, to be punished by death at the stake.

We approve of these arguments, but still consider the bath jokes as genuinely Jewish. We would argue that ritual purifications as prescribed by Judaism, as well as by Islam or Hinduism, do not exclude the possibility that the worshippers remain dirty. The historical argument, especially the reference to early Christianity, is not accurate. The mockery originated at a time when the ghetto-atmosphere was contrasted with the Western civilization that invaded the world of the orthodox Jew.

The point of all these jokes is just that the uncleanliness and the dirt of the ghetto-Jews is put into contradistinction with the habits of the external world, and even with the adopted conduct of emancipated Jewry. I believe that the comical effect of these jokes results just from that contrast and conflict intensified by the conservative and reactionary attitude of the ghetto Jews.

It is best to compare the repugnance and reluctance to the demands of cleanliness, order and hygienic measures with the attitudes of children who recoil from them and have to be educated to be clean and tidy.

The other day I heard that a little boy watched his grandmother dusting the pictures on the wall. "Why do you not do the same to me in the morning? Why do I have to be washed?" It is a similar spirit which lives in the Jewish jokes and one misses the essence of them if one overlooks that the decided resistance against the demands of cleanliness pressed by Western civilization, is similar to that voiced by children who do not want to be washed by mother. The ghetto Jews who lived on the fringes of Western civilization put up a fight against those hygienic regulations as if they threatened the continuation of the old order or of Jewish survival itself.

The misbehavior patterns Jewish wit attributes to the people are of various kinds. There is, for instance, informality, carelessness, ungraciousness at social occasions. I present as an example of such deplorable misbehavior the lack of table manners. Jewish wit describes, for instance, the difference between a

Jewish and a non-Jewish restaurant in a telling contrast. In a non-Jewish restaurant one sees people eating and hears them talking; in a Jewish restaurant one sees people talking and hears them eating.

By the way, in many jokes the impudence of the waiters in Jewish restaurants is illustrated. Here is an example. A guest calls the waiter, after he has been served, and says, "Look, what's wrong with this chicken you brought me? The one leg is much shorter than the other." The waiter replies: "Are you eating the chicken or dancing with it?"

Several sociological and psychological factors will be recognized as determining the origin and the retainment of these misbehavior patterns mocked at in Jewish jokes. Besides those which can be easily understood, there are others which are unconscious and almost entirely unnoticed. I do not doubt that a kind of rebellious defiance or bravado is also operating in many cases of this kind. This desperate obstinacy and continual opposition is, of course, directed against the hostile world surrounding the ghetto in the sense of Shakespeare's line, "Be Kent unmannerly, when Lear is crazy."

JEWISH MOTHERS

Men of all nations glorify their mothers in song and poetry, as do the Jews, but it is a rarity with other people that mothers are made the butt of jokes and of humorous mockery strangely mixed with affection.

It was not for the first time that I became aware of this characteristic of my people when I listened to the report of a middle-aged patient of mine. The man often reported how his mother behaved when he visited and ate dinner with her on Friday evening, how she compelled him to eat more and how she showed her possessiveness in many ways. She invariably told about the various complaints that troubled her. "Every illness she has not got, is rebbach" (gain), commented the son. It was obvious to him that these complaints were described solely to obtain his sympathy and to tie him more to herself. He had also visited his mother the evening before and had asked her how she felt and she had, to his surprise, "regretfully" replied: "Quite well."

When the son occasionally felt unwell she, as so many Jewish mothers, knew a cure-all: chicken soup. In her eyes this was the remedy for all ailments and illnesses from a cold to cancer, and from bronchitis to a broken leg.

There are other characteristic traits. Jewish jokes ascribe to mothers an inclination to stuff their children, and worry that their sons do not eat enough or not the right food. It is as if Jewish mothers tried to make the nutritional symbiosis of babyhood and with it the dependence of the children on them permanent. Their main solicitude is thus directed toward food. In what grotesque forms that concern expresses itself is shown in an anecdote which recently made the rounds in New York. A Jewish gangster walked into an ambush and received serious bullet wounds. With his last strength he climbed the stairs to his mother's apartment and rang the bell. "Mama!" he cried, when she opened the door. But she, unaware of the son's state, said: "Eat first, talk later."

I would like to add some lines here from Heinrich Heine's *A Winter's Tale*, written in 1844. They illustrate this tendency of Jewish mothers as a universal one. The poet traveled to Hamburg to see his mother after an absence of many years.

And when I came to my mother at home,
You could her knock down with a feather.
She shouted "My boy, my boy" and clapped her old hands
    together.
"My boy! It's all of thirteen years!
Let me look, are you fatter or thinner?
Thirteen years: You must be hungry for sure
Now, what would you like for dinner?"

In spite of the domineering attitude many Jewish mothers have towards their sons, they always recognize the privilege of the male and acknowledge his intellectual superiority. Their respect for education and learning as well as their pride in his accomplishment express themselves quite naively. There is the well-known anecdote of the desperate mother who frantically runs along the beach, her arms stretched out to the sea, yelling, "Help! Help! My son, the doctor, is drowning!" The words "My son, the doctor," are almost automatic. That is how the old Jewish woman always speaks of her son. The supreme confidence Jewish mothers have in their sons is beautifully illustrated in a Rothschild anecdote. Once a ghetto-neighbor came to the matriarch Gutele Rothschild. There were rumors of an impending war and the woman whose son had just reached military age was worried and anxiously asked Mrs. Rothschild if she had any news if there would be a war. "War? Nonsense!" said Gutele, "My boys won't let them."

Grotjahn points out that the Jewish mother is different from the Spartan mother, who expects her son to be a hero, whether he is dead or alive. The Jewish mother hopes for victory but accepts defeat, and her main concern is that the son is kept alive.

Another feature in the characterization of mothers in Jewish wit will become recognizable in the following example. A mother gave her son two neckties as a present. The son, who wants to show his appreciation, wears one at their next meeting. Noticing it, the mother says, "What's the matter? Don't you like the other one?"

Jewish mothers show the same unconditional love for their sons as the mothers of other people, yet they have some characteristic features of which the joke makes fun, for instance, their primitive nature, determined mostly by their lack of education. The contrast between this primitiveness and the sons' progressed state provides material for many jokes. In one of the delightful telephone conversations with mother, recorded by George Jessel(24), the son tells her that he is sitting with Wendell Wilkie ("No, mama, not Mendel—Wendell,") who talked about the four freedoms. Mother wants to know what he said about her neighbors upstairs, the Friedmans. The son tells her that he will browse around the art gallery this evening, and had to assure her that this is a respectable place. He promises her that he will bring Whistler's mother home for the living-room, but mother says there is no place there and Whistler's mother would have to sleep with George's sister. The son explains that it is a picture. When he tells her that he picked up a Rubens, she believes that he means Rubin, the delicatessen man. When she is told that Rubens is a painter, she would like to know how much he would charge to paint the kitchen.

As for the sons, the fact that they sometimes make fun of mothers' weaknesses and peculiarities, does not, of course, exclude their deep love for their mothers. It includes it. There is profound tenderness for them in the playful aggression. These jokes are never offensive, but only teasing and full of affectionate and protective compassion. It has been said that true love still loves the object in its shortcomings and weaknesses.

The memory of his own mother will have emerged in every reader. It is now also awakened in me. One of her sayings comes to mind: "Any cow can *become* a mother, but not every woman can *be* a mother."

FAMILYRITIS

When I was a young psychoanalyst Freud told me that one of his early patients was a middle-aged Jewish man from the lower East Side of New York. When Freud first explained to him that most of his neurotic conflicts had their roots in his relationship with his family, the patient was not as astonished as one would have expected. He said: "But I always knew that. We suffer all from mischpochitis." In using the Yiddish word mischpoche (= family) the man coined a new expression, comparable to diphteritis and similar names of illnesses, thus defining the origin and character of his emotional disturbance.

Considering the intimate and insolvable family ties of the Jews, one cannot help but wonder at the fact that they are so rarely subjects of Jewish wit. Perhaps the only exception are the relationships of mothers and children which are sometimes treated in a teasing rather than in a mocking manner. Let me insert here a supplementary story I recently heard. A young woman, who is a social worker, discusses some neurotic clients with her girl-friend and colleague. The old mother who is present at this conversation says to the daughter after the other girl has left: "I know what a mantel piece is. But what is a mantel case?" It is obvious that this story pokes fun of the lack of education manifested in the confusion of the notions of mantel and mental.

Yes, there is even a contrast vividly experienced between the relations with others and those with members of one's family, illustrated by Jewish proverbs. There is that saying: "Gott soll mich benschen; ich soll nicht brauchen Menschen" ("I wish God should bless so that I don't need people," i.e., to help me). Compare this saying with another: "Tie me by all four (limbs), but put me among mine own." This means, obviously, however helpless I am, if I am among members of my family, I know I will be taken care of.

The relationship between fathers and sons hardly ever becomes the subject of Jewish wit. It is as if it were avoided as far as jokes are concerned and as if this disinclination to deal with it in jest reflects the commandment, "Honor thy father and thy mother. . . ." Yet there are flashes of intuitive understanding of the character of this relationship as, for instance, in that proverbial saying that is bewildering at first blush and sounds paradoxical, but which is psychologically profound: "When the father gives to the son, both laugh, when the son gives to the father, both cry." But astonishing general insights such as this are very rarely expressed in jokes about one's family.

If one wants to find the genuine character of a phenomenon like that of Jewish wit, one is justified in exploring not only its peculiar features, but to compare it with similar phenomena and to point out what is missing in the one or the other. One will, for instance, thoughtfully notice that mockery at a crippled condition, physical affliction and ugliness as well as old age, with its many complaints, is amazingly rare as a subject of Jewish witticisms. Here is a psychological check for the jokes, a kind of roadblock in the way of wit. It seems to me that a similar restraint prevents Jews from ridiculing the members of their family, especially the parents. Jewish wit, otherwise without respect, halts here. This restraint has supreme significance. To honor one's parents is not only a religious command, but one of the necessary premises of Jewish survival.

When the Jewish pioneers who worked hard on the desolate soil were once asked, "Is it worthwhile to undergo all the hardships?" they answered, "We may not live so see the fruit of our labors, but our children will live to see them." And how beautiful is the reversal of that answer given by the boys and girls who recently went out to defend the Holy country against the enemy: "Well, we may not see the fruit of our labors, but our parents will." All other human relations are transitory and perishable. Parents prevail.

CURRENTS OF JUDAISM

With the changes brought about by the invasion of Western civilization into the ghetto, the attitude of its inhabitants towards their religion also underwent a radical transformation even to the extent of leaving the faith of their parents. The road often led from agnosticism to atheism with many stations between the point of departure to the point of arrival. Here are two representative samples of jokes reflecting that religious transformation. A Jew comes to an orthodox rabbi and asks him to pronounce his Berocha (benediction) upon the Jaguar car which he had recently bought. The orthodox rabbi refuses to give his blessings to a wild beast. The conservative rabbi whom the Jew then asks for his benediction declines because he refuses to give the Berocha to an automobile. The rabbi of the reform congregation who is finally approached says: "I know what a Jaguar is, but what is a Berocha?" In jokes of this kind the insight emerges that loosening of the ties with the rigidity of the Law inevitably leads to giving up the faith itself.

There is a second story which has the same target and which proves that progress sometimes tends to overshoot its mark. A number of Jews debate whose synagogue is the most progressive. One of them says that in his temple an ashtray is kept near the

Torah so that those who pray can continue to smoke. The
second man says: "We are much more progressive. At Yom
Kippur we serve sandwiches—ham sandwiches, that it." The
third Jew claims: "We are so progressive that we are closed on
the Holy Days." As Martin Grotjahn, from whom I borrowed
this example, remarks, this sweeping statement "neatly finishes
Judaism." There are, as already mentioned, all kinds of transi-
tions from one extreme to the other.

Many Jewish jokes are directed against Reform-Judaism.
An older one has it that a Jew from a distant community came
to the reform rabbi Aaron Chorin, in Arad, Hungary, and declared that he wished to put God on trial because he felt
wronged by Him. The rabbi asked, "Is there no rabbi in your
congregation so that you have to come to me?" "Of course," is
the answer, "We have a rabbi, but he is a very pious and God-
fearing man and he would not dare to bring an action against
God. But you are not afraid of God, therefore I came to you."
That's certainly witty although perhaps we cannot enjoy any
longer the joke as much as the Jewish generation before us. The
point is, of course, directed against the reformatory movement
in the transition-phase.

The allusion to God-fearing is the heart of the story which
attacks the Reform-Jews who are unaware that God to whom
they still pray, got lost. They are contrasted with the Orthodox
Jews who faithfully observe the old religious laws and who fear
God. They fear Him still even when they are inclined sometimes
to protest against Him as once Job did. They remain faithful to
Him even when they feel deserted by Him, and implore Him for
His help, even when they claim that He is not kind to them.
Thus, the sigh of a Jew: "God, help me! You take pity on total
strangers. Why don't you have compassion with me?" Only the
enduring family-ties with God, experienced by this Jew, dif-
ferentiates his pious ejaculation from the reproach that Saint
Theresa of Aquila flung at the Almighty: "You have few friends
because you treat them so badly."

It is not more than a short cultural phase that marks the

distance of young Heinrich Heine from Reform-Judaism which he so often mocked because it saddened him. His attitude during the last years of his life is still closer to the loyal Jews than to the agnostics. Then the poor martyr of the rue d'Amsterdam expressed the wish to put God on trial just as the Jew in the story. The paralyzed poet, tortured by permanent pains declared that he wanted to accuse God of cruelty to animals. When the priest admonished him before his death that he should repent, and God would pardon him, Heine protested with the words: "*Certainement il me pardonnera; c'est son metier.*"

At this point, I will surrender to the temptation to repeat a witticism I recently made. Properly speaking, I did not make the joke; it took me by surprise. I am generally not witty, but the occasion was inviting enough to risk a joking remark. I was invited to dinner by a psychiatrist last September. Only one other guest was present at the informal meal besides myself, an old lady who was a frequent visitor of the family. After dinner we engaged in casual conversation. I cannot remember any more how we arrived at the subject of the Jewish New Year (Rosh-Ha-Shana) which had been observed a few weeks ago. The old lady who was of Irish Catholic descent told us an amusing story of a Jewish acquaintance of hers whom she had known for many years. The old gentleman sent her a greeting card every year at Rosh-Ha-Shana and she always courteously thanked him. It so happened that this year he had run into her as she left her church where she had attended mass a few days after the Jewish New Year. The gentleman, it seems, had been entirely unaware that she was Gentile, and was visibly embarrassed at the encounter, but she tried her best to put him at his ease. "After all," she said, "we all believe in one God." At this point, I was surprised to hear myself say: "At most . . ." "You horrible atheist!", the old lady said, and playfully slapped my arm.

In retrospect it seems to me that I continued the tradition of the infidel Jew in that joke, assuming that the one God is as close as possible to the absence of any deity.

DIFFICULT TO BAPTIZE

One of the favorite subjects of Jewish witticism is the conversion to Christianity and its symbolic rite, baptism. It appears to the Jews utterly incredible that this sacrament should perform the miracle of a radical change. But Jewish wit, directed at this transformation, has more than one arrow on its bow. In the first place, it denies the possibility of a change of this kind and asserts: Once a Jew, always a Jew. The story is told in New York of the banker Otto Kahn and the humorist Marshall P. Wilder who was a hunchback. Strolling along Fifth Avenue. Kahn pointed to a church and said: "Marshall, that's the church I belong to. Did you know that I once was a Jew?" Wilder answered: "Yes, Otto, and once I was a hunchback." The conviction that there is an unalterability about being Jewish is expressed better in this dry sentence than in many treatises. It seems that it is as difficult for the Jew to get rid of his Jewishness as it is for the ancient mariner to lose the albatross.

The time in which baptism was in Heine's words the "entrance ticket to European civilization" is passed. Even then those who became Christians did not deny that turning to Catholicism was done to secure certain advantages. Heine himself remarked, *"Paris vaut bien une messe"* and said, "The few drops of baptismal water dry up quickly." He never tired of making fun of his own and other people's conversion. In a letter (September 26, 1829) he wrote about Moritz Oppenheimer, Salomon Heine's eldest son-in-law: "I do not love him though as a Christian I ought to love my enemies; I am still too young a beginner in Christian love. But Moritz Oppenheimer is an older Christian and should love me . . ."

Very few Jews stated that they turned to Christianity out of conviction and even fewer Jews believed them (an idiom says "Tell that to a Goy!") The remarks of Heine, quoted before, are in the same vein as the words of a very poor client who said to his recently converted lawyer: "I do not know if I should still appeal to your soft Jewish heart or already to your Christian love for your neighbor." There is the story of Mrs. Spiro who, when recognized that the Catholic suitor of her daughter was a son of old Mr. Cohn, said: "I am very happy. I have always wished to have a son-in-law who is a nice young Christian man from a good Jewish family." In the twilight zone of assimilated Jewry the boundaries seem to vanish. Little Ilse Kohn asks her mother: "Mammy, do the Gentiles have Christmas trees too?"

Occasionally a Jew who is eager to receive the sacrament of baptism has to take a nasty rebuff as Dr. Eisenstein who consulted a Christian colleague: "Tell me, please, what do you wear when you are baptized?" The colleague scratches his head, "Well, that's difficult. We wore diapers."

On the other hand, many people who tried to convert Jews to Christianity saw their argument rebutted. More than two hundred years ago a priest called Teller tried his best to convert the famous philosopher Moses Mendelssohn to Christianity. In a humorous allusion to commercial practices of the time in which the son was given credit when his father was still alive in the expectation that the son would pay from the inheritance, Teller wrote Mendelssohn the following verses;

An Gott der Vater glaubt Ihr schon,
So glaubt doch auch an Seinen Sohn,
Ihr pflegt doch sonst bei Vater's Leben
Dem Sohne gern Kredit zu geben.

Perhaps this may be translated as follows:

In god the father you already believe
Thus believe also in the Son,
You are otherwise in the habit
To extend credit to the son while the father is still alive.

Mendelssohn's reply is certainly witty:

Wie koennten wir Kredit ihm geben?
Der Vater wird ja ewig leben.

How could we extend credit to the son
When the father will live eternally?

Moritz Saphir, the Viennese journalist, was born in 1795 as
a Jew, then became a Catholic, and finally a Protestant. Asked
about this astonishing change of faith he gave the following
reason: "When I was a Jew, God could see me, but I could not
see Him (alluding to the incorporeality of Yahweh), then I
became a Catholic and I could see Him, but He could not see
me (meaning the sculptures and pictures of Christ). Now I am
a Protestant and I don't see Him nor He me." In this way he
got rid of any notion of God altogether.

THE MESSIAH

Judaism does not recognize any individual salvation, but
only the salvation of all people, of the messianic time. The
thought of redemption was not alien to Judaism, but concerned
the future in which the wolf would lie down beside the lamb.
The worldly reality remained and should not be despised. The
mysticism of Jewish eschatology also knew an answer to the
question of why they all had to suffer again, the Jews more than
the others. The imminent arrival of the Messiah announces itself
by increased misery and darkness. The coming of the Messiah is
preceded by more bloody injury and depravity, by the "labors
of the Messiah" (Pawle Meschiach in Hebrew). This idea corresponds entirely to the suspense-factor in social or psychic
masochism of the individual as I presented it in *Masochism in
Modern Man.*

How is it to be explained that the coming of the Messiah,
the greatest eschatological idea of Judaism, became a subject of
doubt and even of witticism? It is easy enough to say that the
sense of reality as well as the permanent scepticism contradicted such a mysterious notion. Yet this answer does not reach
to the depth of the question.

Zionism was also a favorite theme of Jewish witticism; yet
it became at least a temporary reality. The argument that the

Messianic idea is roseately and chimerically utopian is not powerful enough to explain why, even within the Jewish ghetto, the idea was treated facetiously. Something at the core of this idea was rejected by the Jews.

Here are a few jokes—examples of this rejection. "Imagine, Chaim," the rabbi says, "the Messiah will soon come." "God forbid! All my relatives would then be resurrected and all would want to live with me!" Another dialogue: "People are saying that the Messiah will come soon. You know, I don't relish that at all. We would have to leave all and go to Israel then. Now, when we finally have a pretty little house." "Don't worry, Moische, God has saved you from Pharaoh, he has protected us from Haman—he will guard us from the Messiah too."

Even the gloomy and atrocious era before the arrival of the Messiah was jokingly seen. A Jew said: "All earmarks of the messianic time are already here: the regime of insolence and brutality—only the ass on which the Messiah shall ride on is missing since all asses have in the meantime become Jewish political leaders."

Enough examples! The Messiah-idea can never become victorious within Judaism as long as it keeps its integrity because the notion contradicts the spirit of Mosaic faith. The Messiah-figure is essentially a special form of a divine son of the deity, of a figure similar to that of Jesus of Nazareth. Once, before the radical religious and social reforms of Moses, in the prehistoric phase before Jahwism, the Hebrew tribes worshipped a similar son-god, equal to Attis, Adonis and Osiris of the neighboring people. Moses, and with him, though reluctantly, the Hebrew tribes rejected the divine son-figure and banned it in the unconscious netherworld until it returned from there in the shape of the Savior. Judaism had become a pure father-religion and has remained so until now. The late notion of the Messiah who will come as the redeemer, not only of Israel, was a breakthrough of the suppressed form of the divine son-figure. As such it was destined to perish, or, what amounts almost to the same, to be postponed into infinity. The notion was short-lived within Judaism and was nipped in the bud.

It is perhaps appropriate to bring these remarks to a face-tious conclusion quoting a recent joke: an Israeli campaigning against Prime Minister Ben Gurion in the elections said: "The difference between the Messiah and Ben Gurion is that the Messiah refuses to come and Ben Gurion refuses to go."

ZIONISM

In a scene of Schnitzler's novel *The Way to the Open,* mentioned earlier, several characters engage in a lively debate on Zionism. The writer, Heinrich Berman, argues with his younger friend, Leo Ehrenberg, who is a passionate follower of Theodor Herzl. To Heinrich, Zionism appears as "the worst affliction that had ever burst upon the Jews." National feelings and religion had always been words which had embittered him with their malignant ambiguity. The notion of fatherland is a fiction, a political idea floating in the air, changeable, intangible. Only the home, not the fatherland has any real significance. Heinrich is quoted as saying that so far as religion was concerned, he liked the Christian and Jewish religion quite as much as Greek and Indian; but as soon as they began to force their dogma upon him he found them equally intolerable and repulsive.

The consciousness of a persecution which all Jews suffered, and of a hatred whose burden fell upon them all, did not link him to men from whom he felt himself far distant. He did not mind recognizing Zionism as a moral principle and as a social movement, but the idea of the foundation of a Jewish state on a religious and national basis struck him as a nonsensical defiance of the "whole spirit of historical evolution." Confronting his Zionistic friend Leo, he asks: "What is your home country, Palestine? A geographical idea. What does the faith of your fathers mean to you? A collection of customs which you have now ceased to observe and some of which seem as ridiculous and in as bad taste to you, as they do to me."

One would think that this is, at least in part as well, Schnitzler's personal view. There is a story that Theodor Herzl once asked Schnitzler to go to Palestine. There the writer would take roots. Schnitzler answered: "What do I need roots for? I have wings."

How does Jewish wit deal with Zionism? The answer is, of course, in various ways. In olden days Zionism was defined as the occasion when one Jew delegates another to collect money from a third in order to send a fourth Jew to Palestine.

There was also the teasing remark of a Berlin Jew that he would like to become ambassador of the new Jewish state in Berlin.

In a recent work, Salcia Landman, an otherwise perceptive observer, contends that the Israeli himself scarcely produces new and original wit(25). She asserts that the Israeli has no wit because he has no use for it. I translate the following passage: "When one attacks the Jews in Israel, he can defend himself instead of the wit again with the weapons, exactly as his ancestors did in Biblical times. The new Israel is therefore witless like the Bible."

But is this true? There are jokes to be found in the Bible, as there is, no doubt, wit in new Israel. Jewish witticisms will perhaps live as long as Israel exists as a separate national or religious group. They are evanescent and ephemeral beings like fireflies and certain flowers, but they are vivid and alive and we enjoy their hustle and bustle even if it lasts only a moment. Jewish wit is an original and surprising statement on life, mostly on Jewish life, but it often opens up wider horizons.

Never contradict a lady, but I utterly disagree with Mrs. Landman who speaks of the "death" of Jewish wit and does not believe that there is a creative production of jokes in the new state of Israel. The changed social and national circumstances will bring about a transformation of the jokes, but the sparks still glow and grow. Here is an example of Jewish wit in Palestine from the time that saw a vast influx of immigrants from Europe(26). A bus running quickly, winds around the hills on its way from Jerusalem to Tel Aviv. A passenger becomes increasingly nauseated. A fellow passenger asks: "May I help? I am a physician." The bus driver stops the car and offers his help. He is also a physician. The sick passenger groans and says: "Leave me alone! I am a doctor myself." The anecdote humorously illustrates the situation about 1930 in Palestine where more than a thousand non-practicing physicians lived. Here is a story from the time when the import of all household utensils of immigrants into the new state of Israel was still exempt from duty. Refrigerators were then still difficult to get in the country and could therefore be sold for much money. An immigrant arrived with wife, children and seven refrigerators. The customhouse officer lets only one refrigerator pass without duty and says, "You need only one." "No," protests the immigrant, "I need one for milk-dishes, one for meat and another for what is neither milk nor meat." "Well, that makes three, but what about the other four?" asks the suspicious officer. "You did not think of Pessach?", replies the indignant immigrant. "Must I not put all dishes and plates away somewhere?" "Well," concedes the officer, "that amounts to three refrigerators, at the most four. What is the seventh one for?" "What for?" says the immigrant astonished. "What for? Is it not allowed to eat a little ham sometimes?"

Here is a newer Jewish story: Joseph Stalin, Harry Truman and Chaim Weizmann discussed the complexity of their respective jobs. Stalin pointed out that there were two million Communist party members, which made his job very difficult. Truman said, "There are 150 million people in the United States and I am responsible to every one of them." "Your job is easy, compared with mine," Weizmann smilingly remarked, "Do you know what it means to be president of one million presidents?"

In a recent anecdote from contemporary Israel, the question is raised why Ben Gurion did not want to be proclaimed king of the country. The answer is; because he did not relish the idea of being called King David II. Jewish wit did not die with the annihilation of the Russian and Polish ghetto. It continues to live in Europe, America and Israel(27).

LOVE

I

It is doubtful that love descends from the gypsies as Bizet's *Carmen* asserts, but it is almost certain that it did not originate in the Jewish quarters. (Yet the theme of romantic love must have sometimes sounded in the ghetto. Where did I hear the song of a young girl?

> I'll run through all streets
> And I'll cry: "Washing linen, sheets!"
> If I can only be with you
> If I can only be with you.)

No, love or romance had no place in the Judengasse. Meeting and mating was the Schadchen's (go-between, matchmaker) doing. Freud has analyzed many of those tales in his book on wit and has shown us that not the lies and the insolence, not the phantastic exaggerations of those poor devils who attack such a thankless job are the subject of those witticisms. The real meaning of the Schadchen jokes is a moral one. The profound sense of those comic tales which all have a similar structure becomes clear when, at the end, the Schadchen admits the truth, or rather when he is taken by surprise telling the truth that he had so carefully distorted or concealed. Reality will out. Man is not made to keep something secret; the hidden oozes out from all his pores.

Yet the deeper meaning of the Schadchen-jokes is the insight that it is really not important for marital life that the partner whom the Schadchen praisingly suggests has weaknesses and failings. Only a sentimental song can assert "I married an angel." No one does. You and I married a woman, which means a human being with failings and foibles, with faults and frailties. The Schadchen finally gives the truth away, lets the cat out of the bag. But that is only the comic side of the story. The other

side is the serious consideration that love and beauty are not
the main things in marriage. A marriage can be quite happy—
if a marriage can be happy—when wife and husband are not in
love. The view of the Schadchen is thus a realistic one. He
knows love is transient and beauty evanescent. He knows: Love
makes time pass, time makes love pass.

Perhaps the best Schadchen jokes do not spring from the
time of the old ghetto, but from the transition period which
saw the inevitable change under the influence of incipient emancipation. Life in the old ghetto was controlled by the spirit of
the strict traditional religion that pervaded not only cult and
service, but all secular activities. The Talmud and the Schul-
chan Aruch regulated the activities of family life and
even sexual intercourse. When the modern spirit of enlightenment began to enter the narrow districts of the ghetto, it also
affected the institution of the Schadchen and many of the jokes
concerning those Jewish matchmakers malevolently criticize not
only their manners, but even their very jobs.

For the men and women of the ghetto, early marriages and
propagation were a moral and religious demand, resulting from
the patriarchal injunction to the Jews to multiply. Within this
framework the choice of an individual mate or of an individual
sexual object had only a secondary importance, if it had any.
The new freedom in that transition-phase not only loosened
the traditional norm, but also brought about a general relaxation
of sexual morals. Marital fidelity, especially for women, had
been a foregone conclusion. A joke like the following would
have been almost inconceivable in the old ghetto: the wife of
the rabbi leans out of the window and one of her husband's
students (in Yiddish, a Bocher) uses the opportunity to slap
her behind as a crude sexual invitation. The woman turns
around and violently abuses him. "You don't want to?" asks the
Bocher. "Who speaks of not wanting? It is only the Chuzpe
(insolence)."

Before that period it would have been equally impossible to
find a variation of the Schadchen jokes like the following story:
a young man for whom the Schadchen had arranged a marriage

insists on it that he has to see the girl nude before he makes the final decision. The objections of the girl are at last overcome and she appears before him stark naked. The young man says: "I don't like her nose."

In that transition-period monogamy itself becomes an object of witty attack and the tendency of men towards variety and promiscuity in sexual relations begins to manifest itself. "How is your wife?" a man is asked. "Mir gesagt," he answers. ("Mir gesagt" is a Jewish magical formula, perhaps translatable as "I wish it could be said about me.") "How come?" asks the other man, and his partner explains, "You know, she has every week a new maid." (By the way, that very formula has been wittily varied. In a scene written by the Viennese satirist Karl Kraus, two men encounter a very pretty girl: "Unter mir gesagt" murmurs one of them—"I wish it could be said that I have her undernearth me." The witty effect is here intensified by the changed meaning of a Jewish colloquialism.)

In the poems of Heinrich Heine, whose ancestors still lived in the ghetto, promiscuity of the male is already self-evident. There is no trace of a transition any longer: the circle has come full around. Modern Jewish writers again and again contrast married life and free sexual relations. The Viennese writer Alfred Polgar once described the paradoxical arithmetic determining the relations of man to woman in the witty epigram, "Many are too little, and one is too much." Another Viennese writer, looking at this problem from the sexual viewpoint, arrived at the daring comparison: "A wife is like an umbrella; one finally takes a bus." (Bus = Omnibus, a Latin word meaning "For all." In this context, of course, a woman for all, i.e. a prostitute.) Karl Kraus described the train of thought of a Viennese woman in these terms: "To sleep with him, yes—but no intimacy whatsoever."

But let's return to love which was not considered a necessary condition to marriage within the ghetto and which became so highly valued in the period of emancipation. Even in that transition-phase the old generation had the conception that love is to be found only in novels and plays. When I was a boy in Vienna, they told the following story: A son declared to his old man

that he wanted to marry Miss Sarah Federleicht with whom he
had fallen in love. The father showed little sympathy and asked:
"What do you mean, you have fallen in love with her? Are you
Sonnenthal?" (Adolf von Sonnenthal, 1834-1909, was the famous
actor who had the leading lovers' parts in the Vienna Burgtheater.)

II

Only at the turn of this century a new theme evolved in the
novels and plays of Jewish writers—the intimate connection between love and death. You will find it a pervasive idea in the
early works of Hofmansthal and Beer-Hofman, but it became a
dominant motif of the novels and dramas of Arthur Schnitz-
ler(28).

After a long interval I re-read *The Way to the Open* by
Schnitzler. Many parts of this novel affect us today as if they
were period pieces, but others are as actual as if they were
written today. At a certain passage in the novel memories in-
truded. One had the impression of hearing the very voice of the
author. I believed for a split second that I was looking once
again into his serious steel-blue eyes and hearing the voice
whose timbre I had liked so much. I remember the first time I
visited him in his beautiful house in the Sternwartestrasse, and
the many conversations we had later on. We met again on the
Semmering, the summer resort near Vienna, a few weeks before
his death. Our conversation had taken a detour over some
psychological topics, and arrived at the problem of death, as so
often before. "No," he said, standing still, "you are mistaken.
One's own death is, nevertheless, imaginable. Yet when we try
to see ourselves dead, we don't see ourselves, but a puppet
lying there."

Suddenly Schnitzler's puppet show *Zum Grossen Wurstl*
comes to mind, the marionette show (the Dutch call it very
nicely "poppenkast") in which Death appears as the last puppet
and makes fun of himself. The last masks drop; the end is a
great *demasqué*. What appeared as a tragic and sinister figure

sometimes assumes a comical aspect in Schnitzler's work. The shadow of death that was cast on this poet's writing, could occasionally jump in grotesque leaps.

It is unmistakable that love and death present themselves to Schnitzler as a single problem, that death bends over every copulating couple. Even in humorous scenes death appears as matchmaker at the door of a bedroom. In *Reigen,* in a bachelor's apartment in the Vienna Schwindgasse there is a transient sexual scene between a married woman and a young man. You hear the following fragment of a dialogue when the woman keeps away the hands of the man which threaten to go astray.

> "The young man: 'Life is so short.'
> The young woman: 'But that's no reason . . .'
> The young man: 'Yes, it is. . . . ' "

Even in the mild dullness of this young man of the Viennese *jeunesse dorée* the elementary power of sexuality makes capital out of the closeness of death. Even over this comical dance macabre Eros and Thanathos form a great arch. The two themes of love and death re-occur in renewed variations and significant elaborations, again and again, and are contrasted and intertwined.

The Way to the Open deals to a great extent with the Jewish problem and most of the figures of the novel are Jewish writers, physicians and politicians. In one of its scenes an older writer who had once been very successful and has now, blasé and disillusioned, withdrawn in retreat, is surrounded by younger ambitious authors. One of them asks him: "By the way, Nuernberger, do you still believe in death? About love I won't even ask any more."

As only few other writers of our age, Arthur Schnitzler, who could thus joke at his ultimate problems, knew that all our thinking and acting is determined by those two opposite drives: by the desire to be loved and the fear of dying.

Some Remarks on Sarcasm

A scholar remarked(29) that the laughter of the Bible "is nearly always an expression of scorn and not of mirth." A recent inquirer, Dr. S. Landmann, contends that the oldest Jewish document—the Bible—contains some amusing stories, but scarcely any wit. She points out that the prophets reject and condemn the scoffer. Yet that did not prevent them from speaking in the most scoffing terms of the gods of their neighbors and from mocking in the most sarcastic manner. Think of Elias' advice to the pagans, of Amos (3/7), of Hosea and Isaiah. There is no more biting sarcasm in the literature of the ancient world. Job's words to his supposed comforters are sometimes full of bitter jeering ("You are the people and wisdom shall die with you").

This particular sarcastic tone also marks a certain type of Jewish wit of later times. To prove its constancy and continuity, we leap across a span of three thousand years and find that sarcastic character again, for instance, in the following scene before the judge who asks the witness: "What's your name?" The answer is: "Menachem Jomtef." Next question: "What is your profession?" "I am a dealer in second-hand clothes." "Your domicile?" "Rzcezow." "Your religious creed?" "I am called Menachem Jomtef, I am an old clothes-man, I live in Rzcezow— I am perhaps an Hussite?"

But let us change the milieu as well as the language in a most decisive manner. We are moving into England, Great Britain of more than one hundred years ago and into the highly respectable atmosphere of the House of Commons. The language we will hear here is very remote from Yiddish jargon, it is the cultured and careful diction of parliamentary discussion(30). The situation that confronts us at about the year 1843 is the following: Sir Robert Peel, who had fought his predecessor Cunnings, dominated the House of Commons after George Cunnings' death. Young Disraeli, who belonged to Peel's party, once appealed to the minister and asked him to see in his remarks not criticism, but amicable frankness. Sir Robert Peel turned disdainfully to Disraeli and quoted some lines by the Hon. George Cunnings:

> Give me the avowed, the erect, the manly foe
> Bold I can meet, perhaps may turn the blow;
> But of all plagues, good Heaven, Thy wrath can send
> Save, save, o save me from the candid friend!

Peel's quotation was not a very happy one, as he had played the role of the treacherous friend in Cunnings' life. Disraeli made no reply, but a few days later he rose again to protest Peel's system. In a gentle, almost monotonous voice Disraeli carefully prepared his attack: "If the Right Honorable Gentleman may find it sometimes convenient to reproach a supporter on his right flank, perhaps we deserve it. I for one am quite prepared to bow to the rod; but really, if the Right Honorable Gentleman instead of having recourse to obliquity, would only stick to quotation, he may rely on it it would be a safer weapon. It is one he always wields with the hand of a master and when he does appeal to any authority in prose or verse, he is sure to be successful, partly because he never quotes a passage that has not previously received the meed of Parliament, and partly and principally because his quotations are so happy. The Right Honorable Gentleman knows what the introduction of a great name does in debate—how important in its effects, and, occasionally how electrical. He never refers to any author who is not great, and sometimes who is not loved—Cunnings for example. That is a name never to be mentioned, I am sure, in the House of Commons without emotion. We all admire his genius. We all, at least most of us, deplore his untimely end, and we all sympathize with him in his fierce struggle with supreme prejudice and sublime mediocrity—with inveterate foes and with candid friends. Some line for example, upon friendship, written by Mr. Cunnings, and quoted by the Right Honorable Gentleman! The theme, the poet, the speaker—what a felicitous combination! Its effect, in debate, must be overwhelming; and, I am

sure, if it were addressed to me, all that would remain would
be for me thus publicly to congratulate the Right Honorable
Gentleman not only on his ready memory, but on his courageous
conscience."

One can understand the tremendous effect this speech had
upon the House. The venomous darts were shot with deadly
certainty. Slowly presented in a soft voice, from the beginning
with feigned humility to its climax in that sentence "The theme,
the poet, the speaker—what felicitous combination!"—here is a
masterpiece of sarcastic aggression. The words are daggers, accompanied by a bow. The effect upon Peel was indeed deadly.

At his farm in Bradenham, Disraeli's old, blind father, Isaac
d'Israeli, seated at his wife Sarah's side, kept repeating, "The
theme, the poet, the speaker."

It is not accidental that those outbreaks of sarcasm are reactions against affronts and insults from an authority. They are
expressions of a fierce vindictiveness. More than two hundred
years before Disraeli's speech, Shylock reacts against the out-
rages of the unnoble nobleman of Venice in the same sarcastic
manner when he asks whether a dog can have money and
whether a dog can loan three thousand ducats. Shylock himself answers when asked of what use a pound of human flesh
would be: "To bait fish withal; if it will feed nothing else, it will
feed my revenge." (*The Merchant of Venice III*).

One can speak of "friendly irony." The expression "friendly
sarcasm" is not possible, since sarcasm is cutting and biting and
goes to the extremity of elementary drives. It is not less primitive
in character when it appears in verbal form. It is deadly also in
words. The very name sarcasm is derived from a Greek word
which means to lacerate or mangle. Ridicule also kills.

THE SPIRIT OF SCEPTICISM

I

The other day I read a cynical sentence of Oscar Levant who
said about Hollywood: "Strip away the phoney tinsel and you

will find the real tinsel underneath." It is not the penetrating
cynicism that is psychologically interesting in such a casual
remark, but its pre-phase, namely the scepticism which refuses
to be impressed by the "face value" of things and wants to look
behind the wings of the phenomenon. This attitude prevails in
Jewish mentality, whether it concerns basic ideas or small things.

That pervasive scepticism is not a fruit of modern times. It
was present when Isaiah describes the pagan carpenter who had
carved a god for himself out of a block of wood, the rest of
which he used for preparing his food. It was there when Hosea
mocked the idolaters who sacrificed men and kissed calves. It
appeared in the grim jocularity of the scene on Mount Carmel
where the prophet Elijah challenged the priests of Baal: "And it
came to pass at noon, that Elijah mocked them and said: 'Cry
aloud, for he is a god; either he is talking or he is pursuing or he
is on a journey, or per adventure he sleepeth, and must be
awakened.'" (I. Kings. 18:27.)

That was in the 9th century before Christ and the god who
was mocked was Baal. But there is no halt before Jahwe and
before the Jewish religion. No doubt, we are living at the twilight of religious belief and the future of this illusion, as Freud
called religion, is not doubtful any longer.

In countless Jewish jokes the teachings of Mosaism and
monotheism are sneered at. It is remarkable that the very dis-
belief becomes frightened of its own courage. There is, for
instance, the story of Yankele, the cobbler, who was a declared
atheist making fun of all religious observances. On the Day of
Atonement Yankele appears in the synagogue, prays and beats
his breast in repentence. The astonished rabbi asks him: "I
thought you don't believe in God. Why are you here praying?"
Unperturbed Yankele replies: "Sure, I am an atheist, but how do
I know that I am right?"

Oftener even is that such scepticisms are fears of the temptation to transgress the severe religious commandments. These are
fears of punishment from the God whose very existence is
doubted. One of those comic stories tells, for instance, that Itzig,
who observes the twenty-four hours of fasting on the Day of

Atonement, feels painfully hungry, leaves the synagogue and goes to a restaurant. He asks the waitress there, "How much is a cheese sandwich?" Just then a thunderstorm breaks out, shakes the house and flashes of lightning appear all over the sky. Itzig, terror stricken, cries "Nu, nu, there is no harm in asking; is there?"

The spirit of scepticism combined with eagerness of inquiry made the Jews enemies of all kinds of superstitions. It started as an energetic rejection of sham and make-believe, as defense against any attempt to impress them by the grandiose appearance of flimsy values. A French saying proclaims that sceptics cannot be deceived.

II

In every fully developed religion there are heresies and blasphemies which defy the official tradition and ardently claim that they are in possession of the higher truth. The Cainites of the early Christian period asserted that the mortification of the flesh must be achieved by plunging into sexual orgy. Another Christian sect glorified Judas because only through his treason was the salvation of mankind made possible, and he was celebrated as Saint Judas. Judaism too knows similar heretics. If one can believe certain Christian dogmatic authorities, the very existence of Judaism is heresy since it denies the divinity of Jesus Christ.

Some Jewish jokes prove that the boundary-line between faith and blasphemy is by no means sharply defined. More than this, they prove that blasphemy or sacrilege is occasionally sanctified and traditional belief abhorred. The Devil sometimes quotes the Scripture and tempts the devotee to believe him. Doubt itself is sometimes put into the service of religious belief.

The point I want to make here—a point driven home by many Jewish jokes—is the following: under certain circumstances the man who breaks the sacred law is to be esteemed higher than those who faithfully observe it. There is, for instance, the story of the chassidic rabbi who is believed to ascend to heaven on Saturday and who is caught chopping wood for a poor widow on the day of rest. By this sacrilegeous action, they said, he ascended even higher. Here charity conquers the Holy Torah.

There is that precious anecdote of the poor Jew who would like to attend the service at the synagogue, but cannot afford the price for the seat on the High Holiday. He asks the sexton at the door of the synagogue to let him enter because he has to give Mr. Eisenstein, who is inside, a very important business message. But the sexton, who knows his people, sternly refuses him entrance: "I know you, you gannif (= scoundrel)! you only want to get in to daven (= to pray)." A mundane and materialistic pretext is here used as a screen in order to make it possible for the poor Jew to pray, which is a duty as well as an emotional need to him. This is, indeed, a pious lie. Only by cheating can he satisfy his spiritual need.

The Jewish proverb knows that violent remorse over a sin is useless and often even harmful, because it is bound to lead to a repetition of the sinful act. The proverb advises, "When you eat *chaser* (= pork-meat), let it be fat." That means: if and when you sin, at least enjoy it. A forbidden act, remorsefully committed, amounts to a double sin. (Nietzsche already stated that remorse is stupid and compared its uselessness to the stupidity of a dog who bites into a stone.)

Not only Jewish anecdotes and jokes justify an occasional infringement of the Torah; tradition itself sometimes glorifies such a violation of the Law. Resh Lakisch, the Talmud records, blessed Moses for his courageous breaking of the tablets of the Law. The great leader who saw the Israelites dancing around the Golden Calf did not want the sacred tablets to fall into false hands and foresaw that the children of Israel would put them to wrongful use. "Praise be to you for breaking them!" All kinds of voices are heard in those stories and anecdotes that express doubt, scepticism, and uncertainty: sometimes even the Voice of voices.

THE WIDE NET OF DOUBT

There are certain neurotic disturbances characterized by a regiment of doubts that pervade through one's whole mental life. These obsessional neuroses show all kinds of doubts that are mostly kept secret and are brought to light in psychoanalytic treatment. Obsessional doubts often concern not the great problems of life, but small questions of everyday existence. The unconscious contents of obsessive doubts are manifold, but can, in psychoanalytic explorations, always be traced back to a few questions of a general nature and reflect the decisive conflicts within the patient. Whatever are the objects of those doubts—and they are many—their center is always doubt of oneself, resulting from a conflict between the demands of one's drives and those of one's conscience. Their frequently trivial character is due to an unconscious displacement onto a small detail.

Jewish jokes often deal with doubts of many kinds, especially with those of a religious and social character. Yet there is no scarcity of jokes that show uncertainties, distrust, and incredulity with regard to everyday life experiences. An example is this dialogue at the information stand of a train station: "When is the train to Pincew going?" "Every day except Sunday at 11:30 P.M." "Wednesday too?" Compare this doubt with that of a neurotic patient who visits a bank to ask how many dollars he would get for changing a certain amount of European bills. After he got the information, he had to ask each teller of the same bank because he doubted that the information was correct.

Another example: a Jewish man in a railway compartment suddenly begins to lament because he has lost his pocketbook. The other travellers help him search for the lost object, but do not find it. Finally a passenger, exhausted from searching below the benches, asks: "Did you also look well into all the pockets in your overcoat?" The Jew, very alarmed, cries: "What did you say there? If the pocketbook is also not in my overcoat, then I am totally lost." The corresponding behavior-pattern, whose character is the avoidance of decisive certainty, will often be found in the symptomatology of obsessional neuroses. A patient plans for several years to write a novel whose outlines are clear to him. He complains that he can write a few short stories and various articles for magazines, but avoids starting on the novel. He has many and various pretexts and "rationalizations" for this avoidance of "the real," as he calls it. He explains finally that he cannot think of writing the novel because if he would begin to write it, then he could perhaps recognize that he is not really a writer and his last hope would vanish. He avoids thus the decisive certainty just as the traveller did not allow himself to search for the pocketbook in his overcoat. The patient himself compares his behavior with that of a man who is in love with a certain girl and hopes that she will return his affection, yet avoids making her acquaintance because he is afraid that she would not like him.

A Shocking Thing To Say

An investigation of Jewish wit would be incomplete without considering the group of jokes which refer to the processes of body evacuation and of sexuality. Those Jewish witticisms often deal with those physical urges in showing them clashing with the codes of Western civilization. Certain elementary and vital physical needs, unchecked in the ghetto, are depicted in their conflict with the proprieties and conventions of another world. In Jewish jokes of this kind you will not find anything of the bawdiness of Shakespeare or of the lewdness of Rabelais. On the other hand, there is no trace of the subtlety and sophistication of modern French wit.

To make the difference unmistakably clear, here is an example: in Anatole France's novel *La Revolte des Anges*, Mr. Arcade and Mr. Gaston visit their friend, the young aristocrat Maurice, who is ill. The gentlemen talk about various problems of religion and philosophy. In the course of the conversation some obscene remarks are made that would have made not only a sergeant, "but even a Parisian woman blush." Let us transpose the situation for the sake of a thought-experiment into the milieu

of a ghetto. It is inconceivable in this atmosphere to make a
witty comparison like Anatole France's and to say the remarks
were so lewd that they would have made not only a sergeant,
but even a Jewish woman of Tarnopol blush. The modesty or
chastity of the woman in the ghetto forbids such a possibility
which is very imaginable in the atmosphere of *mondain* Paris
society.

Crude Jewish jokes confront men of the ghetto with the
conventions of Western civilization especially at occasions when
the need of physical relief in form of evacuation is experienced.
A Jew appears, for instance, for a consultation with a physician
and complains: "Doctor, I cannot piss." The physician offers
him an urinal and asks him to try to urinate. There is no dif-
ficulty and the doctor expresses his astonishment that the patient
complained as being unable to urinate. The Jew explains: "Of
course, I can, if one lets me." On the street of the ghetto he
could satisfy that need unconstrained, but that's impossible in
the street of a great city.

To the same or to an adjacent area belong jokes like the
following: The physician asks the patient: "Do you suffer from
winds, Mr. Eisenstein?" "What do you mean? Suffer, Doctor?"
asks the patient who obviously feels great relief when he can
break wind.

Those are stories which were only told in the company of
men. One of them was told to me by the late Dr. Hans Sachs:
"When you are six, you believe the penis is there only to urinate.
When you are sixty, you know it." Such a joke does not, strictly
speaking, belong to the group of folk-witticisms, but I don't
hesitate to insert it here, because it is of a similar kind. An
observation conveyed to me by a man of advanced age, has the
same character: "When you get old, you forget to close your fly,
and when you get still older, you forget to open it."

Jokes such as the last ones already mark the transition from
the region of urination to the area of sexuality. Here is also a
distinct difference between Jewish jokes originated from the
world of the ghetto and those of emancipated Jewry of the great
cities. Compare the following two examples with later ones:

during a pogrom, the wife of a rabbi was raped before his very
eyes by a Cossack. Afterwards she humbly begged her husband's pardon assuring him that she was helpless and could
not prevent the rape. The rabbi concedes that the rapist was
stronger than she, but he asks: "But why were you shaking your
behind?"

Here is a witty comparison from a comedy *Die glücklichste
Zeit* by Raoul Auernheimer. The play, which I saw in the Vienna
Burgtheater, is dated at the turn of this century when auto-
mobiles were introduced into Austrian society. A man tells his
friend: "You see, with woman it is as with a car. To have no
car is uncomfortable. To have a car is expensive and sometimes
risky. The best thing is to have a friend who has a car." There is
the story of a Jewish widower in his seventies who decided to
marry again and does not listen to the objections raised by his
grown-up children. He consults a physician who gives him a
clean bill of health. His oldest son asked him what the doctor
had said about sexual relations and the old man says: "The
doctor recommends intercourse semi-annually" and adds: "How
often is this in the week?" The following dialogue already reflects life in present-day America: "Don't you take business trips
to Paris? How much do you spend there for a week?" The
answer is, "That depends. When I take my wife, it costs me a
few hundred dollars. When I go alone, a few thousands."

Mephisto in Goethe's *Faust* remarks: "Before chaste ears you
dare not say aloud what chaste hearts cannot do without."
Jewish wit dares to say those shocking things, sometimes in a
cultivated shape and sometimes in a crude form.

THE FACES OF TRUTH

It is very significant that Jewish jokes avoid certain subjects
of jest. Discovering the absence of those themes will sometimes
help the psychological observer more than other approaches
when he attempts to compare the distinctive features of Jewish
with with that of other groups. Jewish jokes almost never make
fun, for instance, of physical handicaps or frailties, almost never

mock at body deformities and ugliness. Beauty is in the eyes of the beholder and so is ugliness. There are no cruel or sick jokes among these people. Let me compare, for instance, the humor of the good-natured Viennese who sometimes joke about physical pains with Jewish witticisms. There is the anecdote about two moving men who have to transport a very heavy piano. On the stairs, the piano slides down and falls on the foot of one of the porters who groans in pain. The other asks, "Since when are you so delicate?" (In the original Viennese jargon: "Seit wann bist'denn so haklig?")

It is very unlikely that one would encounter similar jokes among the Jews, even among the Jewish transport workers of the Saloniki harbor.

But even the same subjects which provides themes for joking and teasing are differently treated in Jewish witticisms. It has been said that nothing is as hard as a fact, and nothing as tenacious or as difficult to deny. Wit makes the apparently impossible in questioning the nature of truth and demonstrating its relativity.

Yet even in this daring doubt there are subtle differences between jokes of the Jews and those of other groups. Take the following French anecdote: In a Paris salon some ladies discuss the age of the playwright Alfred Capus. A few days after the opening night of one of his comedies one lady remarks: "He looks as if he were forty years old," "No," the other says vivaciously "he is already forty-five," and a third woman says, "You are joking, he is scarcely thirty-seven years old." Just then the writer of *"La Veine"* enters the salon and one of the ladies decides to ask him directly. After he has paid his compliments to the hostess, the playwright approaches the group and is asked: "We are very indiscreet, Monsieur, but we have just made a bet. How old are you?" Capus looks at them and answers amiably: "Mesdames, that depends on your intentions."

That sounds, of course, nonsensical at first, because age or the number of one's years is an objective fact. The answer of the writer is utterly unexpected, but we guess that he implies in it that the curiosity of the women has a concealed sexual character.

The sentence has the specific character of Parisian jokes and is coined in the French manner. One can seriously doubt that witticisms of this character would flourish in the Jewish ghetto milieu.

When the moment comes when we have to face the truth, is it the truth we face? That is the question here and Jewish wit raises it again and again. I once saw a cartoon in which a man impatiently tells his mistress: "Stop lying now! I already believe you!" We know that we mortals are not made to accept all truth when we recognize it as such, but can we accept and acknowledge lies, although clearly seen as mispresentation? But this is precisely what the man does when he asks the girl not to lie further as he already believes her lies. According to this sentence, one can unquestioningly believe in a lie if one wishes to ardently enough.

Truth has many faces; so has falsehood, and occasionally truth can be disguised as a lie, as in the anecdote in which two Jews meet at a Galician railway station. The one asks: "Where are you travelling?" "To Cracow," replies the other. "Now see here, you are a monstrous liar!" says the first indignantly. "When you say that you are travelling to Cracow, you really wish me to believe that you are travelling to Lemberg. Well, but I am sure that you are really travelling to Cracow, so why lie about it?" Freud, who analyzed the technique of this "precious story" in his book on wit points out that the joke shows the uncertainty of one of our most common notions. It is not enough to tell the truth if one does not consider the mind of the hearer. One has to concern oneself also with the way the hearer will interpret one's statement, how he will react to it. It is not a person or an institution which is attacked in this group of jokes, but the certainty of our knowledge, the nature of truth itself.

But if this is so, will doubts never cease? If all the statements of one's fellow-men become doubtful, extreme scepticism will not end at the word of God, and the veracity of His revelation may be contested.

REDUCED TO LOGIC

I

Many authors treating Jewish jokes quote a collection which Alexander Moszkowski published under the title, *Der jüdische Witz und seine Philosophie,* almost forty years ago. The writer not only collected jokes, but also tried to shape a philosophy of Jewish humor. He asserted that the Jews are the witty people par excellence, that they, as people, are witty, and he designated the Jewish joke as "the crown" of all witticism. It seemed to him that "the notion of Jewish wit results in a pleonasm, a tautology because the basic elements of this notion cannot in effect be separated. What determines the nature of wit, the contrast, forms also the token of Judaism, in its good as in its bad, in its elegiac as in its comical significance. In the martyrdom of this contrast the burning way of thinking evolved, which emits sparks of witticism."

Love is blind, also the love of one's own people. With the same justification as Moszkowski declared Jewish wit to be the crown of all wit, so the French will ascribe this attribute to *"l'esprit"* and the British will point to the excellence of their satirists from Jonathan Swift to G. Bernard Shaw. We shall not criticize Moszkowski's metaphorical diction and his false pathos ("In the martyrdom of this contrast the burning way of thinking evolved which emits sparks of witticism"), but simply state that while his collection of Jewish jokes is rich, his philosophy is decidedly poor.

There are occasions at which all the rules of logic are ridiculed, for instance, the one in which the timid Jew says: "Sure, I know that dogs that bark don't bite—but do the dogs know?" There are, furthermore, situations in which reality forbids the application of logic; for instance, in the story of the mortally wounded Jewish soldier. A Catholic priest approaches him and shows him a cross with the crucified Christ on it: "Do you know what this means?" But the soldier says: "I have a bullet in the stomach and he propounds a picture-puzzle to me!" The comic effect is clearly connected with aggression against Christianity.

But we wanted to discuss the role that logic, as an object, plays in Jewish jokes. There is an excellent example in the story of the rabbi who has lost his glasses and finds them via a long, logical detour. The chain of his reasoning (here shortened and translated from the Yiddish) is the following: "Since the glasses are not here, they have either run away or someone has taken them. Ridiculous, how could they have run away? They don't have any legs. Since someone must have stolen them, it must be someone who has glasses or someone who has not. If it was a person who already has glasses, he will not take mine. If it was someone who does not have glasses, he was someone who does not see without them. If he has no glasses and sees, what does he need my glasses for? It must have been someone who has no glasses and sees nothing. If he is someone who has no glasses and does not see, how could he then find mine? Since no one took them who has glasses and sees and no one took them who has no glasses and sees nothing, and since they did not run away because they have no legs, the glasses must be here. But I see they are not here. I do see? Thus I have glasses. Since I have glasses, they must be either mine or those of another person! But how come another person's glasses are on my nose? Since they cannot be other glasses, they must be mine. Here they are!"

The chain of acute questions which the rabbi poses and acutely answers himself, always in strict application of the logical principle of the excluded third possibility, led him at last to the missing glasses on his nose.

In this and in many other similar examples it cannot be the triumph of logic or the victory of an ingenious mind that makes us laugh, but the exaggerated intellectual expenditure and what is signified behind it.

Thus the little story shows us that a tremendous expenditure of thinking is wasted in order to arrive at a result that could have been reached by simple perception or by a much shorter thought-path. We understand that the over-wise rabbi, in his search for his glasses, applies the typical kind of deductive reasoning he has learned in the study of the Talmud. Behind the comic facade there is mockery at the tremendous intellectual effort wasted in the study of the Talmud and of other law texts, and of their discussions abounding with subtleties and sophistries.

The argumentation in the search for the glasses does not differ essentially from the kind of detailed and extensive discussions centered upon whether an egg laid on the Sabbath may be eaten, whether one is permitted to pick up a splinter of wood on this day, and so on. That study, whose methods of logic the rabbi had here applied, was directed at ideas that were once of great significance for the Jewish religion and law and which are insignificant for us and the world we live in. The respect which other intellectual Jewish accomplishments of this kind inspire in us, has disappeared because of the insignificance of the objects for which the intellectual effort is made.

Yet, even this humorous story contains a hidden aggression against the Gentiles who attack the religious and legal literature of the Jews having not the slightest notion of how many and how great varieties of subjects are in its study and how many indelible traces they left in the thought and in the feelings of those people who, landless and luckless, carried their portable country with them in the form of a book. It is as if that anecdote wants to say: "You are perhaps right; this whole study is now superfluous and obsolete. It is a useless and ridiculous waste of thought, but do you understand what strict school of thought, of logical and verbal precision this is?" The want of respect with which the talmudic dialectics are treated in this story is compatible with a great concealed pride in its excellent qualities and its advantages, hidden to outsiders.

The Duke of Wellington said that the victory of Waterloo was won in the playing fields of Eaton. The many intellectual victories of modern Jewish scholars and explorers were achieved in the Talmud schools, the Jeschivoh of East Europe, where they, or rather their ancestors, studied.

II

Biblical and talmudic tradition is continued in striking metaphors and droll comparisons of modern times. Here is an example: "Life is like a baby-shirt: short and full of shit." Some reflections on the same subject sound as if they try to anticipate and caricature existential philosophy. Listen to the exclamation: "Life is terrible. Think how you go to bed in the evening as a healthy person and you get up the next morning dead."

In some sentences of this general kind profoundness makes, so to speak, a somersault and results in nonsense. There is, for instance, the meditation: "Life is like a suspension-bridge." "How?" asks someone. "How should I know?" is the answer. This is, of course, self-caricature; it mocks at alleged philosophical reflections. Compare such a saying with a French example. The playwright Alfred Capus runs into a man who explains to him, as if it were the result of long and profound meditations: "My dear Capus, all is in all." The writer says: "And reciprocally." An adverb produces here a *bon mot*. The difference between this kind of esprit with the Jewish analogous examples is that the sarcastic rejection of alleged profundity in that *bon mot* is attributed to another person while the Jew himself makes fun of his dark philosophical speculation.

III

"Why do you Jews answer a question with another question?" a Gentile asks. "Why should we not answer with a question?" the Jew replies. This sounds comic, but, as far as I know, no one has attempted to explain that Jewish peculiarity. It is easy to refer to the manner of talmudic debates which sometimes make the impression of a game of questions, answers, and new questions. But this is no explanation; it rather begs the question.

A significant hint can perhaps be inferred from language. We speak of firing, flinging, hurling questions at someone, of embarrassing, plaguing and vexing someone with questions, and questioning is sometimes used as synonym of grilling. In medieval time, torture was called questioning ("Peinliche Frage").

We can arrive at a satisfactory explanation of that peculiarity only by application of psychological methods. Certain experiences made in psychoanalytic practice taught us that a pronounced kind of question asked by the patient often has the unconscious character of concealed aggression, as though the patient wants to test or to embarrass the psychoanalyst. Sometimes such questions approach a kind of veiled attack.

The best tactics in those cases consist in, so to speak, throwing the ball back across the net, to respond, for instance, in the form of "What do *you* think about it?" There are, furthermore, neurotic cases which react with suspicion to every question. A patient of mine was asked by an acquaintance whom he ran into on the street "What are you doing now?" He suspected that the meaning of the question was to find out if he was still masturbating. Setting aside such pathological cases, many people consider questions that need not be personal, as intrusion.

In quite a few myths, fairy-tales and folktales, the question —motif appears in the shape of propounding a riddle. From the riddle of the Sphinx to Schiller's Turandot a female figure sets a riddle and kills the man who cannot solve it. The aggressive character of this motif cannot be doubted(31).

When we now return to the joke of the counter-question of the Jew, "Why should we not answer with a question?" it will not be difficult any longer to explain that bit of social behavior. The critical or aggressive character of the inquiry is undeniable. The Jew responds to it again with a question, as if it were not only a defense, but also a counterattack. He pays back the Gentile so to speak, in his own coin.

If we now look at the problem, it reveals its character. The Jew suspects in every question an open or concealed attack and takes the appropriate measure of self-defense and counteraggression. He feels that he is under the pressure of certain standards to which he should conform. Those values are alien to

him and he feels scrutinized by the question. Under these circumstances his caution easily obtains the character of suspiciousness. Thus he suspects hostility behind the question and he is
often right. Such real or alleged aggression from the Gentile
often concerns only Jewish social behavior. But there is sometimes more at stake. To be, or not to be: that is the question
for the Jew.

PARADOXICAL

I

A discussion of the use and abuse of logic is perhaps the
appropriate place to mention the notion of a "paradox," that is, of
a statement which may be true, but which seems to say two
opposite things. There is an abundance of such paradoxical
statements in the talmudic and post-talmudic literature, and
any collection of Jewish jokes offers a rich variety of them. The
paradoxical often seems to be the antithesis of reason and, at
first sight, sometimes gives the impression of the unnatural or
nonsensical. Yet it frequently reveals itself as an hidden truth
or one which contradicts all conventional ways of thinking. It
seems to me that one of the essential characteristics of the paradoxical is its surprising character. It may be coarse or subtle,
enjoyable or painful, or even cruel, frivolous or serious, but is
has to be surprising or it loses its quality. This distinctive
feature is more important than its logical or illogical attribute.
There are paradoxical emotions and experiences. Here is an
instance of such a paradoxical feeling that seems to contradict
all our ideas of the typical Jewish attitude. Little Moritz sees an
historical film showing the early persecutions of the Christians.
During a Roman circus scene in which many Christians are
thrown to the lions, Moritz breaks out in sobs and says to his
mother: "Look at that poor little lion there, it has not got any
Goy to eat!" Under the disguise of pity for the neglected beast
is an old hatred and repressed cruelty against Gentiles. It breaks
through here, surprisingly, and reaches the emotional surface.

The situation of the circus reminds me of another anecdote
in which a paradoxical or utterly unexpected feeling emerges. An
old Jew is taken to the circus where he sees an acrobat hanging
by his legs on a high trapeze, his head downwards, and playing
the violin. The spectator instead of admiring the acrobat
remarks: "A Mischa Elman he is not." This surprising statement
shows that the Jew is not very impressed by the spectacle or at
least that he denies being impressed. It is perhaps permissible
to add here that the Jews of the ghetto are easily frightened,
but almost never embarrassed.

In the loose manner of thought-associations a saying of a New
York writer occurs to me in connection with violinists. This
bonvivant stated: "Of the Jewish holidays I observe only the
Jascha Heifetz concerts." This almost sacrilegious sentence replaces the concerts of the celebrated violinist in lieu of the
religious holidays of the Jews and asserts that a performance
by that artist is attended by his Jewish admirers as zealously as
they previouly attended services in the synagogue. It gathers the
Jews, so to speak, into a new collective or community.

I am perhaps allowed to add here some remarks by Freud,
made during a personal conversation with me. We discussed the
case of an American patient whom Freud had referred to me.
The patient's marriage was an apparent failure until his oldest
boy became infected by infantile paralysis and died. Shaken by
this tragic event, husband and wife were reconciled and re-
united. Freud, who had attentively listened to my report, remarked dryly: "The ways of the Lord are dark, but rarely
pleasant."

During the time of the political riots in the last years of the
Austrian Republic Freud told us, his Viennese students, that we
should be careful in treating patients who were political fanatics
of the extreme right or left. The symbolic color of the Socialist
party was red, that of the reactionary Catholic party black.
Freud said to me that it is not necessary to be "red or black. A
man should be flesh-colored."

To come back to Alexander Moszkowski's book, mentioned in
the preceding section, this author attempts to see logic as the

foundation of Jewish jokes. Moszkowski assumes that by a successive narrowing of the possibilities a central notion is precisely grasped. This concentric narrowing of the logical circles compels us to find the central idea with mathematical precision.

But such an interpretation of the Jewish joke just describes its shell and leaves its kernel untouched. It is not from logical deduction that the listener derives the essential enjoyment. This pleasure is present, but it has the character of pre-pleasure and conceals, rather, the deeper sources of enjoyment. Compare, for instance, that kind of enjoyment with the one derived from the elegant solution of a mathematical problem or the pleasure derived from following a system of definitions, axioms, corollaries, etc., such as is offered in the system of Spinoza's *Ethics*. The satisfaction experienced at the examination of logical or mathematical procedures is in its quality very different from that derived from sharing a witticism. It is obvious that the pleasure we feel is determined by the emotional premises of the joke.

An interpretation that is concerned only with the logical facade and does not consider the unconscious emotional processes, does not penetrate the surface and will not recognize the essence of the joke. Let me remind you of the story of the Jew who, when asked if it was true that his face was slapped in the streets of Krotoschin, replied "Krotoschin—some place!" As Moszkowski justly remarks there is a transference from the event to the locality and it is correct, as he says, that this is the only association which promises an advantage to the embarrassed person. But does it exhaust the depth of the joke when we are told that the unpleasantness of the event "vanishes before the prevailing idea that that place cannot be taken into account as a business town?"

Is not the special effect of the joke conditioned by our unconscious identification with the beaten person and in the revenge taken in degrading the town and its citizens? We understand that the meaning of this reaction is typical for Jews, and realize that the only weapon at their disposal towards the brutality of a powerful environment is a fierce and bitter contempt of the violence of the mob.

It is certainly true that in some Jewish jokes a great pride in the power of the mind, especially of logical thinking, is clearly recognizable. Yet it is equally true that in many of them a certain talmudic kind of logic is sneered at and derided. It is true that Jewish wit often deals with the uses and abuses of logic, but it is not really concerned with purely intellectual problems. They sometimes form the facade of those jokes which go to the "heart of the problem."

THE BELIEF IN THE OMNIPOTENCE OF THOUGHT

I

We have often acknowledged that the poets anticipated a great part of the insights that we psychologists acquired later by way of laborious empirical exploration. It has scarcely been noticed that wit also often conveys psychological understanding which is ordinarily difficult to attain. That foreknowledge of emotional and mental processes—a foreknowledge of a special kind, it is true—reaches from the sphere of the unconscious, which can be made familiar to us, to the area of the repressed, which affects us as alien and sometimes even as uncanny.

To be sure, to discover that hidden insight of wit—we often forget that wit and wisdom are akin—it is necessary to look behind the facade of the joke and to analyze its latent meaning. One of the unconscious psychical phenomena that became a subject of Jewish jokes is the belief in the omnipotence of a thought or wish. Psychoanalysis asserts that unconsciously we have a grandiose belief in the power of our own emotional processes and still assume that our wishes govern the course of events in the outside world. This primitive belief in the power of our thought originates in the world of the child, who is first convinced that whatever he wishes will be realized.

Jewish wit sometimes makes fun of that superstition, but not too rarely confirms its existence and efficacy. Take, for example, that jargon-witticism, also quoted by Freud, about the well-known Rabbi N. who once sat in the synagogue of Cracow and suddenly screamed. Asked by his worried students why he howled, he declared, "Just now the great Rabbi L. in Lemberg has died!" The congregation goes into mourning for the famous rabbi. Travelers from Lemberg who arrive in the city the next day know nothing of the death of their rabbi. When they left, he was in excellent health. Finally it becomes certain that he did not die at the time when Rabbi N. in Cracow telepathetically saw his death, but that he was still alive. That telepathic message of his decease was grossly exaggerated. Some Jew from Lemberg uses the occasion to tease a student of the Cracow rabbi about his master. "Your rabbi made a great fool of himself when he saw Rabbi L in Lemberg die. Our rabbi is still alive." "That does not matter," replied the pupil. "The Kück (glance) from Cracow to Lemberg was still grandiose!"

This means, of course, that telepathy, as such, is admirable, whether its result corresponds to the truth or not is irrelevant. Here clearly is a sophistic error, since the value of phantasy and that of material reality are treated alike. It is a cynical or critical joke attacking the belief in miracles as it flourished in Hassidic circles of East Europe. It still bears witness to the tenacity of that belief even when reality contradicts it. A remnant of that superstition is maintained even when the truth must be faced. Freud points this out, but I do not believe that his remarks reach the depth of this joke.

For the psychoanalyst there is still another, psychologically more important aspect to be considered. It is obvious that the explanation of the student in the anecdote is a reaction to the attempt of the other person to mock at the superstitious belief in his rabbi's magical power. That answer is more than the naive admission of the wish to retain the superstition. The student does not take the attack lying down, but says, "To be sure, the rabbi of Lemberg is still alive, although my rabbi has seen him dead. But what do you say to the fact that he has seen his death?" The admiration for the "Kück" from Cracow to Lemberg has its psychological significance, beyond the question of believing in miracles.

In the expression of unconscious processes his answer means:

what an intensive hatred is alive in my rabbi against his Lemberg colleague, what terrible secret storms rage in him that he can see the other man die from so great a distance with visionary clarity?

Here then is the serious, psychologically interesting gist of that Jewish joke. The vision of the rabbi becomes a manifestation of an unconscious wish that the rival should die. What is thought and desired is seen as done and finished, as in a dream.

Psychoanalysts have recognized that the intensity of such a belief in the power of one's own wishes depends also on the depth of the drives which awaken and maintain it. That pupil could have answered, "It is of no consequence that the Lemberg rabbi is still alive. He is really already dead. The power of my rabbi's wish has killed him."

The context of the answer is significant. It is the pupil's reaction to the jeering of the other. When you put aside the manifest content of address and answer and consider its concealed meaning, often unknown to the speaker himself, you will recognize the threatening character of the reaction. From this viewpoint, the student's answer means, "Beware of me! I am a pupil of that rabbi who is so powerful in his hatred." The joke sacrifices the Cracow rabbi as a telepathist, but it proves the intensity of his emotions and drives. In it he is admired as a good hater.

II

We are now in search of another example of wit, one which shows another intensive emotion in connection with the primitive belief in the omnipotence of thought. Two Polish Jews stand in the fourth gallery of the Vienna Opera and are enraptured by the diva Marie J., famous for her magnificent singing and her glamorous beauty. During the intermission one says, "I would like to sleep with J. again." "What?" asked his surprised friend. "Did you already sleep with her?" "No, but I have already wanted to . . ."

Here, too, the day dream is treated as though it were reality, but such a relationship is, in this example, psychologically more comprehensible than the one presented in the anecdote of the telepathic rabbi. The desire which could be fulfilled only in phantasy was so strong that it was conceived as equal to reality with a certain subjective justification of the adorer. For the infatuated man and his consuming desire, his daydreams of sexual intercourse had so much of the character of reality that he could almost not separate its distance from the facts. It is as though he had already enjoyed the favor of the admired woman since he had already vividly imagined it. Here is an identity of fancy and fact.

Another example will lead us beyond the phase presented here and will follow that belief in the power of one's own wishes into the area where it takes the form of belief in the power of the word. To the magic of the imagination the magic of spoken words must be added. Isidor Mayer had apoplexy of the heart while playing cards in a coffee house, and died. There is great confusion among those present, and they deliberate over which one of them shall deliver the terrible news to Mrs. Meyer. Finally, the delicate task is entrusted to one of the players at the card game. Arriving at the apartment, he greets her, "How do you do, Mrs. Meyer? I wanted only to tell you that your husband played poker today in the coffee house and lost a good deal." "He should have a stroke," Mrs. Meyer shouts, full of anger. "He already had it," the messenger quickly says.

The contrast here is between the wishes which we express daily when we are excited, without taking them seriously, and the real meaning and earnestness of the words we use. Is it not as though the woman's words, at the moment they were spoken, became reality, as did those of the Creator in the Book of Genesis? Her husband died earlier, as a matter of fact, but the joke playfully treats with the fantastic and fantasied possibility that he should have died as a result of his wife's evil wish.

The contrast between this rash and unhesitatingly expressed wish and the terrible reality would not result in a joke, if we did not assume that there is another conflict in the woman. Behind the intensity of furious impulses to which, so to speak, the power to become reality is tentatively attributed we can presuppose affectionate feelings in the wife toward her husband. The humor lies in the breakthrough of drives, showing that our impulses, often contradictory to each other, are of a particular intensity and forcefulness.

III

In this and other jokes of a similar kind the exceptional situation that is the premise of witticism approaches an artistic product that seems to be very remote namely the fairy tale. A wish is realized as soon as it is uttered, even as soon as it is thought. You may remember perhaps the fairy tale of the three wishes—a man wishes, in a moment of annoyance, that a sausage should hang on his wife's nose, and must use the only other wish left to him to remove it from there.

In jokes of the kind mentioned above, we see, with terrifying clarity, the potential injuries we would cause, if we, who are inconstant and pulled by so violent wishes, really would get full power over the world events. We are all murderers, but we do all not commit murder—except in our thoughts.

It is not surprising that the Jewish joke which pokes fun at the belief in the omnipotence of thought, nevertheless acknowledges it to a certain degree. Wit itself belongs to the great arch of physical products that leads from neurosis to dreams and to various forms of art, from the fantasies of the insane to everyday life. Like those products of imagination, it disavows—if only for a split second—the unpleasant reality we must face, or tries to improve it in thought. Finally, also, wit, when it mocks the infantile belief in thought-omnipotence of adult persons, can not help but acknowledge—if only reluctantly—the emotions at the root of that belief: the force of hatred and the power of love.

The belief in the power of thought does not express itself only in jokes. There are more subtle manifestations of such superstitions still existing in the Eastern Jews. Echoes of them can be found in their customs and proverbs of everyday life. They tell the story of the old Jew who appears as a witness at court. The judge asks him, "How old are you, Mr. Eisenberg?"

"Seventy-two till a hundred," replies the witness. "What do you mean?" asked the judge, astonished, "till a hundred? How old are you really?" The man repeats the same information. The judge becomes impatient, but the attorney for the defense says, "Your Honor, please let me ask the witness." "How old are you till a hundred?" And Mr. Eisenberg answers: "Seventy-two."

The phrase "till a hundred" is, of course, a customary superstitious formula and is directed against the potential evil wishes of the listener. As a measure of defense similar to those applied against the evil eye the formula should prevent others from wishing that the life span of the person be shortened. The Jew protects himself by pronouncing the formula "till a hundred" against the power of evil thoughts that could reduce his life expectancy, expressing the wish that he should live until he reaches a hundred.

The helpful attorney did not practice magic when he asked the Jew adding this formula "till a hundred;" he only made use of the superstitious belief to get the correct answer.

Comic Curses

The story of Mrs. Meyer quoted in the preceding section, seems to confirm the unconscious belief in the magical power of the spoken word. As the Old Testament shows this conviction was an integral part of Hebrew religion and manifested itself in its clearest forms in the belief in the inevitable efficacy of blessing and cursing. The curse was a prayer or invocation of evil fortune to befall a certain person or thing, and had emotional dynamic certainty. Word and fact were united in it. In the Bible it is especially forbidden to curse God, the parents, the authorities and the helpless deaf. Later on it was assumed that the undeserved curse has no effect and may be turned by God into a blessing. (Prot. 22:23, 26:2, Dt. 23:5). The rabbinical tradition finally prohibits to curse any human being.

C. Leviacs points out that the Orientals have a tendency to curse even at the slightest provocation in daily life(32). It was not easy for the highly temperamental Jew to surpress his propensity for cursing and he often failed in the attempt at self-control.

There is nothing funny about curses. Yet some of them are unquestionably comic, for instance, "You should be like a lamp, hang during the day and burn in the night." The funny character of such sayings is to some extent determined by the ardent imagination that creates such images. Another emotional factor achieves or multiplies the comic effect, namely the amusing exaggeration in some curses. A curse I heard in Holland says "You should wear out an iron schiva-stool!" (In the original Dutch "Jij zult een ijzer schive-stooltyje verslijten!") "Schiva" denotes the time of seven days of mourning for a near relative. During this week the person in mourning must go barefooted or in socks and must sit on low stools. The meaning of that curse is thus that the execrated person should lose so many dear relatives, must sit so often schiva that he wears out an iron stool.

The only example of cursing I remember from my childhood was that of an old Jew who visited my grandfather and who furiously swore at a certain person: "You should have a stroke on your most beautiful yomteff!" The expression yomteff was known to me; it means holiday or joyful day. The meaning is thus: you should have an apoplexy of the heart on the most joyful day.

This example turns our attention to a new factor or to another kind of cursing, namely to those forms in which the evil fortune that is invoked on a person is contrasted and combined with an occasion otherwise considered especially fortunate. I was reminded of this kind of curse when I attended a performance of the play *The Tenth Man* by Paddy Chayefsky. This highly original drama has as its scenario a very poor orthodox synagogue. The first act takes place on a very cold winter day before the morning-prayer. Two men, Schlissel and Zitorsky, both in their early seventies, come puffing into the synagogue. Here is a fragment of their dialogue. Zitorsky says: "My daughter-in-law, may she invest heavily in General Motors and the whole thing should go bankrupt!" In a later scene Zitorsky voices the wish: "Ah, my daughter-in-law, may she eat acorns and may branches sprout from her ears!"

Is it not remarkable that those wildly fantastic and drolly farcical curses are all hurled at daughters-in-law who are generally liked by fathers-in-law? One would guess that both old men are by circumstances compelled to live with their daughters-in-law and that these women have treated them badly or have shown little consideration for them. This is, of course, mere conjecture, but there is at least a bit of psychological circumstantial evidence for its justification. In the same scene, Schlissel casts another curse upon his relative: "May my daughter-in-law live to be a hundred and twenty and may she have to live all her years in *her* daughter-in-law's home." This furious curse also contrasts and combines the two elements previously mentioned, a good wish and a condemnation. But do we not feel the bitterness of a disappointed expectation in those words? It seems to me that there is still a trace of what the French call *"dépit amoureux,"* of the hurt disillusionment and desperate defiance of a loving father.

Alfred Kazin, returning to Brownsville, his childhood home, remembers how mothers rammed great meals down the throats of their helplessly kicking offsprings(33). He still recalls hearing Jewish women cursing their children. "Eat! Eat! May you be destroyed if you don't eat! What sin have I committed that God should punish me with you! Eat! What will become of you if you don't eat! Imp of darkness, may you sink ten fathoms into the earth if you don't eat! Eat!"

His Own Physician

There are quite a few Jewish jokes on physicians and illness. Here is an example: "When a Goy has much thirst, he drinks a few pints of beer. When a Jew has much thirst, he goes to the doctor to be examined for diabetes." Such a concern about one's health is contrasted with a kind of indifference towards illnesses, often based on ignorance. Here is the counter-example: After careful examination, the physician declares to the patient: "Mr. Lefkovitz, I regret to tell you that you have cancer." Old Lefkowitz says: "Cancer, schmancer—main thing is that one is healthy."

Here is an example in which the magical belief in prayer competes with religious faith. Pious Eastern Jews prayed, in emergency situations by reciting the text of the Psalms. Such reading or reciting of the Psalms was called, "to say Tephillim" in Jewish circles. A Jewish mother comes to the rabbi and laments that her child suffers from diarrhea that cannot be stopped. The rabbi tells her, "You must say Tephillim." Three days later the Jewess appears again at the rabbi complaining that the child now suffers from the opposite symptoms. The rabbi recommends: "Say again Tephillim." "But Rabbi!" cries the horrified woman, "Tephillim are constipating."

Freed from such superstitions, Judaism still considered life the highest good given to men. The absence of a belief in a beyond made life and survival the more desirable. In that transition-age from the ghetto to modern times the traditional reverence for life was never retrenched. The mother of the founder of the banking-house Rothschild once consulted a physician to whom she spoke of the various complaints she had. The doctor told the very old lady, "Well, I cannot, alas, make you younger." "Doctor," said the old lady, "I want only to become older."

Even in the cynicisms of emancipated Jewry that ancient belief in the value of life is still persistent and profound. The famous impressionistic painter, Max Lieberman, met the well-known Berlin banker, Fürstenberg, and asked him: "Have you heard who died today?" Fürstenberg replied: "To me, everybody is welcome."

REVERENCE FOR LIFE

The Viennese had a saying reoccuring in their songs: "You live only once." Implied in this was, of course, the exhortation: "Enjoy, enjoy!" The Jewish Viennese writer Karl Kraus, parodied that sentence, remarking "You don't even live once!" In spite of such occasional pessimistic utterances the Jewish joke proclaims again and again: "Live and let live!"

It shows a determined abhorrence of the urge to kill which so often appears in the words and deeds of the Germans. The pervasive reverence for life manifested in so many Jewish jokes, is very rarely missed in Jews all over the world. It is as if it were inherited although it is certainly an attitude that is the result of individual education through many generations.

We can follow that reverence for life from the Bible to the sayings and jokes of the ghetto and from the rituals and ceremonies to the everyday life of Eastern Jews. We recognize it as an immanent part of the *Weltanschauung* of the emancipated Jews of Europe and America.

Here are two examples: A Jew in Galicia warns a Jewish policeman that a dangerous criminal was seen in one of the dark sidestreets. "Thank you!", says the policeman, "I know how to protect myself."

Here is another ghetto story. A policeman orders a Jew to pick up litter he has just dropped in the middle of the street. The Jew walks on as if he had not heard. "Pick it up or I take you to the station!" shouts the policeman, but the Jew pays no attention to him. Finally the policeman harshly orders: "By the life of your children, pick up the litter!" Whereupon the Jew says: "Since you come at me with force . . ." bends and picks up the papers he had thrown away.

In the first example the policeman thinks only of his own life when he is told about a killer. His attention is directed to self-preservation first, not to protecting others, not to the abstract idea of execution of the law. First things first!

The other joke stresses another aspect of that reverence of life. The Jew who is abjured on the life of the children gets frightened and obeys the policeman. The original Hebrew conception of life comes here into vivid expression, the conception of the commandment: "Honor thy father and thy mother that thy days may be long upon the land which the Lord thy God gives thee." (Ex. 20:12) Not individual life is meant here, but

the life of generations following each other. Reverence of life is
here professed in the devotion for the family and implied in it
for the survival of the ancestors in their descendants. It is the
same basic conception that sings wonderfully in the last lines in
Richard Beer-Hofmann's *Lullaby for Miriam*(34).

> "Are you asleep, Miriam, my child?—
> We are like rivers; now calm and now wild,
> And deep within us an ancestor's seed,
> Their pride and their pain, their vision, their deed,
> Their past now returning to children and heirs.
> You are not alone, and your life is theirs.
> Miriam, my life—my child, good night!

To return from the area of jokes to that of *Weltanschauung:*
Albert Einstein wondered, as a recent perceptive biographer
reports(35), "where his reluctance to shed blood and his unwill-
ingness to inflict suffering originated and he realized that he had
another trait in common with other Jews—respect for the living
of every living creature."

MESCHUGGE

For many Jewish jokes a glossary of Hebrew and Yiddish
expressions would be necessary in order for us to understand
and appreciate them fully. Yet some of those words have become so familiar that their meaning is immediately clear to
everyone. They have found entrance into everyday language,
into the European and American vernacular. The Hebrew
word "meschugge" belongs to this group. Usually it is used in
the sense of "crazy." Yet the meaning of the word covers such
adjectives as mixed up, confused, mad and insane, from eccentric or neurotic to lunatic and psychotic. To illustrate the verbal
ambiguity of the expression, a comical question, a kind of
proverbial phrase, will be remembered. When it is mentioned
that some man is meschugge, another person who is sceptical
may ask: "If he is meschugge, why did he not kiss the hot stove

instead of the beautiful girl?" Then the explanation will, perhaps, be given: "So meschugge he is not." When you apply the word in the sense of insanity, there are certainly psychotic and neurotic cases of serious masochistic character whose self-destructive tendencies make them kiss the hot stove rather than the pretty girl.

The same verbal uncertainty is met with in another proverbial saying: a person whose near relative behaves capriciously or foolishly will sometimes react to the amusement of others in a typical manner and say: "I would laugh too, if the fool did not belong to me." That is to say, the foolishness of that man or woman would amuse me too, if he were not a member of my own immediate family, a fact that fills me with worry and grief.

The Jews of the ghetto generation generally have a tolerant attitude toward mentally deranged persons and also bear fools gladly. There are even collections of jests and tricks of buffoons or over-sophisticated rabbis which resemble the stories of Till Eulenspiegel. Tomfooleries and nonsensical actions such as German folklore reports of the citizens of Schilda are told of the natives of the small Polish town of Chelm.

The majority of witticisms dealing with persons who are meschugge have another humorous aspect. In telling them, the Jews enjoy revealing the secret motives and purposes of the so-called "meschuggene" person. There is, for instance, the anecdote, told in several variations, of a Jew in a mental asylum who insists that he must have food according to the dietary laws prescribed by the Torah. Finally the director of the institution complies with the urgent requests of the patient. The next Saturday the director sees the patient who is taking a walk in the garden and smoking a cigar. The director indignantly cries: "You are so religious that you have to have kosher food and now you are smoking on the Sabbath?" Whereupon the patient replies: "What am I meschugge for?"

Freud told me this anecdote when I reported a case of a compulsive patient who suffered from fear of infection ("*délire de toucher*") and used complicated means of protection or de-

fense to disinfect all objects which he considered contaminated
with dangerous germs, for instance the seats of the family-car
in which an allegedly infected person once sat. His continual
complaints about such incidents finally became so intolerable
that his parents acceded to his appeal to buy him a car of his
own. Freud pointed out to me that the patient used his neurotic
infection-fear to win an obvious advantage. Psychoanalysis calls
such unconsciously wished for advantages from neurotic disturbances "secondary gains." The question, "What am I meschugge for?" reveals a similar secret tendency.

GESTURES

I don't believe that the Jews, living for many centuries in
Italy, Spain and other mediterranean countries, were very much
aware of the fact that they accompanied their talking with ani-
mated gestures. Only the contrast with the behavior of the
Nordic people and the mockery and imitation to which the
Jews were exposed made them pay attention to their gesticulations. When their demeanor in this direction became conspicuous, Jewish wit dealt with the vivid and expressive gestures, so
characteristic of Jews in a self-critical way. The fully American-
ized David Levinsky, in Abraham Cahan's story(36), still strug-
gles hard against the habit of "Talmud gesticulations" which
worries him like a physical defect. Another man in the same story
never opens his mouth when it is so dark that his hands cannot
be seen. Mandelbaum reads the theatre advertisement and asks
his friend: "What is this: a pantomime?" "Noo," replies the
friend, "that is simple. People talk together, but they don't say
anything."

In reality, gestures form a language of their own and they
say a good deal. Charlie Chaplin did not learn this language
in the London East End, he only brought the gesticulation that
was natural to his people to the highest artistic expression. In
employing gestures, he went through the gamut of emotions
from the desperate to the jubilant and he could depict an
absent object with a few movements of his hands.

Jewish witticisms do not comment on the habit of employing gestures, but rather on their indispensability. "You are a bore today," says a friend to a man, "Why don't you say something?" "In this cold I should take my hands out of my pockets?" is the counterquestion.

Krotoshiner who comes to a big city the first time, watches a policeman directing traffic with the movements of his hands. Finally he approaches him and asks: 'You stand here entirely alone. Tell me, to whom do you talk all the time?"

Gestures are a means of communication, originally as important and even more important than words, but they were later relegated to a secondary rank. The Jews brought their gesticulation with them from their Oriental past into Western civilization, together with their changeable facial expressions. Gestureless talking was originally as rare with them as a poker face. To understand Jewish jokes, you have to be all ears and all eyes.

Two Contemporary Men of Genius

In the following paragraphs I quote the humour of two men who influenced the thought and *Weltanschauung* of our time more than any other thinkers, Albert Einstein and Sigmund Freud. My personal contact with Einstein was restricted to a few occasions during the thirty years that I was Freud's student and friend. Both men of genius could be witty in conversation. As far as I know, they rarely indulged in humor in their writing. Both men enjoyed Jewish jokes and could laugh aloud at them. In a lecture, Einstein once discussed the mathematical procedure of Verjüngung (rejuvenation) which is used in Tensor calculus and added: "Since I have treated the subject of rejuvenation so often, I was many times confused with Steinach." (The Viennese biologist Steinach whose method of rejuvenation once caused a great sensation.) On another occasion, when Einstein was already at an advanced age, he was asked why he never visited Israel. He gave good reasons for missing the opportunity, adding: "When I was young, I wanted to go there

and look at the people, and now I am afraid that the people
there will want to look at me." In this joke, which uses the
technique of reversal, it is palpable that his fame was not always
a source of pleasure for the great man. In old age he sometimes
spoke of himself as a "has-been."

I could report many examples of Freud's witticisms, but
will, for reasons of symmetry, only mention two of them here
Freud's earliest students were mostly Jewish and he himself
liked to tell Jewish jokes. (I remember some meetings of the
Vienna Psychoanalytic Society which took place forty years ago
where Ernest Jones sometimes appeared as a visitor. Dr. Eduard
Hitschmann, who sat beside me murmured "Boruch ato Adonoi,
here comes the honor-Goy.")

When Dr. Dorian Feigenbaum, the New York psychoanalyst,
gave a guest-lecture in the Vienna Psychoanalytic Society, he
spoke of the seemingly nonsensical language of schizophrenic
patients and showed that even their "word-salad" has, if examined with psychoanalytic methods, some reason. At the end
of the ensuing discussion Freud mentioned that the absurd
phrases some people utter while card-playing also make some
sense, if psychoanalyzed. He added: "It seems in general very
difficult to produce consciously complete nonsense, while the
books of many German scholars are full of effortless unconscious
nonsense."

At another occasion Freud told us, his students, that in order
to be convinced of the truth of many psychoanalytic insights it
is necessary to fight with them and to overcome one's resistances
"Convictions and women we can easily conquer are not highly
appreciated by us."

The achievements of these two great men belong to the
world, but their witty remarks, made in the circle of their family
or friends, will contribute to the picture of their personalities
which had a perceptibly Jewish flavor.

CULINARY

I

Jewish jokes cannot be understood as an isolated phenomenon, but have to be seen in their social and historical context.
Even the geographical situation can become important here.
Jonathan Swift once remarked that a certain joke might be very
witty, but its point is gone with the wind as soon as it is
transplanted. There are jokes, he says, that ought not transgress
the area of Covent Garden, and there are witticisms that are
only understandable at the corner of Hyde Park.

Wit, says Freud in his mentioned book, is, so to speak, "the
contribution to the comic from the sphere of the unconscious."
He obtained the best insights into the dynamics of wit by comparison with the technique of dream-work, but he did not omit
to point out the radical distinctions between them. In some
ways, wit is akin to obsessional thoughts in the later phases of
their development where the forbidden thoughts and impulses
finally break through the wall of conscious censorship.

Many obsessional thoughts cannot be understood, if one does
not trace them back to their infantile origin. Similarly, some excellent Jewish jokes can be understood and appreciated in their
deeper meaning only when one explores their historic or even
prehistoric premises.

This and the two following two essays present some examples
of this kind of Jewish anecdote as illustrative material. They
are introduced here to demonstrate the way in which psychoanalytic interpretation reaches the core of Jewish wit by penetrating its surface and by reconstructing its concealed historic
and prehistoric foundations. I hope that the three analytic in-
terpretations presented in the following chapters will also show
that depth-psychology which differs from other types of exploration, can accomplish a kind of understanding not accessible to
other methods.

II

The customer ahead of me in a delicatessen ordered: "Give me a pound of kosher ham." Without saying a word the sales-clerk weighed a pound of pastrami for him. That very harmless jest will serve as the first bar to the melody of Jewish cuisine, of *the* food-preferences of this people and of the specialties *de la maison d'Israel.*

Jewish food-preferences have been treated in jokes for some centuries and Heinrich Heine has devoted many witty para-graphs of his prose and many verses to it. In his book on Boerne, published in 1840, Heine lets Boerne deplore the fact that the Christian church, which has borrowed so many good things from ancient Judaism, did not also adopt the schalet. He guesses that it kept this borrowing for future use. "When things should go badly, when its most sacred symbols, even the cross itself, should lose their force, then the Christian church should turn to schalet, and the people who had slipped away should press back into its bosom with renewed appetire. The Jews, at least, would then adhere to Christianity with conviction—for as I clearly perceive, it is only the schalet which keeps them to-gether in their old covenant." Boerne even assured Heine that "the apostates who went over to the new covenant needed only to smell the schalet to feel a certain nostalgia for the synagogue. The schalet is, so to speak, the homing-call of the Jews."

Heine shares this enthusiasm for the dish and parodies the first lines of the solemn Beethoven-hymn into:

"Shalet, schoener Goetterfunken,
Tochter aus Elysium."

Shalet, thou spark from flame immortal,
Daughter of Elysium.

Heine introduces a renegade, the Knight Don Isaac Abar-banel of an old Spanish Jewish family into the historic novel

The Rabbi of Bacherach. In this story of medieval Germany,
Don Abarbanel functions as Heine's representative. The knight
confesses that it is the fragrance of the Jewish restaurant that
lures him again and again to the ghetto. He has forsaken the
religion of his fathers, but "my nose kept the faith." He has "no
special liking for the company of God's people, and really, it is
not to pray, but to eat that I visit Jew street."

It was also "tasty childhood memories" that arose in the poet
when he visited his mother in 1844 in Hamburg, and he describes what mother gave him to eat.

> Es stand auf dem Tische eine Gans,
> Ein stilles, gemütliches Wesen.
> Sie hat vielleicht mich einst geliebt
> Als wir beide noch jung gewesen.

> There stood on the table a German goose,
> A creature of gentle demeanor.
> Perhaps she once loved me in days gone by
> When we both were younger and leaner(37).

Goose was a favorite dish not only of North-Germany, but
also of Viennese Jews before Hitler. It was always eaten with
certain vegetables. When I grew up in Vienna, they told the
anecdote of Mr. Feigenbaum, who comes into a delicatessen to
have his dinner, as every evening. He is not in the best of
moods. He says to the waitress: "Bring me breast of goose."
The waitress asks: "With red cabbage Mr. Feigenbaum?" "No,"
replies he, "with a breastpin." The sarcastic answer says more
than the words express. Not only does the question appear to
him stupid and superfluous since breast of goose is always served
with red cabbage, but as in the lines of Heine, quoted before,
the goose is for a split-second revived and changed into a
woman. The answer of ill-humored Mr. Feigenbaum says: "You
are a stupid goose." It is as though he arrived, in the way of
loosened train-associations, from breast of goose to the idea of
breast of woman and then to the notion of a pin. The tendency

of his sentence is obvious: it is aggressively directed against the waitress who had asked him a nonsensical question. What is specifically Jewish in that joke? It originates in a customary combination of certain dishes than can well be called national or religious dishes.

At this point, a new general view reveals itself and we are confronted with a question, almost never asked. Is the comic effect, the laughter it evokes, the only test for deciding how good a witticism is? There is a considerable number of Jewish jokes whose effect is less intensive than enduring, jokes which linger in our mind and which awaken not only laughter, but give us food for thought. Laughter is only the noisiest and most conspicuous reaction to a good joke. It need not be the only one. Some of the best Jewish witticisms are those in which other emotional or mental reactions follow upon laughter and which produce a long after-effect.

III

To remain within the area of the problem that occupies us, here is another Jewish joke: Mr. Knoepfelmacher who was baptized not long ago, comes once again into the delicatessen where he enjoys chopped breast of goose and sighs regretfully: "And from such a religion one should seperate oneself!" This sentence sounds at first bizarre or ludicrous, but makes sense on second thought. It reminds us also of Heine's figure of Don Abarbanel who comes to the ghetto "not to pray, but to eat."

Is here really a contrast and conflict or is there some sense in Mr. Knoepfelmacher's regret in having deserted "such a religion"? The answer is evident: not merely culinary interests of little importance, but matters that were once of greatest religious and national impact are disputed here. An echo of ancient food-orders and prohibitions, of that which once formed the unity and community of the Hebrew tribes penetrates here the world of emancipated Jewry of the West. In the last analysis, the special food-taboos lead us back to the primitive tribal religion and organization which we know as totemism. A great number of climatic and social factors have transformed the originally sacred character of totemism. But a residue, a survival of the ancient, primitive totemistic religion is maintained in food preferences and avoidances.

There is still a trace of that primeval view in the caricature that depicts the German eating Sauerkraut and sausage, and the Englishman as a beef-eater, while it shows the Hungarian preferring peppery bacon. In such displacement to the detail of food-preferences the old totemistic religion continues to live. Still recognizable in its original character, food-preferences remind us of common meals in which certain dishes and combinations of them were preferred. In a similar way people were reminded of their original totemistic meals in which the tribes established and renewed their community. Robertson W. Smith wrote in his book *Kinship and Marriage* published in 1885, that "identifications which lie at the root of clan-feeling rest upon the recognition of a common substance and may even, therefore, be brought about by a meal in common." Yes, that common totem meal was in the early childhood of mankind the only religious and social ritual.

Traces of primitive evolution are indelible. They even reach into as deep a region as the tastes of people. When that Jew who became a Catholic eats goose breast in the delicatessen and regretfully says, "And from such a religion one should seperate oneself," he has said more than he realizes. He has, for a split-second, regressed to a primeval phase in which common meals and religion were almost identical.

THE FAINT RESONANCE

I

It is now more than thirty years since I lived in the Hague in Holland, and heard the following comic Jewish story while visiting my home town of Vienna. In the middle of the night, the janitor of the Spanish ambassador's house is awakened by

the repeated ringing of the palace bell. He finally opens the
door and finds two well-groomed, very dignified gentlemen outside, who vividly repeat one sentence. At first he can not understand what they say, but he guesses from their gestures and
from the names they mentioned that they wish to speak to the
Spanish ambassador most urgently. The single sentence both
excitedly repeat sounds to him like genuine Yiddish. It is "Wir
zyn zwo Spanish Granden." (= we are two Spanish grandees.)
The plain-spoken Viennese janitor has the impression that the
two men want to make fun of him, and enraged he is about to
send them away. But their urgent demands to see the ambassador make him uncertain, and he finally awakens the ambassador's secretary to whom he reports the appearance of the two
gentlemen and their strange manner of expression. The official
greets the two men with great respect and the astonished Viennese janitor hears them converse with the secretary in pure
Castilian. They are really two Spanish noblemen of high rank
who have brought an important message from the King. Asked
about the funny sentence, they explain that they had run into
a Polish Jew on the train from Madrid. They had made him
understand who they were and asked him what they should say
when they arrive at Vienna, since they could not speak German.
The Jew taught them to pronounce that sentence to introduce
themselves to the Viennese janitor.

After my return to Holland, the memory of the comical
anecdote soon faded, but it was revived on two occasions. On a
bus in Amsterdam a few weeks later, I could not help hearing
two Sephardic Jews talk about the approaching holiday. When
they separated, they wished each other "Buenos Festos." I
wondered about the phrase that had certainly been used by the
ancestors of these men many hundreds of years ago, and about
the tenacity of language custom. Soon afterwards, I read a
history of the Sephardic Jews, written in Dutch. It treated
in detail the vicissitudes of the Jews in Spain. At a certain
point the memory of that comical anecdote emerged and from
then on often accompanied my reading at a distance, like a
court jester in a splended procession. What did it mean that the

echo of that comical story resounded in me? I had been amused by it, but now it appeared to be odd rather than funny.

During another visit to Vienna I told the anecdote to Freud who disclosed its concealed meaning to me. It becomes transparent when one sees the two Spanish grandees in their intimate connection with the Polish Jew whom they had encountered. In other words, when one assumes that the two Spanish noblemen were descendants of Sephardic Jews, one sees that there was a hidden affinity between them and the Jew from Poland. The impression of Freud's interpretation became stronger when I returned to the Hague and continued to read the history of the Spanish and Dutch Jews.

In the vicissitudes of the Jews in the dispersion during the centuries they lived under Moorish or Castilian sovereigns, is one of the phases reaching from the highest to the lowest point. In this connection, the proverb *"Quien dice Espana, dice toda"* is meaningful. From the pages of the book I was reading, the image of one of the most splendid periods of medieval civilization emerged. Planets shining forth slowly follow their course and comets traverse the night at extreme rapidity. Not only under the sovereignty of the Almovides and Almohades, but also under the Castilian and Arragonian kings, Jews were appointed to the highest posts and lived in intimate intellectual intercourse with the kings and with the nobility. They were highly thought of on account of their talents and their scholarliness, because of their diligence and their moral conduct.

In the Castile of the Reconquita, the Jewish cultural centers of Cordova and Seville fully blossomed again. When the Jews, greeting King Ferdinand in the city, presented him with a silver bowl bearing the inscription *"Deo abvira, Roy entrara,"* (God will open, the King will enter), a happy period began for the Jews of the Hiberian peninsula.

The great figures of medieval poets and thinkers, of Jehuda Halevy, Ibn Gabirol, and Maimonides emerge; with them, and after them, a sequence of scholars and researchers, of statesmen and financiers. Most of them are at the court of the Spanish kings or close to them in friendship. There is, for instance,

Josef Benveniste who, as administrator of the treasury and confidant (privado), directed, together with two noblemen, the politics of the young King Alfonso XI. He lived like the other Castilian grandees when he feasted at his home. When he went to see the king, whom he counselled, an escort on horseback accompanied him. The treasurer of Petro the Fourth, was Samuel Helevi Abulafia; the physician in ordinary of His Majesty was Abraham Zarzah. The friendship of Petro for the Jews was so great that people sometimes said that he himself was a Jew. His rival Heinrich exclaimed when he saw the vanquished Petro, "There he is, this Jew, this son of a bitch who calls himself King of Castillo." Even today a street in Toledo is called "Calle de Samuel Levi."

There, in a palace inscribed with Hebrew letters, the minister of finance lived, the minister of Alfonso VI, who called himself the sovereign of the kingdom of two religions ("severano de gente de dos religiones.") In the City of Seven Hills, Abraham Ibn Erza was born, one of the great thinkers of Judaism; here Jehuda Halevi wrote his passionate poems. Here are the synagogues Santa Maria In Blanca and El Transito, world-famous monuments of medieval architecture. In the same city the grandees took up arms to protect the Jews, when in 1212 French crusaders attacked them. Here Alfonso VIII, the lover of beautiful Rachel, often stayed. He liked and appreciated the Jews; he really could have spoken the sentences which Franz Grillparzer put in his mouth:

> There is, Garceron, something great
> In this tribe of wandering, fugitive shepherds,
> We others are of today, but they reach
> Back unto the cradle of creation
> When God, still manlike, walked in Paradise,
> When Cherubim were guests of patriarchs,
> And the only God was judge and lawgiver.

Alfonso X worked here with the astrologist Don Zag Ibn Said on astronomical tablets and asked the Jewish scholar to render the works of Galen accessible to the West. Yet through the Via Dolorosa of that city thousands of Jews were dragged and burned on the Grand Plaza. Together with the tunes of the pious psalms sung by the priests of the Santo officio the spectators heard the "Schema Isroel" of the dying Jews.

A walk through the Juderia of Cordoba, where a street is still called "Calle Maimonides," and through some quarters of Granada and Seville, awakens recollections of a great period of Spanish and Jewish culture. Yes, many Jews were grandees in this period.

Many of them had all the faults and bad habits which they so easily adopt from their surroundings and which they so often unconsciously caricatured by the exaggeration of significant features, in their conceit, vain-gloriousness and boasting, in the empty desire of luxurious ostentatiousness and in many formalities.

The Maranos, who had submitted to baptism, but remained secretly Jews, were related by marriage with the highest circles of society, with the court and the church. Yes, many of them were themselves noblemen and priests. Gentile and Jewish blood had, for three centuries, been mingled when the Inquisition began to destroy Judaism. Then one began to explore with the help of genealogical registers who had Maranos or New Christians in his line of descent, and one demanded the certificate of pure blood (the "certificado de limpeza de sangre") for any office. Is not history repeating itself?

The family ties knitting Jews with the highest social ranks had become inextractable. The Marquis of Pombal, one of the most distinguished statesman, who broke the power of the Santo Officio and enforced the civilian equality of rights for the Maranos, once sent to Josef II three great hats of the kind the descendants of the Maranos had to wear, according to royal order, to signify their differences from genuine Christians. When the king asked him for whom these hats were, the Marquis answered: "The first is for me." "And the second?" "For the Cardinal." "And the third?" "The third is . . . , for your Majesty."

The blood of the *conversos* flowed together with that of

Spanish and Portugese high aristocracy and Jews were grandees with all the attributes of Spanish chivalry. They also maintained a good part of that grandeeship, remained proud, ambitious, stubborn, and often narrow-minded, when they became refugees. An echo of that phase is still heard in many of their descendants, in the Sephardim who arrived in Holland and England, in North Africa and America. The dignity and noble demeanor of the grandee or the hidalgo, as well as his striving for glory, still appeared in Josef Hasi who could call himself "Prince of Naxos" and "Duc of the Aegean Sea;" in Menase Ben Israel who negotiated with Oliver Cromwell; in Lord Beaconsfield (Disraeli); in Uriel Acosta; in Baruch Spinoza and Josef Caro.

The great grandsons of tortured and persecuted Jews who had died at the stakes of Spain, still clung for a long time to that noble bearing and adhered to the language of the country that they had once called their home.

II

It is often stated that the effect of wit depends always on an unexpected contrast. If we tentatively agree with this view, what is the contrast which brings about the comical effect of the joke about the two Spanish grandees? We immediately think of the sentence "Wir zijn zwo Spanish Granden." The content of that statement is bewilderingly contradictory to the Yiddish expression. Here we find the element of surprise common to all wit. If what I asserted in a psychoanalytic theory is true(38), namely that surprise of such a kind represents a reaction to the emergence of something unconsciously expected, we would guess that the comic statement of the two gentlemen contains a confirmation of something we had unconsciously foreseen.

The confirmation must be contained in the fact that the two Spanish grandees speak Yiddish. The secret significance of the scene is now easy to guess. The Spanish grandees are really Jews. More accurately, the ancestors of these grandees were Jews and a part of their glorious past continues to live in their descendants. The core of such a joke is disclosed when one dares to treat its absurd or grotesque assertion seriously. We see that the suspicion of the Viennese janitor is somewhat justified; these Spanish grandees are Jews. In this allusion, the confirmation of an unconsciously expected thing we presupposed reveals itself.

If we attempt to replace the Yiddish sentence by one in high German, not the slightest comic effect remains. The introduction of jargon in this context is necessary to produce the full effect. It is as though the use of jargon measures the distance separating the Jews of the present in their humiliating situation from the glory of their ancestors.

Now another minor element of the comic anecdote attains significance. In the story two gentlemen appear. If one is convinced of the strict determinism of little traits within the realm of the psychological, this trifling fact also becomes significant and has to be fitted into the situation. The two gentlemen represent, so to speak, the two main groups of the Jews, the Ashkenasim and the Sephardim.

Here an objection can be anticipated; does the one gentleman really represent the Ashkenasi, the Jews who late came from Russia and Poland to Germany and to the West? That group of Jews is very different from the Spaniards. Their ancestors never resided on the shore of the Ebro. Their behavior shows nothing of the grandeur and the grandezza of Spanish nobility. Yet it can not be irrelevant that the Polish Jew functions as a kind of interpreter for the grandees nor that we encounter them on a trip to the East away from home. It is as if the geographical distance becomes meaningful, symbolizing the abyss between, and the connection with, the ghetto. Eastern Jews and the Jews of the Spanish court—both belonging to the Diaspora and both of a proud heritage. Here it becomes obvious that what the facade of the joke reveals is unimportant, in this case that the two gentlemen are Spanish grandees. Only the inner story of the anecdote is meaningful, that they are of an older nobility, belonging to that true aristocracy which only spirituality and civilization give to their bearers.

As in our example, the Jewish joke sometimes presents in its facade the contrast between a glorious past social situation and the actual misery of a poor minority deprived of elementary civil rights.

The core of this and similar Jewish jokes is disclosed only when one recognizes that the contrast does not exist in reality, that here a people justifiably claims to belong to the earliest upholders of civilization, and that their forefathers were members of a spiritual aristocracy in their efforts and in their accomplishments. The contrast reveals itself in the analytic penetration of this kind of Jewish joke often as the disguise of a hidden truth.

III

A separate group of jokes, made by Jews or about Jews, belongs to this group. The Duc of Lign, the first Jew to be made a peer, who was wittily called *"le premier baron du Ancient Testament"* in Vienna, certainly did not have any idea of what that scornful attribute really referred to; that the Old Testament tells of kings, priests and heros whose aristocracy is not only older, but at heart more incontestable than that of the oldest European houses of high rank. This sarcasm could only be justified if it concerned that striving for outside and superficial honors which mean so little compared with a cultural achievement that is of greater weight than weapons, coats-of-arms, and other decorations of a relatively new upstart level of society.

Here is a comic story, but is it the whole story? The degradation of one's own people, so conspicuous in the contrast of the joke facade, conceals an unsuspected pride in a past that need not be conscious to the individual. When you look behind the facade, you see a stage peopled with kings, priests and sages.

IV

To prove that the story of the two Spanish grandees is no isolated case and represents in its facade and in its concealed core a whole group of Jewish jokes, another example of such stories, to all appearances from a remote area, should be added here. The old Elkan Zuckerfarb takes a train in Cracow with a second class ticket, but enters the first class compartment. He remains undisturbed there until the train reaches the station Prerau. There is great excitement because the Archbishop of Olmütz is expected to travel to Vienna. The first class compartment was reserved for the prince of the church. Zuckerfarb is found contentedly smoking his pipe. "You have to get out here," the train official shouts, "this compartment is reserved for the Archbishop!" "Bishop?" Zuckerfarb smoking replies, "who said that I am not the Bishop?"

After having laughed at the witty surprise of the story, you realize that its hidden significance is also there to be recognized only when one dares to take seriously what it says. Indeed how can the train official know that the old Jew wearing a caftan is not the high dignitary of the church? At first we laugh at the insolence of the Polish Jew and do not wonder at his unperturbed sang-froid. His reply sounds, of course, ludicrous if one takes it literally and pays attention only to this superficial aspect. But this sound changes when one listens to the undertones of his sentence.

There were Jews among the first bishops of the church, when it was first established. The twelve apostles, the bearers of salvation to whom Christ entrusted his treasure to be handed on to posterity, were all Jews. The thread of tradition was not broken; the medieval revival and even modern times saw a number of baptized Jews on the episcopal seat. However funny it might seem, however all external signs might contradict such an assumption, the apostles and the first guardians of the early Christian community must have appeared similar to the Polish Jew on the train. (Again, the train as a symbolic hint of a remote past?) Those who listen to the joke think only of the present and are perplexed by the situation in the compartment. But he who listens with the "third ear," perceives that the joke took wing and crossed the abyss of two millennia.

We learned from Freud that wit—also Jewish wit—inevitably gives expression to repressed and disavowed drives and impulses.

In the two examples quoted here the element of subterranean
drives emerging from their recesses is easily identified. It mani-
fests itself in the grotesque absurdity of the Yiddish self-intro-
duction of the two grandees and in the suggested possibility that
an old Polish Jew could be a bishop. Absurdity in dreams as
well as in obsessional thoughts means, as psychoanalysis has
proven, unconscious mockery. (Are you now thinking of the
scene in Shakespeare's play in which the Prince of Denmark
makes monkeys of the courtiers through absurd statements and
comparisons?) The hidden meaning of such Jewish jokes can
be understood only if one brushes aside the objections of so-
called "common sense" and takes seriously what appears as
absurdity in the manifest content of the wit. The psychoanalytical observer will penetrate to the core of the joke when
he tentatively accepts the ridiculous or foolish statement as true.

Superficially seen, the two Jewish stories make fun of the
Jews and of their predicaments, but in their deeper aspect they
mock the Gentiles who have forgotten that they owe some of
their best cultural achievement to the people of the Bible.

Beside the emergence of repressed impulses in Jewish wit as
it has been represented in the two examples quoted here, other
emotional factors appear which have been entirely neglected in
the literature on the subject until now. When we penetrate all
the veils of such Jewish wit, we enter a territory of deepest
shadow, the realm of unconscious memory traces. Did we think
upon hearing the two stories that they contain memory traces
of a forgotten past which emerge from dark recesses and are
reawakened? The application of psychoanalytic methods of research results in tracing back the latent content of jokes of this
kind to a historic, unconscious or repressed recollection. Here,
memory carries us far back into an historic past whose glory
stands in striking contrast to the constant misery of present Jewish existence. The thought play of contradictions which results
from the simultaneous presentation of past and present, gives to
Jewish wit of this kind its manifest comical, and its concealed
tragical character.

Unconscious memory traces thus mark Jewish witticisms of this kind, pointing to a past that is not in conscious reminiscence. The pleasure-effect of such jokes is not only determined by the disguised breakthrough of repressed drives, but also by the re-actualization and reanimation of unconscious memory traces. As in the psychoanalysis of certain obsessional thoughts and of compulsive symptoms, a deeper insight into the nature of this genre of wit is not accessible without tracing its content back historically.

Unconscious memory traces of a common past tie men of the Jewish community more intimately together than the conscious tradition. They produce a feeling of solidarity which is not horizontally, but vertically determined by the vicissitudes of successive generations whose heritage is handed down to the individual. That subterranean feeling of a community of destiny, of which the individual is not always aware, can not refer to possession of a country or to a share of a nation. The Jews can not proudly say "My country, right or wrong," nor refer to their nationality when they claim their rights. Their quest for identity has to answer not only the question of who they are, but also, who they were and where they are going.

BACK TO THE ROOTS

In a previous section, I tried to analyze the Jewish story of the two Spanish grandees, and I hope I have succeeded in demonstrating that a deeper understanding of the anecdote is only possible if one traces its context back in history. There are, although rare, Jewish jokes which reach still further back into history, even into prehistory, into the primeval time of Hebrew mythology. A beautiful example of this remarkable kind of joke concerns a peasant who got along quite well with his Jewish neighbor. He became seriously ill and made a vow that he would make a crucifix from the tree in front of his house if he would recover. He was restored to health and kept his vow. The peasant once observed that the Jew did not take off his hat before the crucified Savior and called him to account for it. "But my dear friend," said the Jew, "I already knew him when he was still a tree."

Superficially seen, this explanation amounts to just a derisive remark, and one is justified in taking this for an explanation. The person, however, who likes to go right to the depth of a joke, will dig beneath that surface and reach a surprising conclusion.

In a psychoanalytic book, *Myth and Guilt,* published in 1957, I tried to prove that the character of original sin must be understood as a crime against God, who was first conceived of as a tree-totem. Adam's fall was originally a break of the laws of tree-worship of the ancient Semites: he ate of the tabooed tree of life, which, in the oldest religions of the ancient Orient was conceived of as a deity. Devouring the God in His original form of a tree-totem is a substitute for a brutal cannibalistic art. Christ is again and again called "the second Adam," he redeems mankind and releases it in taking the original sin upon himself ("For as in Adam all die, even so in Christ shall all be made alive" I. Corinth 15,22). The Tree of Life is not contrasted with the Cross, but the two are originally identi-cal. The deepest meaning of Christ's crucifixion becomes clear when one follows the line that leads from the totemistic tree-god, disguised as the Tree of Life, to the cross, which finally became an object of adoration. Jesus Christ died on the Cross, which is a late descendant of the tree-totemistic god.

The Jew who remarks that he knew the crucified Christ when he was still a tree returns, without knowing it, to the origins of the Semitic religions. In the joke one recognizes a remnant of the earliest tree-worship of the Hebrews in the same manner as one sometimes sees traces of a baby's face in the features of a very old man.

LEAVENED AND UNLEAVENED

One is often surprised to find that religious holidays are evaluated quite differently in childhood than in later life. In our own fantasies and thought-associations as well as in those of our neurotic patients, holidays have an importance of their own, independent of the religious meaning teachers and priests of the various denominations attributed to them later on.

I found a new confirmation of this fact when reading the autobiography of Gertrude Berg(39), one of our beloved television and stage stars. She clearly remembered the Friday Nights, but besides those, of all religious holidays her favorite one was, when she was a young girl, Passover. "There was something inexpressible, an excitement, a rushing that led up to Passover . . . To a child, the Passover celebration meant a party with the whole family together, laughing and singing songs and staying up late."

In accordance with this different meaning of these holidays, they appear more or less frequently in the jokes made about them. The Day of Atonement and New Year's Day are rarely the subject of Jewish witticisms. There are, of course, jokes in which these holidays also are dealt with facetiously. There is, for instance, the story of the old man warning a younger man who beats his breast incessantly while he confesses his sins during the holy service: "With violence you will not achieve anything with the Lord!" There is the other story connected with the commandments to ask friends and foes for forgiveness on the High Holidays: after the service a Jew reconciles himself with his worst enemy, telling him: "I wish you everything you wish me." Whereupon the other Jew indignantly replies: "Do you already begin again?"

But to return to Mrs. Berg's autobiography, besides the Sabbath and the Passover celebrations, other religious holidays are scarcely discussed in her often delightful memoirs. Philip Goodman recently published a "Treasury of wisdom, wit and humor for the Sabbath and Jewish holidays"(40). There is no scarcity of jokes on other religious celebrations, but the Passover festival makes, no doubt, the greatest impression on the children. Their imagination is stimulated by the stories of the Exodus from Egypt which is commemorated by the eating of matzoth and other food different from that of every day, and by other features of the Seder. There are the four questions to be asked by the youngest child, beginning with the query: "Why is this night different from all other nights?" "(Manishtanah?") Whereupon the narrative of the Exodus is begun.

In Jewish jokes echoes of those ceremonials often resound. There is, for instance, the modern anecdote of a Jew who after many years of sexual relationship with a certain girl finally married her. A friend sent him a congratulatory telegram on the wedding night adding the ceremonial question: "Mahnishtanah?" (= "why is this night different from all other nights?")

A good example of thought-associations connected with the Passover food is contained in a comical pun which can be interpreted as a slip of the tongue, yet is more likely to be conceived of as witty aggression. One of the singers of the Metropolitan Opera who has broken off all ties with Judaism had to sing in her early teens in Jewish restaurants. When once those early years of the singer's career were discussed, an old Jew of the lower New York East Side remarked "Oh, she had already then a beautiful matzoh-soprano."

It seems to me that further confirmation of the strong impression the Passover ceremonies made on children is established by the frequency of thought-associations alluding to them.

Let me add here as a kind of vignette some little memories from my thirty years with Freud. When I functioned as secretary of the Vienna Psychoanalytic Society, a guest-psychoanalyst once gave a lecture which, although treating his subject extensively was rather boring and did not offer anything stimulating or original. Freud slipped a little paper over to me sitting at his left. On it was written: "It has as little taste as matzoth." Another example of this kind: I once asked Freud which of two ways of psychoanalytic procedures was preferable in the treatment of a certain patient. His answer was: "One can eat leavened or unleavened bread."

Another memory: Freud, in his lecture on the primitive phenomenon of Taboo alluded to the Seder-celebration in an aside which is not to be found in his book, published later on. (If memory serves me, this lecture was given in the Vienna

Psychoanalytic Society late in 1911.) In discussing the displacement and transferableness of taboo Freud quoted from Frazer's
Golden Bough the story of a Maori-chieftain who will under no
condition blow into a flame because his sacred breathing would
convey his power to the fire, this to the pot put on the fire, the
pot to the dish cooked in it, the dish to the person eating of it.
Thus the person had to die because he has eaten from the food
cooked in the pot that stood in the fire into which the chieftain
had blown with his sacred and dangerous breathing.

Freud turned to me and said: "Does that not remind you of
the Had Gadya?" He alluded to those Aramaic verses recited
at the Seder-evening. In this tale a father buys a little kid. The
cat came and ate it. Then came the dog who bit the cat, the
stick came and hit the dog, the fire burned the stick, water
quenched the fire, an ox drank the water, the slaughterer killed
the ox, but the Angel of Death killed the slaughterer. Finally
God destroyed the Angel who has slain the slaughterer that
killed the ox that drank the water that quenched the fire that
burned the stick that beat the dog that bit the cat that ate the
kid. The refrain is Had Gadya (= an only kid).

Freud was reminded of these old Aramaic verses by the
taboo-fear of primitive races. In his thought-associations a half-
forgotten past walked into our meeting.

THE OLD COVENANT AND THE NEW COVENANT

I

In the conflict between the synagogue and the church which
has lasted for almost two thousand years, many different weapons have been used on both sides. At first the Jews, who were
on the defensive, had to control themselves and to exercise a
dignified restraint against so powerful an adversary. They confined themselves to mock humility and to parrying the blows
that ceaselessly descended upon them. Such a defense was sometimes made in witty forms as we see in the Hebrew literature
of the first centuries of triumphant Christianity. In the satirical

writings of early medieval times, Jews became more courageous and sometimes ventured to counterattack. We can follow this development to modern times in which Jewish witticisms are directed against Christian dogmas and rites.

Let me quote as a modern example of such a witty attack a sentence of the great statesman Isaac Adolphe Cremieux (1796-1880) whose ancestors were accused by Christian adversaries of murdering Christ. Cremieux replied "In order to do away with this affair, we will allow you to kill our God as well when you meet Him." About the time, when Cremieux parried the blow of his antagonists in France, the German philosopher Lazarus Geiger answered the question of a Catholic priest who asked him, "When will you finally give up the old prejudice and also start eating pork?" Geiger replied: "At your wedding, your Reverence." (Henriette Herz the wife of Dr. Markus Herz, the famous Kant student, was at a party and suddenly had to yawn. Her neighbor, a count F., said "Please, don't eat me up!" "Don't be afraid," said Mrs. Herz. "We Jews don't eat pork.")

There were various facetious ways to discredit the basic dogmas of the new covenant, droll ones and funny ones. There is, for instance, the old anecdote of a conversation between a Catholic priest and a rabbi who decide that they want to found a common religion. This was to be accomplished by concessions and compromises on both sides. The priest demands changes in the ritual such as having the service conducted in Latin instead of Hebrew, and that Sunday instead of Saturday should be held as the day of rest. Instead of Pesach, Easter has to be celebrated. The rabbi grants this and many other reforms without objections. Finally the priest asked the rabbi what changes he demanded. The Jew said: "Only one: Jesus Christ has to be radically taken out." All the other reforms and changes, according to this joke, are irrelevant, but, if the figure of the Savior is removed, what remains but genuine Judaism?

In another joke, a rabbi and a Catholic priest talk about the future careers of the young generation. The priest's nephew attends a theological seminary in order to become a clergyman. The rabbi inquires about the possible future career of the young man. "Well," says the priest, "He can become a chaplain." "And then?" asks the Jew, "He could even become a cardinal in time." "And then?" "Well, he can even become a pope." "And then?" "What more do you want? Do you imagine that he can become God?" asks the priest, impatiently. "Well," replies the rabbi, "One of our boys made it."

Not as coarse as this joke, Heinrich Heine's rabbi in the poem "Disputation" discredits the fundamental religious doctrines of Christianity in his quiet and biting sarcastic refutation of the Franciscan monk who is his opponent(41).

> "Unbekannt ist mir der Gott
> Den ihr Christum pflegt zu nennen.
> Seine Jungfer Mutter gleichfalls
> Hab ich nicht die Ehr zu kennen.
>
> Ob die Juden ihn getötet
> Das ist schwer jetzt zu erkunden
> Da ja das Corpus delecti
> Schon am dritten Tag verschwunden.
> Dass er ein Verwandter sei
> Unsres Gottes ist nicht minder zweifelhaft
> So viel wir wissen,
> Hat der letzte keine Kinder."

> Quite unknown to me is the God
> Whom you call the Christ, good brother,
> Nor have I ever had the honor
> To have met his virgin mother.
>
> That the Jews, in truth, destroyed Him
> Is difficult to show
> Since the delicti corpus
> On the third day vanished wholly.
> It is equally uncertain
> Whether He was a relation
> Of our God, who has no children
> Not, at least, in our recollection.

Not moving at the height of abstract debate, but closer to practical, everyday life, another Jewish joke makes fun of Christian rites. A Jewish housepainter is sent to a convent to do some work there. The Mother Superior of the convent shows him what and where he should paint. After the major part of his work is done she tells him that she is satisfied with the job and asks him to continue, but adds: "Remember please, to take off your hat when you are working in the church. Do not wash your hands in the holy water and say 'Mother Superior' to me, and not 'Mrs. Shapiro.'" The degradation of the Christian ritual implied in the house painter's behavior in church is, of course, only superficially seen, naive. His actions leave no doubt of his intentions.

There is the story of the Catholic priest who tells a rabbi: "You have a funny religion. Explain to me why your synagogues are so dirty while our churches are kept very clean?" "Oh, that's simple," replies the rabbi, "you have a housekeeper who scrubs and sweeps them, but our God has no wife who could do this in His house." "Tell me," the priest continues, "why you shout so loud when you address your god while we pray in a low voice?" "Our God is already old and He does not hear very well any longer. On the other hand your God is young and has good hearing." "Tell me why your funerals are so gloomy while there are flags, statues and flowers in ours?" "That's true," concedes the rabbi, "our funerals are mournful and yours are rather cheerful. I therefore prefer to witness the burial of a goy." The rabbi turns at last from defense to attack. We perceived with him the aggressive tendencies in the questions of the Catholic priest. The rabbi answers as well as he can in protecting himself and his faith, to parry the thrust, but finally he strikes back at the Gentile.

II

I have, so far, endeavored to cut short every long Jewish story, but the following anecdote is an exception to the rule observed in this book. A Jew was grazed by a truck and pretends to be seriously hurt. He sues the truck-company for damages claiming an exorbitant amount since he is paralyzed by the accident and unable to work. After careful investigation, the insurance office of the truck-company pays him a huge amount. He was warned that he will be carefully observed in the future. If he is able to walk a single pace, he will be persecuted for perjury and fraud. He says to the insurance-adjuster: "I already made arrangements to be picked up by an ambulance and brought to the air-port. I will be flown to France. Afterwards another ambulance will transport me to Lourdes." He then finishes the description of his plans with the words "Boy, will you see a miracle then!"

The Jew who ostensibly hopes that the virgin of Lourdes will work a miracle for him simultaneously mocks at this belief. He laughs sarcastically at the miracle and the Christians who believe in it by sarcastically agreeing with them.

VIOLENCE

A clinical psychologist recently made an inquiry into the psychological differences between Gentile and Jewish college-students and published some of his interesting results. He found, for example that the majority of Jewish young men showed a distinct aversion to violence. This dislike or even abhorrence of brutal force cannot have been a primary attitude of the Jewish people. The biblical stories of their early period, especially of the period following the invasion of Canaan, show not a trace of an original strong aversion to violence. As a matter of fact, these early phases are filled with the outrageous and brutal deeds of the Jewish tribes whose temperament was certainly like that of other Semites of antiquity.

It seems that only with the great Mosaic religious reform and even more effectively with the teachings of the prophets did the original inclination to violent action slowly give way to a reaction against blood-thirstiness and murderous drives. It is difficult to estimate how permanent such emotional reaction-formations are, but it is certain that relapses into a primitive and elementary

attitude occur under certain sociological and psychological circumstances. If one can trust the news reports from Israel, retalia-
tive and vindictive actions of the new generation of Israeli,
murder and brutality as revenge for Arab aggressions are no
rarity.

There are, however, differences in the form and extent of
brutal actions between the average Gentile and the average
Jewish man. We will compare them by contrasting a typical
Viennese anecdote and a sentence spoken by a Jew. When I was
a boy, there lived, in Vienna, an athlete and wrestler, Jagendorfer. One evening he told his friends about an event of the
day: "Imagine, when I came to my coffeehouse this afternoon
and wanted to play billiards, my cue was not there. I searched
for it everywhere but I did not find it. Then I saw a man playing
on another table and he was using my cue. I go over there and
say: 'Mister, that's my cue.' Says he: 'No, it's mine.' Says I:
'Mister, give me the cue, I told you it belongs to me.' But the
guy does not want to deliver it and keeps saying it's his cue.
After they washed him with vinegar, I realized that it's really
not my cue." This is a humorous story rather than a joke. Our
first impression is that the coarse giant who knocks down an
innocent person on account of such a bagatelle is a clumsy
blockhead.

Let us try to rephrase his tale. "When I knocked him unconscious and people tried to revive him, I realized: . . ." There
is still a bit of the comic left, but the witty effect hangs on the
omission of words, on the ellipsis, the skipping of words and
with it the jumping from one situation to another without considering the intermediatary step. The following sentence then
contains an allusion to the omitted content, to the blank left in
the story.

We compare the Jagendorfer tale with a witticism which
originated in Vienna in the same period. Karl Kraus, the witty
and bellicose editor of the Viennese polemic magazine *Die
Fackel*, often attacked powerful and influential people in articles
full of biting irony. Sometimes the aggressor was physically maltreated by those he had attacked. Once, when the rumor of a

new misdeed of one of Kraus' old enemies was spreading in Viennese circles, someone said: "When Karl Kraus hears of this his face will be slapped again."

Our initial bewilderment at such a non-sequitur soon disappears when we guess what was omitted here. When Kraus hears of that, he will write one of his malicious articles and his victim will retaliate by slapping his face. The technique of this joke is, of course, also elliptic.

But we wanted to point out that there are differences between the Gentile story and the Jewish witticism. In both physical violence are the subjects of the joke and we laugh in both cases because we are saved from feeling pity for the victim of a violent attack. Yet in the Jagendorfer anecdote the aggression is of a very brutal, unjust and exaggerated nature. The witty remark about the predicted maltreatment of the Viennese writer by the offended person points also to a violent act, but of a less coarse and brutal one—besides that the maltreatment has at least a semblance of some justification. Both deeds or misdeeds are, however, drastic measures in which physical force is used.

Their common basic character is more obvious than their differences. Here the question could be posed: what happened to those aggressive and violent drives of the Jewish people after they were energetically repressed by the religious commandments and the ethical teachings? This oversteps, of course, the bounds of our inquiry marked by the psychological exploration of Jewish wit. We will, at least, attempt to refer to one of the transformations of those aggressive tendencies, to a change which appeared in Jewish jokes of a certain group.

Here are two representative examples, the one, related before, from the ghetto-milieu, the other from the transitional level to emancipated Jewry. A Jew asks the other if it is true that he got beaten up in Rzezow in the middle of the market place? "Pah," answered the other contemptuously, "Rzezow—also a town." Instead of giving the information, the victim disdainfully dismissed the place in which his face was slapped as insignificant and despicable. In the other anecdote a Jew comes to a party and greets

the guests: "How do you do, gentlemen! Please strike me already!" The men, astonished, ask him why they should do this
and he tells them that the day before yesterday he had been at a
social function. Politics had been discussed and he was asked to
which party he belonged. He answered; "I am a Liberal." Everyone had then shouted, "Strike him." Yesterday he had been at a
party where the same question was asked and he had answered
that he belonged to the Conservatives and the men had yelled,
"Hit him." "Here I am today," he added, "so I say: Why so many
questions? Hit me already!"

We will ignore here the one aspect of the joke that demonstrates that the Jew will be hit whether he professes to the one
or the other conviction. What interests us here are the experiences of the Jew's aggressive and sadistic drives. The two jokes
say it clearly: those violent and cruel tendencies were turned
inside and transformed into a masochistic inclination, into a
kind of unconscious satisfaction in suffering and occasionally
even in the provocation of punishment, of injuries and insults.

It seems that the Jews have learned during the terrible time
of the dispersion that it is better to suffer persecution than to
persecute. Overshooting the mark, Christianity proclaimed that
the attacked person should turn the other cheek.

By Any Other Name

In primitive thinking, an object and the word representing it
are inseparable. For preliterate people, and for children, the
name of a person is as substantial a part of him as his body. A
change of names therefore means that it is not the same person
but another one. A prominent psychologist who studied the
character of infantile thought-processes stated that for a child
to think means to deal with words. "Until the age of six or seven,
names come from the things themselves"(42). Here are two
examples of such childhood conceptions of the significance of
names. My son Arthur who is now forty-six years old, does not
remember any longer that as a little boy he wondered about the
fact that one of his playmates was called Herman. It was incon-

ceivable to Arthur that a little boy should be called *Herr* and *Mann*. Arthur, who has been interested in music since early childhood surprised us once with the question: "Is he called Mozart because his tunes are so *zart?*" (zart in German==tender, delicate).

The inseparableness of name and individual, so characteristic of primitive thinking, explains why we unconsciously attribute a high significance to the name of a person. The psychoanalytic study of dreams and neurotic symptoms shows that we still unconsciously believe that the name of an individual is as near to him as his skin.

In old times Jewish names were patronymic. A man, for instance, was called Moses Mendelssohn and a descendant of his, Felix Mendelssohn. Other names like Cohn, Levi, Rabinowitz, etc. point to religious traditions. Only in the beginning of the 19th Century were Jewish family-names finally determined by Gentile officials. Some of the new names were harmless. The German officials chose labels from the countries or cities from which the person originated, for instance, Oesterreicher, or Hamburger. The officials, especially those of the Austrian-Hungarian monarchy, often chose ridiculous or even vulgar names so that the new name-giving sometimes amounted to name-calling. Jewish wit often used these names as material for satire. In countless jokes the witty effect is tied to the very name of the person of those stories.

Let me quote an example from my own experience. Several years ago I was invited to give a lecture at the psychology department of Adelphi College. When Dr. Donald Milman, a lecturer on psychology at that college, picked me up, we drove past a great number of beautiful cottages on Long Island. I expressed my astonishment about the well-kept suburban houses. Dr. Milman said: "Yes, these people try to keep up with the Cohens." The witty effect of the sentence results from the variation of an American phrase. In substituting "Cohen" for the colloquial name "Jones," Dr. Milman alluded to the fact that most of the residents of that suburb were Jewish.

The name of an individual thus became the token, by and

by, of belonging to a religious community. In a scene of a now forgotten play, (if memory does not fail me, Max Bernstein's "Herthas Hochzeit") a person says "That's as certain as the Gospel." The partner of the conversation bows and says: "My name is Rosenthal" and thus indicates that he is Jewish. Let me insert here a comic anecdote which centers around a name. A married couple visit the exhibition of a famous modern painter. When they enter a room, the wife points to a picture and says "That's a nice portrait." The husband contradicts, "But that's a landscape." They walk nearer to the painting and look at its title which is "Nussbaum an der Riviera." "Did I not tell you," says the woman, "that it is a portrait?"

The mockery in many Jewish jokes is directed to the more or less successful attempts of many Jews to change their names in order to be assimilated into Gentile society. Derisive laughter is provoked by this kind of protective mimicry in which the individual tries to disavow his Jewish origin. In an American example, the singer Rosen introduced himself to the director Conried of the Metropolitan Opera. "Where did you leave the Feld in your name?" Conried teasingly asked the singer. The artist replied "At the same place where you found the Ried of yours." The allusion in the director's question suggests, of course, that the singer was originally called Rosenfeld, and the answer of the singer hints at the possibility that the name of the director was at first most probably Cohn or Cohen.

Bruno Walter whose family name had been Schlesinger was teasingly called "Herr Schlesinger von der Vogelweid"—an allusion to the line "Herr Walter von der Vogelweid, der ist mein Meister gewesen" from Wagner's *Meistersinger*.

A full change of the original name does not protect the person from suspicion. They tell the following story from old Hungary. In a train compartment four gentlemen get into conversation during which they introduce themselves. "Kamory" says the first, "Kemeny" says the second, "Kratvany" the third. "My name is also Cohn," says the fourth.

Another tale from Hungary shows that the possibility of a new name began to haunt Jewish people. A friend shows Sammy Fischer around in Budapest. The two men come to the monu-

ment of the famous Hungarian poet Alexander Petöfy. Sammy
Fischer listens to the biographical sketch of the writer given by
his friend, and asks: "What was he called previously?" Here are
two recent variations on the old theme: Once a Guernsey and a
Holstein breeds were crossed and produced a Goldstein cow.
Instead of saying "Mooo!", the descendant of the interbreeding
says "Nooo. . . ?" Finally an anecdote from the new state of
Israel. At a social party, some officers of the army introduce
themselves to each other. The first says: "Jacob Shulamith,
formerly Edelstein," the second: "Jacob Kadera, formerly
Katzenelbogen." A major of the Israeli army who is present
remarks, "What Israel needs, is a *Who* Was *Who*."

The old belief in the magic qualities of a name continues to
live in Jewish jokes of this kind. Romeo's question "What's in a
name?" invites the Jewish answer: The very person.

The Echo of the Proverb

To my sister Margaret

I

It was rather strange how we felt, my younger sister and I,
whenever we overheard a proverb in the conversations of the
grownups. When someone said "However you throw a cat it
always falls on its feet," the meaning was quite clear. We knew
that, for we ourselves had tried the experiment time and again.
But why was this proverb used when one of the partners in the
conversation would obstinately keep coming back to the same
point? What had that to do with the acrobatic agility of a cat?

Many proverbs were quite unintelligible to us and remained
so for a considerable time. For instance, what was the significance of the phrase, "Drag me; I am so happy to come!" That
sounded absurd. Only much later did we understand that here
was an allusion to the behavior of a girl who plays hard to get
and just loves to be conquered. How peculiar and utterly funny
for us children was the proverb "Every mother is a mother."
Naturally, every mother is a mother since she has a child.

Today the sentence sounds as though it had anticipated Gertrude
Stein's stylistic mannerism "A rose is a rose is a rose." We did
not then realize that the saying did not refer to the actual state
of motherhood, but that the psychological importance of motherhood was driven home by the obviousness of the remark.

For simple folk as for children it is, I think, but one step
from the unusual and incomprehensible to the farcical and
funny. We just laughed at some of the Jewish proverbs and
sayings which we heard at an early age. We laughed at them
as we did at a jest.

The dissimilarities between a joke and a proverb are so
evident that we are tempted to shut our eyes to the fact that
both phenomena are neighbors with respect to their actual
origin and result. There exists a genetic connection of a distinct
kind; many a proverb can be proved to have crystallized from
a comical anecdote or a joke. "Rotten fish and a thrashing to
boot," was an occasional saying. Its origin, obviously, is an
anecdote or a funny tale of a man who buys worthless goods,
and, voicing his discontent, gets a thrashing into the bargain.

On the other hand, a number of jokes owe their popularity
to a witty presentation or distortion of well-known proverbs
and phrases. We heard, for instance, the phrase "He has a cap
for riding." This was said of someone who was in no way prepared for a certain task, but had provided for himself only a
superficial attribute, like a jockey who has no horse or saddle,
only a cap.

In Jewish everyday life, the line of demarcation between the
contiguous phenomena of the proverb and the joke often becomes indistinct. There is evidence of the fact that proverbs and
precepts of Biblical and Talmudical times were subjected, later
on, to farcical applications or variations. It might be argued at
this point that we should add to the momentary emotional
effect the decision whether the matter in question be a proverb,
a funny story, or a witticism. But even this criterion becomes
uncertain. What we are dealing with is, for instance, an otherwise reputable proverb which has been disguised by a fool's cap,
or merely a joke pretending to be didactic and posing as a

proverb. We smile, as if the difference were but of little importance. And sometimes we don't even smile. My grandfather used to say that a baby is born with clenched fists and that a man dies with his hands open. It sounded like a metaphor expressing the idea that the infant wants to grasp the whole world and that he finally lets it slip out of his hands as if it had been nothing. It did not sound very funny to us children.

Most of the Jewish proverbs we heard, however, seemed to us funny. Was it not funny to be told "Wash my fur, but do not wet it?" (It was, of course, at a time when other chemical cleaning processes were unknown to us.) However, as often as not the fun left an aftertaste, for we found many of these sayings detestable. They were sometimes in strange contrast to our feelings, as well as to the moral views imparted to us at home and at school. There was, for instance, the phrase "To kill a chicken and not hurt it." To us children it meant, of course, not to inflict pain on an animal unnecessarily. It was only many years later that we found out the real meaning of this phrase: that to attain a definite goal one must not have an exaggerated delicacy of feeling. Qualms must not deter you if you are bent on success.

Another phrase seemed even stranger. A person who was generally disliked was being discussed, and somebody said "If God is so fond of him, He had better take him." This was utterly incomprehensible. There was nothing peculiar in that God should take to Him some person He was fond of, but why was it said in such a strange tone? We realized much later that it was the euphemistic expression of a desire for the person's death, and we took exception to it, all the more because it was uttered in connection with "our Lord."

We also strongly objected to the saying "He who is kind to himself, is kind to others." We had been taught not to try to promote our own welfare, but that of others, and to suppress in their favor our own self-seeking interests. This proverb recommended almost the reverse. It took us a long time to comprehend the psychological justification of the words. The study of one's own life and of the lives of others proves that it is impossible to neglect one's own interest to an excessive extent in favor of that of others. Too much consideration for others, a tendency to self-sacrifice, must lead to an inordinate desire to revenge one's self on those others for such self-denial and sacrifice that were too great. Unconsciously, free play will then be given to evil and revengeful impulses.

However, such a maxim must by no means be mistaken for a pronunciation of "*sacro egoismo*." It is rather a reactive egotism which crops up, a warning originated from the inner perception and coinciding with the findings of psychoanalytic practice. Human nature being what it is—our own including—we must be tolerant towards our egotistical impulses, too, to a certain degree, lest we treat our fellow-men badly.

Well-considered self-interest was also served in the advice we heard given: "One must not push anybody away, only gently put him aside."

We paid exceptional attention to proverbs which referred to the family—most of them also incomprehensible or contradictory to our childish feelings. For instance, it was said of a couple who were eternally quarreling, "They do not really quarrel with each other; it is their 'dalles' that quarrels." The Jewish word "dalles" which we had often heard before meant poverty, indigence, actual want. Life showed us later how great a part a strained financial situation played in the origin of conjugal conflicts.

Some proverbs brought food and health in intimate connection. One was told, for instance, "You ask an ill person, and you give a healthy person," which means to give whatever food there is to someone who is healthy without asking him if he wants it; you only ask an ill person if he might want certain dishes. Puzzling was the saying, "When a Jew eats a chicken, either the Jew is ill or the chicken is ill." We ate sometimes, though very rarely, chicken, and we got it although we were not ill and we were convinced that mother would not cook a chicken that was ill.

What was the meaning of a proverb: "That suffering which a man inflicts on himself, not ten enemies could do to him?"

There was a phrase: "Kowed on the left, money on the right." The Hebrew word "Kowed" meant honor, appreciation, even admiration, and the phrase implies that often honor bestowed upon one can well be accompanied by poverty, or that it is advisable not to strive too ambitiously for appreciation, but to look for a comfortable life. (How often did I remember that saying in later years!)

We sometimes heard proverbial phrases about maids, for instance, that they are "paid enemies," which astonished us since they always seemed to be our friends. In this connection the hypothetical possibility of God having a family surprisingly arose. It was said "If God's sister were a maid, she would not be better than this one," which meant that you have to keep up with the present maid; the next would be the same.

On the whole, it was astonishing what a strange part God played in these proverbs. There sometimes appeared the complaint, "God should not lay as great a burden on a person as he is able to carry!" One phrase seemed to confirm the Lord's omnipotence when it said, "If God wills it, a broom will fire shots." A broom functioning as a gun was, indeed, a funny idea. After all, it was not quite clear why God should use a broom when He was able, in His omnipotence, to make a gun or a revolver go off. On the other hand, there was a phrase which seemed to express serious doubts about God's omnipotence. It sounded like a sigh: "All right, God will help, but who is going to help me until He does?" Who but Himself should give help, in the meantime, if need should arise?

III

In recalling those proverbs and many other phrases heard in early youth, the memory of the people who used them is easily evoked. Many beloved phantoms rise up from the shadowy past, and many hated ones as well. These proverbs were uttered on various occasions by our parents, relatives, friends and acquaintances, but most of them, by far, came from our grandfather. I must now relate a few things about him.

In my memory he lives as a very tall, old man, with white hair, which was always covered by a small cap, and with spectacles, over the top of which he looked at us. I can still see him in his old-fashioned, somewhat untidy dressing gown, slouching through the apartment, as often as not taking snuff out of a small, black snuff box, and talking or shouting in the Jewish-German idiom. It was told later that he was a well-known, even a famous Talmud scholar. I, myself, can remember Jewish scholars and pious men coming to see him frequently in order to study or to argue with him. We could hear, in our bedrooms, their loud and excited voices which they made no effort to lower, until late in the night.

Our grandfather had spent the best part of his life as a business man and Jewish scholar in a village near the Austrian-Hungarian frontier where there was still a sort of ghetto. We children had frequently spent our holidays there (Nagy-Marton, today called Mattersdorf, in Austria) and we had often wondered at the strange practices and habits in the small Jewish community. Our grandfather encouraged us to take part in the religious rites which we could only follow imperfectly, but by which we were deeply impressed. Passover, New Year, the Day of Atonement, the beginning and end of the Sabbath, left their lasting marks on our minds. Very ancient choral music, which I then heard in the synagogue, comes sometimes, surprisingly, to my mind.

After his wife's death, grandfather, already old and frail, found himself alone, without sufficient means of subsistence. He moved to Vienna to live with us in our rather small flat. I well remember the day of his arrival, because his first action upset us children a good deal. There was a marble bust on the sideboard representing either Jove or Apollo. Our grandfather must have been upset by it when he first walked through our rooms. He seized a chair, climbed on it rather clumsily, and with a hammer struck off the bust's nose. This incomprehensible act had, of course, a religious motive: my grandfather, who was fanatically devout, would on no account tolerate images in rooms inhabited by him, since those images were strictly forbidden by the Jewish commandments. ("Thou shall not make unto thee any graven images.")

This act was the beginning of a bitter struggle, lasting for many years, between grandfather and father, interrupted only by shorter or longer truces. Violent debates were fought out on religion, its object and justification, its attitude toward modern civilization and progress. There was no bridge from the one shore to the other—from the standpoint of a God-fearing prose-lyte to an agnostic, from a medieval to a modern mind.

But the point in question was not merely theoretical. Many excited discussions were held with regard to the observance of the dietary laws in the kitchen, and my grandfather insisted, with obstinacy, upon its ritual strictness. Since his son-in-law would not submit to his dictatorship and since there was but one kitchen, it was extremely difficult to keep a strict division between "kosher" and "treife." It was almost impossible to prevent plates for meat coming into contact with those for milk, and not even the slightest of any such transgressions escaped my grandfather's relentless observation. Each such discovery ended in a scene in which he tried to enforce his despotic will upon the household.

My father, revolted by this tyranny and yet pitying the old and lonely man, could not forego his advanced views. In the conflict between her father and her husband it was my mother who suffered most. Yet she could not make up her mind to send the old man to a home for old people. We children gradu-ally began to detest our grandfather. Yet there are memories from our earlier childhood which show, that in spite of all, we loved and admired him, and that his affection, often clumsily shown, must have found an echo in us.

It did not always happen that the disputes between grand-father and father took a violent turn. Now and then the two men had peaceful, even friendly conversations, and I know that some of the funny or witty sayings of the old man made my father laugh heartily. But generally the contrasting views brought about, all too soon, a rupture in the discussions.

If matters came to this point it would frequently happen that my father felt upset and declined to talk to his father-in-law. In that case the two men who, after all, felt the need of expressing their views, would live like strangers side by side. Our grandfather then remained in his room for the better part of the day, moodily playing the part of King Lear. His sense of guilt and his wish for reconciliation must apparently have been fairly strong, for he always managed to make my father, who was irritable, but good-natured to the extreme, start talking to him again. I remember during one of these periods of a temporary breaking off of diplomatic relations, we happened to hear strange sounds in my grandfather's room. He was walking up and down talking to himself, "ba, ba, ba, ba . . ." Mother and we children rushed into his room crying: "What is the matter? What are you saying?" "Nothing," he replied, "I am giving myself some practice in order not to forget how to talk altogether. Nobody will talk to me."

I can still see the figure of the old man at the hour of my father's death. Praying aloud he entered the room where the man, by so many years his junior, was lying in his last sleep. In accordance with the religious rites my grandfather first of all covered up the mirror and opened the windows, so that the soul of the dead man might ascend towards heaven. After that event he seemed to have grown more laconic and gloomy. He died a few years later in a persecution mania full of religious delusions. It was from this tyrannical, detested, and yet much admired grandfather that I heard a great many of these Jewish proverbs. It was much later that I understood their poignancy or charm.

IV

Something said in passing often reappears after many years like a delayed echo. The proverbs and idiomatic phrases heard by us children long ago were quickly "forgotten." They sank down into the recesses of the soul from where they sometimes surprisingly emerge. Just as mysterious as the causes which de-

termined their disappearance were the motives which forced
these phrases to the surface again. Frequently no connecting
link was discernible in the actual situation. Our memory does
not remind us that we have searched for these sentence. They
simply turned up. The after effect of such proverbs heard in
childhood may prove more significant than the effect itself, the
echo more important than the original sound.

Here is an example. There is a conflict between strong im-
puses emerging for biological reasons and opposing forces caused
by the development of civilization and bent on surpressing and
displacing the former. In this conflict the forbidden impulses
have provided for themselves an unconscious outlet. Under the
effect of the two opposite forces there arises a possibility of
recognizable utterance and expression. They form a compromising manifestation, an unconscious admission of those surpressed impulses. That emotional tendency breaking through by
such compromising actions I have called compulsion to confess.
Their compulsory character became evident, for the most part,
from the instinctual nature of the original, repressed impulses
and also from the strong pressure of the sense of guilt reacting
on them. The striving to give expression to the surpressed impulses have, under the influence of certain cultural factors, led
to the development of an unconscious compulsion to confess,
which clearly exhibits all characteristics of its origin and presents itself as something intermediate between concealment and
representation.

Some time after I had formulated my analytic experiences
and views in a book *Geständniszwang und Unbewusstes Straf-
bedürfnis*, published in 1926(43), I suddenly remembered one of
those sentences frequently used by my grandfather. We often
heard this phrase when my father, hurt by some of grandfather's
remarks in one of those excited discussions, left the room. The
old man would sigh deeply and utter: "When we are alive, we
are forbidden to talk. When we are dead, we cannot talk." We
children laughed secretly, since we only understood the literal
sense of this saying, which we considered a platitude. We did

not realize that from this statement followed the question: When, after all can one talk? When are we free to express our views?

It was that phrase which prompted me to recognize the development of my theory of the compulsion to confess whose character takes the form of a compromise owing to the cooperation and opposition of biological and cultural factors.

Late resounds in us what early sounded. We do not show enough surprise, I think, when phrases from the time of our childhood turn up again after a long interval, when all at once we utter expressions heard in years long gone by and never heard again, when sentences unfamiliar to our conscious thoughts and proverbs that we had entirely forgotten and for which we should have searched our memory in vain, come to mind. It is as if we had unexpectedly met, after a very long time, a childhood friend. It is as if somebody else uttered those words and yet it is the Ego, a part of the self, that has become estranged to us.

Asleep for many years in unknown depths they return more and more frequently the older we grow. They demand that we listen to them and act upon them. What is their purport? To remind us of our childhood, of our parents and grandparents who once upon a time pronounced them? They are a reminder that we are to set out on the path travelled by our forefathers. They summon us to our forebears before we are gathered to them.

THE VOICES OF OTHERS IN YOU

I

In the preceding chapter the question was raised why long forgotten proverbs that we once heard often continue resounding in us. They often surprise us by their reemergence and we are sometimes tempted to brush them aside. Yet most of them are meaningful in the context in which they occur. It is only necessary to lend them your ear without interfering, to recognize them, when they resound. (An Irishman recently asserted that his wife has the last word even to the echo.)

Not only proverbs, but also jokes and funny or peculiar phrases, long forgotten, reappear in this way. It is as though they come as messages from an alien territory, but it is not alien, only alienated. They form a background music to our thinking. It is interesting to examine the occasions in which they occur. Here are a few of them: during a theater performance a Jewish joke suddenly came to mind. On the stage a heavy hail-storm broke forth. Looking at the scene I remembered the anecdote in which a Jew tells another that he has insured himself against fire and hail. The other says: "Fire I understand. But how do you produce hail?" The meaning is quite clear. It is an allusion to a future design to cheat the insurance company by burning up his house and then cash the amount insured. But how can he follow such a procedure in the case of damage by hailstorm? The emergence of this joke is determined by my wondering what technical trick is employed to produce hail on the stage. Behind that astonishment must be, of course, some sort of mockery, a reluctance to accept the illusion created by the stage-manager. The nature of thought-associations bringing up the memory of that joke is in this case quite clear.

Here is an example of a proverb of which I had not thought for many years and which I suddenly remembered during a psychoanalytic session. Quite a few years ago I listened to a neurotic patient who for many hours described the shame he felt of his family. He said that since boyhood had felt embarrassment that they, immigrants from Russia, could not speak correct English and remained orthodox Jews observing all religious holidays. Later on he had changed his name because it sounded Jewish. The same patient complained that he had bad luck in his profession, that his marriage had been a failure and that his friends had deserted him in a critical situation. As I listened to him, apparently from nowhere the following lines occurred to me:

> Wer sich schämt von seiner Mischpoche
> Auf dem ist ka broche

Mischpoche is the Hebrew word for family and broche means blessing: the saying would thus mean: Whoever is ashamed of his family, has no luck. The proverb connects—in a religious or metaphysical sense—misfortune with shame of one's family. There is good psychological sense in this saying: One can choose one's friends or one's mate, but one cannot choose one's parents or ancestors. One must accept them with their good qualities and weaknesses and cannot escape from them. A permanent feeling of being ashamed of them must lead to some unfavorable characterological consequences: the person will not accept himself, since our parents continue to live in us, are introjected in us, and are part of our personality. Thus a kind of flight from oneself begins. Connected with it is the resulting unconscious guiltfeeling which leads the person to spoil his own changes in life, to sabotage himself, and unconsciously to stage manage his own bad luck. Those impressions must have run through my mind while I listened to the patient and found their crystallization in the emergence of that long forgotten proverb.

Another proverb, suddenly remembered during a consultation, surprised me. I had seen the patient several months previously and had referred him to a student of mine for psychoanalytic treatment. He had come back for a consultation during which he complained that his psychoanalyst had an aloof attitude, rarely gave him encouragement and did not help him solve the serious conflicts into which he had been drawn. At a certain point two lines I had not remembered for a long time, ran through my mind:

> Einem Stein soll man's klagen,
> Nur nicht bei sich soll man's tragen!

I must have heard these lines in childhood. They mean, freely translated:

Better pour out their troubles to a stone—
But don't carry them within yourself.

In this situation this means: it is better to have this silent and
seemingly indifferent psychotherapist than cope with emotional
difficulties alone, without confiding in anyone. In spite of his
complaints I must have observed in the patient some improve-
ment which I attributed to the freeing, cathartic effect of the
treatment.

Here, for a change, is a Jewish joke that came to mind during
an analytic session. The patient had described an attitude that
had once puzzled him: on the evening of the day on which his
wife was buried he suddenly felt engulfed by a wave of sexual
excitement and visited a prostitute. At this point the Jewish
anecdote occurred to me: the husband of a woman whose funeral
is about to take place, is nowhere to be found. His brother-in-
law at last finds him in the room of the maid, with whom he had
just had sexual intercourse. Full of indignation and rage, the
brother-in-law abuses him for such conduct. The husband defends himself, saying: "Do I know what I do in my mourning?"
This half-serious memory of that anecdote certainly occurred to
me as a kind of psychological interpretation of the patient's
behavior.

II

All the preceding examples are explainable as results of a
train of thoughts accompanying my conscious reflexions while I
listened to my patients. Memories of Jewish proverbs and jokes
of which I had not thought for a long time, formed, so to speak,
running comments to the reports of the person who told me
about his experiences. Our knowledge of the laws of thought-
associations are sufficient to explain the emergence of those half-
forgotten sayings and anecdotes. There is nothing mysterious
about those cases. The occasion when they occurred, their associative connection with the subject under discussion and their
meaning present enough psychological data to understand their

emergence. The phenomenon is not very different from a situation in which I suddenly remember that I have put a book I had missed for some time in this or that place.

We now look at cases of surprising emergency from another point of view. Not the occasion of the reappearance, but the original source from which that anecdote or that joke came puzzles us. I have said in the preceding chapter, that I had heard many of those proverbs or sayings from my grandfather or from other relatives. In some cases, however, the origin of those reoccurring sentences or witticisms remained enigmatic. The other question, as to why they reappear just when they do is sometimes easily answerable, but where do they come from, where and from whom have you heard them first?

While writing about jokes in which Jews make fun of their own misconduct, I, to my own surprise, thought of a sentence that, in spite of its incompleteness, was connected with that theme. There was the name of a place or of a city which eluded me, but the continuation of that sentence was a question: . . ."Is that not the city where they have geganved (Yiddish=stolen) an engine?" I was only able to remember that I must have heard that said when I was a little boy and that I had wondered about that sentence later on. It was certainly before I was four years old, perhaps not more than three and a half years old. I tried to remember who the person was who had said that, and who the other was to whom it was said. I remember only that it was in some street in Vienna, and I see myself as a little boy standing close beside the man who asked that question in his conversation with another man. The reconstruction I attempted never went beyond that point, but I know that neither of the two men was my grandfather or father. Perhaps it was another relative who had taken me for a walk. I do not know why, but I have the impression that the other grown-up person laughed at that question. I seem to have taken the story that the Jews in P . . . had stolen an engine seriously. Laughter was, perhaps in my view, an inappropriate reaction.

I understand, now of course, that the grotesque story that the Jews of P. had stolen a locomotive, was a gigantically exaggerated allusion to the dishonesty of the Jews in that city, but I am almost sure that the moral side of the tale was of no interest to me as a little boy. I listened as someone does to an interesting piece of news.

We compared those other cases of the emergence of forgotten jokes and proverbs to the situation in which a person who had forgotten where he put a certain object, a book for instance, suddenly remembers the place where he left it. The case just discussed is very different: only after I, so to speak, caught that phrase in my inner ear did I remember that I must have heard it once, almost seventy years ago. To continue with the comparison used; it is as though we find an object, a book, for instance which we never knew we possessed. Let me give you an illuminating instance of this kind, also connected with writing. I wanted to quote a few lines from Friedrich Hebbel's play, *Gyges and his Ring*, but was not sure if I had kept the text correctly in my recollection. I took that volume of Hebbel's works from my library and searched for that passage. I had not read the tragedy for many years, but I knew that the lines are spoken by Kandaules, king of ancient Lydia. Searching for this passage in turning over the leaves of the book I found, to my great surprise, a money-order to me, dated almost twenty years ago, which I had never cashed. More than this, I had, during all this time, never remembered it and did not recognize the name of the sender. I just did not know that this money-order existed and was somewhere in my possession. Such a case is psychologically quite different from the other in which you misplace an object and do not remember where you put it.

In the case of the engine-story the occasion when it reoccurred is obvious. I had just written the paper on jokes about Jewish misconduct (included in this book). Also the associative link in thought is known, but who are the two persons in that conversation? And what was the significance of that phrase, that had sunk into oblivion for perhaps seventy years, for me, then a boy of four? Until now we were concerned with the nature of the mental process by which such memories are revived, but we paid almost no attention to the emotional side of that reemergence. Yet there must be some emotional tendencies which help them to cross the threshold of the unconscious and those determinants are perhaps more important for the understanding of their reappearance than the laws of thought-association. We shall soon revert to this subject.

III

John Keats wrote in a letter to Fanny George and Georgiana Keats, dated May 3, 1819, the following sentence: "Nothing ever becomes real till it is experienced—even a proverb is no proverb to you till your life has illustrated it." Our parents sometimes quoted a Jewish proverb "The love of the parents goes to their children; the love of these children goes to *their* children." Only the first part of this sentence made sense to us children. The notion of children of our own was unfathomably nebulous. Only after we became parents and grandparents ourselves, were we able to understand how true and profound that proverb was.

In *The Secret Self* I described fully a scene which presents a vivid example of such an experience in which a proverb became alive for me. Proverbs which the French writer Joubert once called "abridgments of wisdom," are not results of intellectual efforts, but of amusing or melancholy experiences made through the generations, and a profound understanding of their meaning can be obtained only by experience lived by a person who not only sees the truth of the proverb, but is also surprised by its depth and veracity.

The quintessence of that scene was that one evening I felt unappreciated and hurt by my daughters, then in their teens, ruminated over it, and could not fall asleep. Then I caught myself suddenly murmuring: "Kleine Kinder, kleine Sorgen— grosse Kinder, grosse Sorgen." I was taken aback by what I had said. Was it I who had said or thought this or was it another's voice? Suddenly I had a very vivid image of my father as if seen in the center of a Rembrandtesque illumination. There must have been other persons at the fringes of that picture, perhaps an aunt of mine to whom my father spoke. I was certainly there. My father must have complained about me, (I was then at the age my younger daughter was at the time of the experience). There was an immediacy of reference to the boy, myself, who has caused his father grief and had disappointed him. The image lasted not more than a moment, but I distinctly heard the voice that resounded in me.

It was a moment of personal discovery. The emotional turmoil vividly experienced had ebbed away suddenly, and its place had been taken by that visual image and that voice. It was undoubtedly the voice of my father who had said "Kleine Kinder, kleine Sorgen—grosse Kinder, grosse Sorgen"—it was even the timbre of his voice and his slightly Viennese pronunciation. Yet I knew that I had murmured that meaningful sentence containing the essence of the experience with my own children.

For a moment the past was resurrected and the voice of my father was the voice in me. Do our parents continue to live through us and in us long after they have died? The self has some depth-dimension of which we are not aware and in which the undying past dwells, and in it the personalities of those who molded our character.

More than ten years have passed since the experience in which I heard myself say that Jewish proverb. The emotional disengagement that marks the aging process has swept aside so many experiences, but I still know that that hour has helped me in my growth to personal identity. *"Nous mourons tous inconnues,"* Balzac had once remarked. Really, we all die as unknown persons, unknown even to ourselves, but flares of self-understanding such as I experienced at that moment in which the forgotten proverb re-emerged sometimes flash through the darkness.

IV

I would like to revert now to that funny remark about the stealing of an engine I had heard when I was a little boy, but I can do this only on a detour.

Alexander Moszkowski once tried to define a Jewish joke:

Ein jüdischer Witz
Mit jüdischim Akzent:
Was ein Goy nicht versteht
Und ein Jud immer schon kennt.

A Jewish joke
With a Jewish accent
Which a Jew already knows
And a Goy doesn't understand.

In this sense that question about the place where the people have "geganved" (= stolen) an engine is not a Jewish joke, but a teasing jest allegedly asking for information.

To bring the character of that story into sharpest focus, you must imagine the Jew asking that astonishing question. He and all other Jews telling jokes do not only tell them, but act them. They play a solo-scene acting the part of the schnorrer or rich banker, the Talmud-student and his hosts, the matchmaker and the young man or young woman involved, and so on. We should not speak of the teller of Jewish stories, but rather of their actors.

What is the psychological process that takes place in this actor, who, to speak with Shakespeare "in his time plays many parts?" Is it simply an identification with the various characters who appear in his story? Does he renounce his identity and assume another in place of it?

Yvette Guilbert, the famous French diseuse, wrote Freud, who was not only one of her admirers, but also her friend for many years, that she planned to write a book in which she wanted to explain the secrets of her dramatic presentation. She thought that her technique consisted of banishing her own person and of replacing it with the character whom she represented.

In his answering letter(44), Freud says that he know little about this process and can therefore make only a few suggestions. That concept of the psychological mechanism of the actor's art has been almost universally claimed, but had never quite satisfied him. That idea "of the obliteration of one's own person and its replacement by an imagined one" gives too little information about the process and does not explain why one actor succeeds so much better than another in achieving that aim. Freud rather suspects that an element of the opposite mechanism operates here: one's own person is not obliterated, but "parts of it—repressed desires and traits that haven't a chance to develop—are employed to represent the chosen character. This hidden part of one's own personality find expression in acting and gives the stamp of realistic truth."

In another letter(45) to Yvette Guilbert's husband, Dr. Max Schiller, Freud defends his theory. He refers there to the great artist Charlie Chaplin whom he admired. Chaplin always plays the same part, the poor, weak and clumsy fellow. "Now," asks Freud, "do you think he has to forget his own self in order to play this part?" No, he plays only himself, namely the self of his grim youth; he reveals the impressions of that time, its humiliations and deprivations. Freud thus maintained that the achivements of an artist are conditioned internally.

A possible argument could be taken from the fact that Madame Yvette plays with equal mastery all kinds of characters, saints and sinners, coquettes and hausfrauen, criminals and apaches, etc., but Freud asserts that this testifies only to an unusually rich and adaptable psychic life of the actress and is inclined to trace back her whole repertoire to experiences and conflicts of her early years.

This piece of tentative theory—Freud refers in this context to his essay on Leonardo da Vinci—is, of course, incomplete, and should be continued, but what is said in those letters is sufficient to shed light on the nature of the teller or rather on the actor of Jewish jokes who plays many parts while he relates them. Certainly, his acting and telling are also determined by his own childhood impressions, vicissitutes, repressions and disappointments, but I am inclined to go beyond this point of Freud's theory in two directions. I would assume that in his representing different characters, the schnorrer and the banker, the rabbi and the poor widow, he not only actualizes experiences of his own early childhood, but also the vicissitudes of people who were near to him whom he incorporated or introjected into himself. I would guess, furthermore, that in the characters he depicts in his stories, and whom he vividly portrays in gestures, modulations, manners of speech and facial expressions, he brings to life many potentialities, various vicissitudes, that were not lived out, possible attitudes and actions that were not taken, but could have been taken. Many of those potential attitudes and actions were disavowed or repressed, sunk into oblivion. I would not hesitate to theorize that the story-teller or actor, in playing those many parts, revivifies vicissitudes of his ancestors among whom were certainly schnorrers and rabbis, Talmud-scholars as well as criminals a.s.o. But this is a far country and I must break off at this point.

Another aspect of the representation of various characters by the teller of Jewish jokes must at least be mentioned. His telling or acting is in most cases highly realistic, but sometimes an undercurrent of mockery in it is undeniably perceptible. If my theory is correct, this feature would amount to a self-caricature. But this is a delicate problem that deserves a treatment of its own.

Now the way back to the psychological investigation of the story of the stolen locomotive is paved. We have said that the boy took the bizarre tale at face value and believed that the Jews of that place had really stolen an engine. More than this: he perhaps admired the thieves and identified with them. This means that he probably wished to be in their place and be able to steal a locomotive. It did not occur to the little boy why and for which purpose the Jews would have appropriated the machine. It is significant that he never thought what the thief would do with it. I can, in retrospect, conjecture why this question never occurred to me then when I was not yet four years old.

Like so many boys of this age, I passionately wished to be an engine-driver. No conscious memory of this wish is preserved. Is there any circumstantial evidence for its existence and its psychological affect? There are two facts whose psychoanalytic interpretation would allow to arrive at a legitimate conclusion.

My father was an official of the Austrian railway-management and I still remember that in my thoughts I brought this position in intimate connection with trains. At about that time my brother, twenty years older than I got a job on a section of a railway-line and I listened to his stories about it with a kid brother's admiring interest.

The second fact possibly to be used as psychological circumstantial evidence was the occasion when the forgotten phrase about the stolen engine reappeared in my memory. It was while I read Zola's novel *La Bête Humaine*. In the final scene of this novel a driverless engine rushes on and on at top speed. "Like a maddened wild animal, head down," the runaway train flashes through the country at full speed, sweeping toward the catastrophe. While reading the grandiose scene, I experienced for a split-second the exaltation a boy feels who identifies with the powerful running engine.

The result of the analytic interpretation of the meaning that bizarre question had for me as a little boy is that I had wished to steal an engine, to do what allegedly the Jews of that place had done. There was no astonishment about that theft, nor were there any moral scruples connected with that wish.

V

A proverb I had frequently heard as a child came back to me twice during the same evening. The first time, while I listened to a patient in a psychoanalytic session: he bitterly complained about several external circumstances, for instance his financial situation, the character of women with whom he kept company and so on, which he made responsible for his failures. He finished his complaints with the words "Well, it's the white man's burden. Go fight City-Hall!"

I felt like contradicting not his implied statement that it is vain to fight the municipality, but his view that those various external factors were to be blamed for his misfortunes. I felt like reminding him of how much he himself unconsciously contributed to his failures and thought of some constitutional factors operating that could not be changed. I did not, of course, express that opinion, but when he said "Go fight City-Hall" that old phrase, long forgotten and heard as a child, came to mind. When I was a little boy, I sometimes complained unreasonably about something, and my grandfather said "Schlag' dich mit Gott herum!" (= go, fight God). There is thus a contrast between City-Hall and the deity. Common to both of them is that it is vain to try to change their will, but the contrast is that God is the higher instance whose will has to be accepted.

A few hours later I listened to a performance of Johann Strauss' operetta *Die Fledermaus* (The Bat) on the radio. The aria

> Glücklich ist, wer vergisst
> Was nicht mehr zu ändern ist

> Fortunate is he who can forget
> What cannot be changed any more

followed me and was accompanied by the recurring phrase "Schlag dich mit Gott herum." The tenor of that sentence as well as of the aria is, of course, the same, namely that the final outcome of human endeavor must be resignation.

CHAPTER III

In Search of Characteristics

INTRODUCTORY REMARK

The second part of this book presented an admittedly incomplete typology of Jewish jokes. What should now follow, is a survey of their characteristic features, of the manifest and latent peculiarities that differentiate them from the witticisms of other groups. No such systematic presentation has, as far as I know, been attempted until now. The best characterization of Jewish wit is contained in the comments which Freud made in his analysis of their technique and their relations to the unconscious. Ernest Simon recently distilled the essence of those inserted observations of Freud's and could define certain psychological peculiarities common to Jewish jokes. We shall return to Simon's valuable essay later on in our sketch of the psychological literature on the subject.

Occasional characterizations of Jewish wit after Freud's book did not open any new aspects and may be disregarded here. The only notable exception is Martin Grotjahn's article on the masochistic character, to be discussed later on.

Is it possible to discover other characteristic feature of Jewish wit, unnoticed or not yet psychologically evaluated? One has said that dissatisfaction with the status quo is the life-source of invention. It is also the source of new psychological discoveries as, for instance, of unnoticed characteristics of Jewish peculiarities. Dissatisfied with the results of psychological inquiry obtained until now, we shall search for characteristics not yet recognized.

This search is not undertaken for its own sake. It should only pave the way and facilitate the approach to the centre of this book, namely to new insights into the psychology and psychopathology of Jewish wit.

The following chapters present a number of distinctive prevalent characteristics that to my knowledge have not been demonstrated until now.

THE INTIMACY IN JEWISH WIT

I

It gives me great satisfaction that Freud appreciated a small book entitled *Nachdenkliche Heiterkeit*(1) (published in 1933, not translated into English), as a valuable complement to his theories on wit. Not only a letter he wrote me(2), but also a conversation that I vividly remember, proved that he found in the little volume some original thoughts that continued and complemented his own conceptions.

In a previous chapter of this book the telling story of the Jew saying "Asoi!" is extensively discussed. We heard that Arthur Schnitzler, referring to this anecdote, found its essence in the lack of respect in the social intercourse of Jews. The anecdote does indeed show that once if it is recognized that the other person is also Jewish, one needs not "behave," one may drop all conventions and launch out freely. It may well be that the story delineates the intercourse of Jews among themselves, but is it significant for the general character of Jewish wit as a specific notion? One is inclined to deny that there is any representative characteristic in this particular anecdote. The story, thus it seems, represents one group of Jewish jokes, the one illustrating the relations within the Jewish community, but there are many Jewish witticisms dealing with other subjects, for instance, the stories which treat the relationship with other groups or those which present and often expose peculiarities of the religious and professional life of the Jews. An investigation which endeavors to determine the psychological earmarks of Jewish wit, will aim to recognize the characteristic features which are valid for all groups, or which are at least to be met with in the inquiry of as many examples as possible.

I am inclined to make use of the latent content of that anecdote ("Asoi!") in a way that surpasses the significance of this particular example. I am of the opinion that that joke, chosen at random, contains at its core one of the most significant distinctive feature, namely a kind of intimacy, common to all kinds of Jewish jokes. The notion of intimacy is, it is true, ambiguous and it is our task to define what is meant here. When you speak of intimacy, you generally mean a closeness, immediacy and human warmth of a relationship. But this quality also exists, for instance, between the parishioner and his father confessor, between the patient and his psychoanalyst, sometimes even between a pupil and his teacher. No, that's not the kind of intimacy we mean and which we would like to define as a mark of Jewish wit.

We heard from that Schnitzler-character that the special kind of intimacy specific for the social intercourse between Jews excludes the feeling of respect. We need not unconditionally surrender to this view, but we will admit that that statement is the result of accurate observation. The intimate relationship of parishioner and priest, of student and teacher includes a certain measure of respect. In fact, it is even scarcely imaginable without it. It is decidedly another shade of intimacy which must be attributed to Jewish wit.

When we now attempt to find in Jewish joke that token of democratic thought, we will certainly be able to refer to many examples, but that general character is not the distinguishing and decisive mark which denotes Jewish jokes. The wit of the Americans is in its premises and its character democratic also, but no one would say that it is precisely this democratic way of thinking which is its most essential, outstanding feature.

We will perhaps come closest to the nature of that intimacy, when we compare it with the kind of confidence and cordiality

existing between members of a family. The feeling of belonging-
ness and closeness between members of a Jewish family has
often been observed. Is it that atmosphere of familiarity, this
awareness of common descent and of the same fate that gives a
special mark to the Jewish wit? We got the impression that there
is something correct in this suggestion, but we are ready to meet
objections that will be voiced against it.

Jewish wit is characterized by a merciless mockery at the
weaknesses, faults and failing of the Jews. It sometimes seems to
aim especially at exposing their weak spots, at detecting all the
flaws of their character. In which family will a person try un-
ceasingly to subject the others to a cruel criticism and make
great endeavors towards degrading those near and dear to him?
To be sure, the variety and intricacy of family relations makes it
possible that occasionally such cases are also to be found, but
we will agree they do not represent the average manifestations
of family-life. We already thought that we could define the
character of intimacy in Jewish wit as originating within the
family, but the factor of persistent aggression peculiar to it
makes such an assumption very doubtful.

There only remains the possibility of searching for the characteristics of that intimacy just where it is most conspicuously
in the wrong place because it is obviously paradoxical, namely
in the area of aggressiveness. Freud has emphasized that there
are few people which so unsparingly and mercilessly ridicule
themselves as the Jews. It is the sort of mockery directed against
one's own people that is remarkable. It is a demonstration of
their faults and failings coupled with a certain "family"-pride.
It will bewilder us that that aggression can solder together
continuous and cruel criticism with an unmistakable affection
for its maltreated object to form a united expression. That kind
of aggression is painful. Yet it does not loosen the ties with the
other person and it does not diminish the feeling of belonging-
ness. It rather acknowledges the existence of these ties in the
very manner of the attack and caricature.

It would be better not to discuss the question in abstract,
but to make a test by a selection of jokes of this kind. The first

example of a witticism representing this group is an anecdote of two journalists I knew. Egon Erwin Kisch who has moved from his earlier domicile in Vienna to Berlin some years ago, meets his friend Anton Kuh, who came to Berlin only a short time ago. The two journalists want to make an appointment for one of the following days. Egon Erwin Kisch says: "Wait a moment; on Thursday I have an appointment, on Friday we have an editorial meeting at the office, but perhaps on Even Sunday? . . ." "Even Sunday?", Anton Kuh interrupts him astonished. "Even Sunday? I already knew you when you did not yet call it even Saturday . . ." In Germany people often called Saturday "Sonnabend" which sounded affected to Austrian ears. In Vienna where both journalists lived many years before one called Saturday "Samstag." The aggression in Anton Kuh's remark will, of course, mock Kisch's too quick and artificial adjustment to the capital of Berlin and its manners and does this effectively in choosing a detail of the language he now speaks which is used as a projectile. Kuh's linguistic remark means to say: "Where we both come from, my friend, that day of the week had a name that was much closer to its Hebrew origin. The name Schabbeth should sound more familiar to you. Don't pretend to be a native of Berlin, born and bred in Prussia." The aggressive intention, the tendency to unmask and to humiliate the friend is unmistakably there, but it does not want to push he other away, but, strangely enough, it wants to pull him closer to oneself.

We are aware that we are approaching the core of that intimacy whose character we tried to define. Yet we cannot grasp its peculiarity. It is clearly implied in the anecdote that the expression of derision is not bitter hostility and estrangement, but confidence and intimacy. More than this: if we can trust our impression, it is precisely that familiarity which results in the courage to criticize, to attack. But how about that? Intimacy as a premise of aggression? That is psychologically difficult to grasp. The faint insight that seemed to rise to the surface threatens to become submerged again.

II

When you explore the type of intimacy experienced in Jewish wit you will first think of jokes with a certain tendency. Harmless witticism does not flourish well among Jews. In the erotic jokes which have to be considered here besides the aggressive ones, we meet, of course, that intimacy too. Yet there is a remarkable psychological difference: in the sexual jokes intimacy is a natural consequence of the content and the character of the witticism, in aggressive jokes it is in opposition to it. In the first group, intimacy tallies with the direction of the sexual drive which tries to pull the object closer, in the latter group intimacy is in opposition to the direction of the impulse.

Attack as well as vehement criticism wishes to remove the object. In the Jewish witticism, however, aggression does not produce estrangement, but puts an end to it, cancels it. A pathos of distance will not be tolerated in this group of jokes. Yes, Jewish wit often attains its strongest effects by the manner in which differences of social, religious or other distances are bridged. Again we are faced with the paradoxical state of affair: Human closeness is not only a supposition of this kind of joke, but its attainment or regainment is an essential aim of the aggression.

Let us return for a moment to the two jokes, to the "Aesoï" story and to the Even-Sunday anecdote. The aggressive tendency is felt in both of them, but goes into opposite directions: in the journalist anecdote fun is made of the artificiality of assimilation to an alien milieu. In the train-joke the tenaciousness with which Jews cling to an old familiarity is ridiculed in its annoying by-products. Here the intimacy between the one Jew and the other is presented, but is also made a caricature of. That joke says: that familiarity goes too far. That is an intolerable impudence. Yet even this boldness is only an unpleasant manifestation of an intimacy that is experienced.

At this point that contradiction we noticed is at last solved, the paradox begins to make sense. We made a mistake in assuming that that intimacy is there from the beginning, but Jewish wit tries rather to restore a familiarity that threatens to get lost, to tighten again the bonds that begin to loosen. The intimacy is, so to speak, the result or the effect of this humorously presented endeavor, of the successful attempt at spanning an abyss.

We now realize that a social difference plays a certain role in those jokes. There is, of course, the distinction of poor and rich in the Schnorrer-anecdotes, but this is not the only and not the most significant inequality presented in Jewish witticisms. Much more important seems to be the difference in the individual attitude to Judaism and to the other national or religious groups. The gentleman in the train-anecdote has been fully assimilated to Western civilization. There is nothing in his appearance and conduct by which it could be guessed that he is still a Jew. What the story drastically and with necessary exaggeration presents is the overcoming of all conventional boundaries in the moment the Polish Jew recognizes in the other man a correligionist.

The impudence then manifested is subjectively not meant as boldness, but is rather an expression of confidence, a demonstration of fellowship in taking certain liberties. There is certainly an aggressive tendency in the joke. But if an aggressive or offensive intention would be its main motive, the witticism would necessarily have another text. The impudent behavior has as its aim not injury nor insult to the partner, but his lowering in the sense of equalization, in putting him on the same level as oneself. This is not meant as degrading, but rather as downgrading to bring the other nearer to oneself. The Polish Jew tries to make the other like himself, to treat him as an Alter Ego.

I will not pretend that these remarks succeeded in pentrating the core of that quality of intimacy. It is easier to express its character in negative terms than in positive description. That familiarity does not exalt oneself at the expense of the other person, nor does it degrade the other at the expense of the self, but it does bring the other person to the same level as one's own.

The process is psychologically akin to another that belongs to a very different area of social life. There is, as Freud has shown us, a certain type of men those peculiarity makes it impossible to have successful sexual intercourse with a woman who is considered chase and virtuous. This group of woman, often unconsciously compared with the mother or sister of the man, become untouchable. They stand too high to conceive of them as sexual objects. In order to transform them into objects of sexual satisfaction, many men, belonging to this type, have to degrade them first in words or actions so that they can be some sexually approachable.

A neurotic patient I treated was impotent with his wife except when he first addressed her in vulgar sexual terms. In this downgrading, an emotional mechanism similar to that in the Jewish jokes, is performed in order to bring the object closer to oneself. The significant difference is that in this case the aim is sexual in its nature, while in the Jewish joke social intercourse is facilitated or rather made possible by such levelling.

III

The common level maintained is first of all determined with reference to Judaism, no matter if it is conceived as a religious or national community, or as a relation for mutual support, or as the dependance of the individual on others. All those factors are results of the social situation of all Jews, their common, greatly afflicted past and the persecutions to which they were and are subject. Here the necessity becomes obvious to study Jewish wit with regard to its origin and development from certain social and psychological situations. It will be understood that its character was modified by various transformations in accordance with the changes in the destiny of the people. Direction and content of Jewish jokes have been altered several times in the last two hundred years although their essential character remained the same. Thus Jewish wit becomes a true reflection of the cultural evolution, of the social turns as well as of the changes of attitude towards one's own people.

In its revolutionary phase, Jewish wit turned against the many restrictions and privations making life in the ghetto determined by religion and tradition. Wit was thus an attempt at blasting holes in the ghetto-walls from within, to relinquish the long isolation and to find the way to a common cultural life with other people. The rebellious tendencies of this kind of joke are above all directed against the traditions and authorities that demand complete faithfulness to the Torah, which means to the foregoing of all enjoyment of life.

Not many examples of this kind of wit are left in Western civilization where Jews are emancipated. The jokes of the assimilated second or third generation of Jews retain only echoes of this kind of wit. It belongs to the social level which strives from ghetto life to modern civilization.

Yet those echoes resound deeply and still haunt a phase in which Jewish emancipation had already been achieved. They voice a late protest against obsolete and strict prohibitions while revealing a strange kind of affection for customs and laws long in disuse. In many saying is still a residue of that Jewish solidarity. Sometimes a nostalgic affection for the community one has forsaken wells up as in that sigh of a baptized Jew enjoying his dinner at a kosher delicatessen: "And from such a religion one should divorce!"

The jokes of the second or third emancipated generation are often directed against those who cowardly withdraw from a community of destiny or who pretend to belong to it no longer. They ridicule the flight from a group from which one can withdraw only officially. In those jokes is a mocking reminder of the common descent or of the social level once shared and which has now been disavowed.

We have already said that degradation is not the object of such witticisms, but serves only as an instrumental means with which to restore the missed intimacy. It tears down a barrier between persons rather than demolishing the partner.

A comical phrase I heard mocks in a similar way, the exaggerated claim, the two great measure of consideration, that is expected among the Jews. A Jew watching his chess-partner move a piece to attack said with facetious reproachfulness: "Thus you play with a good acquaintance?" Superficially seen the phrase seems to belong to the non-sensical talk that often accompanies games. Content and modulation of the sentence complain: "So unfeelingly or with so little consideration you treat an acquaintance!" or "How can you proceed so unhumanly or mercilessly with a friend?" This reproach sounds with regard to the moves in a game of chess absurd or cunning. The serious core of that automatism is the witty mocking of those exaggerated claims in social intercourse among members of the same group. The sentence, which could express a really justified reproach in another context, is here displaced to an area where it is clearly meaningless. What makes it comic, is precisely this allusion to another aspect of life.

IV

That kind of intimacy, or rather the endeavor to restore it, may be a valid analysis of the jokes, but is it the essential character of all Jewish wit? Well, some will say, there is frequently the expression of a desire to reach emotionally other people in the same social situation as the Jews. Schnitzler points to the analogy of prisoners in the same jail. But what about the considerable group of Jewish jokes which deal with other national or religious groups? In the one group of witticisms a basic attitude or frame of mind in social intercourse is characterized. In the other group of jokes dealing with Western civilization, we can not see the psychological premises for such an intimacy. We have to be prepared that the introduction of this new element will perhaps alter our concept of that social peculiarity of Jewish wit.

We will again preface the following remarks by pointing out that the nature of Jewish jokes had not remained the same; there have been decided changes in their content and accent during the last two centuries. There are, indeed, several witticisms originated in the first generation, in which nothing or very little of that special intimacy can be perceived.

The stupidity or dullness of the Gentiles rather than one's own superiority is, in those jokes, put in the foreground. It is, for instance, reported that a Jew, who had left the ghetto and stayed in Lemberg for some years, wrote a book entitled *The Goyim, their customs and manners,* as if the Gentiles were a native tribe with strange peculiarities and odd morals. But such contemptuous observations become very rare with the end of isolation.

In the jokes of the following decennial, that particular feature, the striving for an emotional intimacy, is there despite all expectations to the contrary; the alien and different character of the Gentiles is presented and the very distance between them and the Jews is often the subject of the joke. In most cases, the demasking of the other person is also here performed to bring him closer, to put him on the same level as one's own. The tendency of aggression and mockery in those jokes is too obvious to be elaborated on. As far as I know, it has not yet been recognized that simultaneously with those derisive intentions —better said, through them—the concealed tendency to restore the intimacy of feelings is operating.

We are not at a loss for examples of this kind. Instead of examples as they appear in published collections of jokes, I will chose a comical story, an account of an occurrence that I heard reported in prewar Austria. It has the advantage that the sentence I will quote was not meant as a joke and yet can claim to be very witty. An East Galician business man sent a car filled with wares to Poland. They got lost and the Jew demanded that the management of the railway line should give him full compensation. The management refused his request arguing that all records and proofs of booking the goods were missing and that he had obviously lost them. His answer pointed out that this assumption was not correct and he enclosed the bill of consignment, the dispatch notes and the other official certificates, proving the loading. His letter ended on a note of triumph, saying that the obligation of compensation becomes clear from the enclosed documents. The last, poignant sentence of the letter was the question: "How are you going to feel now, honorable management?" The original text I happened to see is almost untranslatable: "Wie wird Ihnen, löbliche Direktion?"

The comic effect of this true story results from the presupposition of an intimacy with the railway management. We laugh not only at the unexpected introduction of a jargon phrase in a letter of legal claim, but also because the man addresses an abstract office in a direct and informal manner as if he were speaking to a certain person. The sneering note connected with this address intensifies the comic effect. At all events it does not diminish the presupposed familiarity. The letter gives the impression that it deals with a personal quarrel between two individuals although there is no biting and bickering, but a legal question and although not a person, but an office is addressed and attacked.

It is difficult to characterize the special kind of intimacy in Jewish wit. It is even more difficult to define its nuances and shades. That familiarity reaches from an almost naive kind of intimacy to impudence, to a demonstrative sidling up to the other person.

There are few "harmless" jokes in the Jewish milieu of the West, but even in those the special kind of intimacy I claim as a mark of distinction of Jewish wit is still recognizable. In them too, the laughter results from an appeal to a human community whose nature and foundation is to a great extent unconscious. Even where that wit speaks in terms of the first person singular, it embraces all and means "We."

Here is an example of such rare harmless joke: There was, in Vienna, a delicatessen whose proprietor was called Beel and whose food was highly appreciated by its Viennese-Jewish customers. A board in this restaurant carried the following inscription:

> Already Hamlet asked,
> To Beel or not to Beel, that is the question.

In the original:

> Schon Hamlet sprach, so geht die Sage,
> To Beel or not to Beel, das ist die Frage.

This witty use of a word play in the service of publicity—notice the double meaning of the word "to"—attains its effect, at first, by the surprising connection of the English quotation with the name Beel, familiar to Viennese Jews. There is, no doubt, some parodistic intention in the use of Hamlet's soliloquy, but the specifically Jewish quality of the inscription is the atmosphere of intimacy into which the creator of the witticism pulls the reader, who encounters here to his surprise, the name of the delicatessen store in connection with the famous quotation from Hamlet. For a moment the memory of the melancholy prince emerges, but the question of fate which he poses is pushed into the bacgground by the question whether one should go to Beel or not go to Beel. The advertisement says, of course, that the Danish prince had already known the restaurant, but it proclaims, perhaps, in this context, something else: Hamlet should have been preoccupied with the more important question whether he should have dinner at Beel's. The witticism builds a surprising bridge between Shakespeare's profoundness and the food-preferences of Viennese Jews.

V

I do not feel competent to inquire into all the sociological and psychological presuppositions of these peculiarities of Jewish wit—the less so since it would need a careful and painstaking study of the history and sociology of the Jews in the diaspora and before that. Only the most conscientious exploration of that soil of Jewish mentality would enable research to attain penetrating insights into the origin and development of Jewish wit. What I do hope to contribute to the solution of the question is a psychoanalytic attempt to characterize that social peculiarity, the emotional intimacy, in Jewish wit.

Let us return again to the behavior of the Jew in the train-story ("Aesoi!") and to the letter of the business-man about his claims for compensations. The intimacy in both cases is of a kind of ill-mannered display of familiarity and has the unmistaken character of impudence. That nuance of intimacy is certainly not to be found in all Jewish jokes, but it is not a rare occurrence. It should be tempting to search for the sources of this insolence for which the Jews have a special name (chuzpeh). Is there in it a striving to overcompensate an original intensive feeling of inferiority? The factor of social distance or of cultural difference gives such a deduction a great psychological plausibility, as, for instance, in the train-anecdote ("Aesoi!").

The core of those inferiority feelings which we suspect are one of the sources of impudence, has other roots than physical handicaps or social differences. The democratic way of thinking which Freud attributes to the Jews in his remarks on their wit, does not exclude, but rather includes a high appreciation of the moral and intellectual qualities of the individual and this evaluation would contradict a high esteem for socially elevated position. Let me point only to an East Jewish joking question: "How grows man? From below to above—because below all people are alike, but above the one is taller and the other smaller." The acknowledgment of individual differences, especially those of intelligence and morals, is implied in such jocose remarks.

One comes closer to the comprehension of that effrontery in Jewish wit when one compares it, for instance, with the cheek of Berlin witticisms, with the coarseness of Austrian peasant fun or with the *"blague"* of Parisian jokes. The insolence that makes us laugh in Jewish wit has something provocative and demonstrative. It does not only arouse bewilderment, but also awakens the impulse of immediate reaction and defense. The attacked person experiences intense feelings of annoyance and hostility. In general, that impudence is not as harmless, stupid and sly as that of the peasant, but rather sophisticated and perceptive. It keenly observes and discerns human nature. It is also not poker-faced and controlled, but accompanied with vivid facial expressions and dramatic gestures.

It is not possible to conjecture from those characteristics the dynamics in that attitude, but when one uses insights from psychoanalytic practice, one guesses that that impudence is itself an expression of unconscious impulses that want to annoy and want to provoke abuse and punishment. This paradoxical assumption appears likely when one remembers the psychoanalytic explanation of the individual masochistic attitude. In many cases that particular insolence is not the cause, but the effect of an unconscious guilt feeling originated in the repression of aggressive drives. The vicissitudes of the Jew have provided an abundance of occasions to awaken such evil and vindictive tendencies, but the severe religious and ethical laws of Judaism banned them into the netherland of the unconscious. That demonstrative and provocative impudence is, thus, the expression of an unconscious need for punishment which reacts to one's own suppressed hostile and aggressive impulses.

We already pointed out that there is another psychoanalytic assumption that has to be put alongside the one just discussed and has, it seems, the same value. That intimacy is destined to bring the other person down to one's own level. The analogy with the sexual behavior of a certain type of man, previously presented, is very impressive. The unconscious purpose of that strange behavior in which the love object is degraded in thought is to make the woman available for sexual gratification. External and, especially, inner hindrances prevent the man from desiring the woman sexually because she seems to stand too high for such an appetite. He will, then call up crude sexual or excretory phantasies to overcome his inhibitions, to remove the notion that woman are made from "sugar and spice." The degradation of the object that has been too highly esteemed thus becomes a psychological precondition for imagining that the woman is sexually available. Only the conquest of that distance in the sense of humiliation establishes an intimacy which is a requisite for sexual satisfaction.

The differences in the situations exclude, of course, a conjecture that the same tendency could be discovered in Jewish wit. Yet a similar unconscious tendency must operate in the formation of that striving for intimacy. Its aim is, in general, to span a gap which makes it impossible to experience feelings of fellowship with the other person.

It is irrelevant whether the wit concerns a person from an alien culture or a Jew who seems to disavow his Jewishness. The intention is to approach a person, to make him give up his aloofness or emotional remoteness. The aggressiveness in this group of witticisms is a clumsy attempt to awaken his interest and can even be an expression of desexualized affection. Intimacy in Jewish wit is thus a means to establish or rather to reestablish a human closeness. Those jokes try to build a bridge to another human being even if he is an enemy.

VI

In certain cases the intimacy of Jewish wit soars up to the height of a smiling love of mankind. The bitter mockery recedes, and the impudence vanishes. What remains is an expression of sublimated love of man and sublime humaneness. One of the witticisms which I include in this group is a beautiful example of that surprising quality of intimacy which appears to me as a primary ingredient of Jewish wit, but that joke also reveals a hidden feature; in this particular case that all men are conceived as love-objects. In 1914, at the beginning of the First World War, a Jew came by chance upon a territory on the Russian border which was guarded by a sentry. The soldier raised his gun when he saw the man approaching and shouted: "Halt or I shoot!" The Jew made an irritable gesture and said: "Are you meschugge? Put the gun away. Don't you see that here is a Mensch?" It is obvious that the story shows how alien war and warlike actions are to Jewish mentality. The Jew cannot imagine that the other would really shoot and thus ridicules more than militarism. In his truly sublime lack of comprehension, in the disavowal that one could kill a person because of a national difference, he exposes the inhumanity and barbarousness of war more efficiently than pacifistic manifestoes.

That intimacy, which does not want to acknowledge a deep and insurmountable gap between one man and the other, that intimacy, which tears down all that separates people from each other, has found here its most natural expression. The sentence of the Jew is not less witty because it is more than a witticism. It too proclaims "All men become brethren" and it sounds not less impressively and forcibly when it is heard, not in the solemn chorus of Beethoven's hymn, but in the singsong of Yiddish jargon. That sentence trails an echo in which the voices of the biblical prophets resound, swell and vibrate. The impression that remains is that of the seriousness of such humor.

A last glance at the Jews who produce and tell such stories: here are indomitable figures in Kaftan, creepingly marching through the centuries, underground rebels with a cause whose impact upon mankind surpassed all others. The present and the past, the trivial and the enduring swirl together in a series of their jokes.

THINKING IN ANTITHESES

I

There are quite a number of scholarly papers on the psychology of the Jews, especially on their mental processes in comparison with those of other people. Such comparative explorations are very illuminating and fruitful, the more so when they inquire into the isolated facts and the full details of a particular area. After scrutininzing the abundant evidence, especially the linguistic material, some psychologists have arrived at the conclusion that the Jews, since ancient times, are a people rather of the ear than of the eye, that they belong more to the *"type auditif"* than to the *"type visuel."* In other words: that their impressions as well as their memories are founded rather on auditory than on visual perceptions.

This peculiarity is particularly apparent in a comparison of the literature of the ancient Hebrews with that of the Greeks. The Hellenes love colors and forms, the Jews prefer the sounds of words and sentences. Not the play of images, but the play of thoughts is often the centre of their poetry. It has been demonstrated that the Hebrew language, compared with that of the Greek, is poor in descriptive terms for forms and colors, that certain nuances can scarcely be denoted. Jewish wit also, in contrast with the jokes of other people reflects this characteristic feature.

Ernst Simon, in a thoughtful essay(3), pointed out that Jewish witticisms show characteristics that depend on certain peculiarities of the Semitic language. Take, for instance, their ability to construct extraordinarily rich formations from a few word-roots in such a way that the significance of ancestor-roots is very different from that of their descendants. This multiple significance is often used in Jewish jokes. It takes the speaker of a word, so to speak, at his word. This is palpable in a witticism such as the following: At a dinner, religiously forbidden food was presented to Lazarus Geiger (1829-1870), and the hostess, Freifrau von Bethman, told him: "Please serve yourself." The philosopher said: "No, I can master myself."

Ernst Simon's essay demonstrates that in Jewish witticisms the technique of Talmud-interpretation and argumentation is often employed. The Talmudic texts treat punctuation and sentence structure very casually, so that a statement can be read in a positive or negative sense, can express an assertion as well s a doubt or a query. The reader or student must find this meaning himself and he is helped by reciting the text, speaking it in singsong instead of reading it. The melody of the sentence thus replaces the punctuation.

To give an example of the use of this talmudic peculiarity in Jewish humor a witty definition is quoted: "What is consistency?" "*Today* this way, *tomorrow* this way." "What is inconsistency?" "Today *this way*, tomorrow *this way*." Here it is not the text, but the accent put on the words which reveals the meaning of the sentences.

The ambiguity of the Talmud-dialogue can also explain, for instance, why in Jewish jokes a question is so often not meant as a question but as an expression of a doubt or even of an opinion. The sergeant asks the recruit: "Why shouldn't a soldier walk around in the barracks yard with a burning cigaret?" The recruit answers: "Right you are, Mister Sergeant, why shouldn't he?"

The particular manner of Talmudic discussion is still perceptible in the fact that many Jewish jokes do not follow a comparison through to its end, but go off at a tangent. They do not consider the point, but the context from which the motive of the comparison was borrowed. To illustrate this procedure, the following fragment of a dialogue is offered: "Buy this horse! It is vigorous and quick. When you mount it now, you can already be in Pressburg at four o'clock in the morning." "Good God! What shall I do at four o'clock in the morning in Pressburg?"

What I would like to add to Ernst Simon's just observations, can be defined when we start from another peculiarity of the most ancient languages, namely from the fact that a word often has two opposite meanings and can simultaneously denote a certain statement and its opposite(4). Compare, for instance, the Hebrew word 'kodausch' whihc means the sacred, but also the sacrilegious, and which has a connotation similar to the Australian expression taboo. The oldest word-roots in the Egyptian language also show an antithetic meaning. Imagine, for instance, that the same expression denotes light and darkness. But if there is such a primal contradictory or ambiguous significance to a sentence, if the same expression within a sentence can affirm or deny something, how can the hearer recognize what is really meant? The Egyptian had "determinative" pictures behind the letter to direct the reader and to decide the meaning of the words. Karl Abel guesses that the Egyptians had accompanying gestures in speaking which together with facial expressions and modulation indicated what the speaking person meant(5). We assume that the sentences of those long vanished primal languages generally had such a contradictory meaning and that this kind of archaic expression was transformed only much later into another one in which words and sequence of words had but one meaning. Traces of such an ambiguity are still to be found late, for instance in such English words as "without."

I conjecture that at the root of many expressions of this contradictory kind there was, perhaps, an originally ambivalent attitude to the object or to the action they designate; that the notions in these expressions awakened hostility and awe, temptation and fear. Ambivalence is an emotional constellation manifested in the behaviour of an individual to the object or rather to an action regarding it. On one side the individual has a strong impulse to touch the object, but he is forbidden to carry out this action. The prohibition is, in most cases, conscious while the pleasure behind the temptation to touch remains unconscious.

Let me insert here an example of a Jewish joke which not only shows the use of that ambivalent attitude in wit, but also provides a hint of its original character. In the first decades of this century a certain female type was known in literature and society as the "misunderstood" woman, called the "unverstandene Frau" in German plays and novels. The Viennese writer Karl Kraus stated in joking seriousness: "There are no women who are not understood, only women who are not grasped." (In German, much funnier: "Es gibt keine unverstandene Frauen, nur unbegriffene.") In this meaningful wordplay almost the same expressions evolve and evoke different meanings.

This thinking in opposites does not mean that the result will be a paradox, but only that it will be surprising. The essential character of this way of thinking is best described as an alternation from one position to its opposite. Here is a representative example: the same writer Karl Kraus, contended that a certain official of the old Austrian-Hungarian monarchy took bribes so small that he almost approached incorruptibility. Another Viennese writer, Alfred Polgar, summed up his experience in Hollywood, where so many writers are not occupied, but paid, in the sentence: "Hollywood is a paradise above whose door is inscribed: 'You who enter, abandon all hope"(6). The contrast and the opposition in thought is here, of course, provided by the reference to Dante's description of the entrance to Hell. Take another sentence by the same writer: "The freedom which is most advantageous to a woman, is the one which she takes away from a man(7)."

If we want to prove that this thinking in antitheses has been an unrecognized but essential and pervasive characteristic feature of Jewish witticisms we have to demonstrate its existence and comic effect following them from the typical ghetto-joke to the modern witticisms of contemporary writers. Let us just take examples from Jewish jokes in their narrow sense, such as they flourished in the atmosphere of the Polish and Russian ghetto. We need not make a careful choice, since that feature is supposed to be in any example taken at random. The rabbi shouts indignantly in his sermon "You don't want to pay the taxes for the congregation, but to be buried in the Jewish cemetery, that you like fine!"

Take another example from a more emancipated period: an engineer comes to a little town in Galicia and orders a pair of trousers from a Jewish tailor. When a few weeks have passed, the trousers are still not ready; the engineer has to leave. When he returns to the town after seven years and the tailor brings him the pair of trousers, the customer says, "God has created the whole world in seven days and you need seven years to make some trousers?" But the tailor gently stroking his work replies: "Yes, but look at the world and then look at these trousers!"

One of the nicest examples of that antithetic kind of thinking is provided by the following story: the tenant of the first floor of a building often complained about the terrible noise made by the children of a family living above him. The children danced and tramped around with heavy shoes all day and constantly disturbed the tenant. On Tischa Beaw, the day of religious mourning for the destruction of the Temple, pious Jews must go bare-footed or in stockings. A passage in the letter of complaint the tenant wrote was: "You will even succeed in making Tischa Beaw a day of joy for me." Here is clearly a reversal into the opposite.

But let us turn from the striking antithesis which the tailor and this tenant put into words, to an example from the pen of the wittiest Jewish writer of the 19th century, Heinrich Heine, in whose prose you will encounter expressions of antithetic thinking at every turn. After a German journalist visited Heine in Paris, the poet was asked about their conversation. He said, "We had an interchange of ideas and now I am utterly stupid."

Take an example from our own time. When there was scarcely any doubt any longer, in the First World War, that Germany and Austria would soon be defeated, Karl Kraus described the difference of mood in the two capitals as follows: "In Berlin the mood is serious, but not desperate, in Vienna desperate, but not serious." The same writer once wrote about old Austria that her highest officials treat the citizens amiably, while the office messengers in the best of cases, behave condescendingly towards them. As in many witty sayings of this writer, the humorous effect of the antithesis is connected with the surprising reversal of conventional roles.

We did not forget that this inquiry into the characteristics of Jewish wit was not undertaken for its own sake, but as a contribution to the comparative psychology of the Jewish people. It fulfills its purpose only in so far as it reflects the peculiarities of the Jews and of Judaism. What, if anything, can we learn from this antithetic kind of thinking about their character? This interests us more than the technique and the major themes of witticisms.

A certain antithetic contrast of ideas is common to all, not only to Jewish wit. Madame de Stael once gave the following definition: "Wit consists in knowing the resemblance of things which differ and the difference of things which are alike." But the Jewish jokes go beyond this general characterization. They seem to proclaim a principle of reversal, turn everything upside down and demonstrate that things are the opposite of what they seem. Do we dare to search for the emotional and mental factors that determine this special kind of antithetic thought manifested in Jewish jokes?

II

We discussed above the ambivalent attitude that is at the root of the ambiguity of words and sentences in Hebrew, but this characteristic feature is common to the eldest languages we know and cannot provide a psychological explanation for the thinking in contrasts that we recognized as typical of Jewish jokes. It can only supply the background setting for that special form of thought-process.

If we want to find out what determines the typical alternation of position in Jewish witticisms, we must search for its psychological presuppositions in the singular and unique vicisstudes of this people. Even before recorded history, their destiny took them away from their original home and transplanted them into other countries whose inhabitants had advanced in their civilization more than two thousand years and were thus the superiors of the nomadic Hebrew tribes. The Israelites, fiery and proud, were only partially assimilated and retained their identity and independence although they had to yield again and again to their more powerful neighbours.

Later on, dispersed into European countries and surrounded by Western civilization, they found themselves in a permanently defensive state. They could not help being impressed by the many cultural and material advantages the Gentiles enjoyed and remained aware of their minority state as well as of their singular religious and ethical mission. They also clearly recognized the drawbacks and weaknesses of the people among whom they lived and who were their irreconciliable enemies. This emotional situation between attraction and dislike did not essentially change when the emancipation freed the Jews from many external restrictions.

Among the weapons left to the Jews was wit, since the use of force was denied them, due to external as well as inner conditions. Torn between admiration and repugnance, their criticism of the weak spots of Western civilization expressed itself in jokes. Jokes of this kind were actions in words, a form of verbal attack in disguise. Freud defined thoughts as actions in small quantities.

Since other kinds of critical and aggressive actions were impossible, the inquiring tendencies of the Jews endeavored to express themselves in antithetical terms when dealing with the culture pattern of the people among whom they dwelled. A certain kind of contrariness in thought evolved in satiric contrast to their values. That lack of *verecundia* (= awe or respectfulness) which Arthur Schopenhauer attributed to Jewish mentality, expressed itself in veiled terms in their jokes about their enemies. The antithetical form of thinking was thus put into the service of Jewish wit.

I would like to quote Freud to show the 'typical' in this situation. Freud said, "Because I was a Jew, I found myself free of the prejudices which restrict others in the use of the intellect; as a Jew, I was prepared to be in the opposition and to renounce agreement with the majority." This singular position within a hostile invironment thus favors an intellectually independent and critical attitude which is the opposite of conformity and of inner submission to authority. It was not accidental that Freud could prove in his psychoanalytic research that the things which we rate highest are subterraneously connected with those which we hold in abhorrence.

This critical attitude, this lack of reverence originally shown in Jewish jokes about the high evaluation of certain aspects of Western civilization, does not stop before one's own religion and culture. With the onset and the extension of emancipation, old traditions of Jewish belief and ritual became re-evaluated and critically scanned. That lack of awe towards authorities came, by and by, to the fore.

Thinking in antitheses has become an iradicable habit; it was and still is the ear-mark of the Jews whom a scholar in his quest for the meaning of Jewish history recently called "the world's adamant dissenters"(8).

Since Jacob wrestled with God, they continued to challenge their deity towards whom they remained unfailingly recaltricant. God called them "a stiff-necked people" and His prophet said to them "They neck is as an iron sinew" (9).

Here is perhaps the secret of their endownment akin to that of the original genius who is in Gilbert Murray's observation "at once the child of tradition and a rebel against it." The Jewish people cling to their essential traditions and their spiritual heritage in spite of their insurrection against them. Dispersed and scattered from one end of the world to the other, they still insist upon their rights against all worldly authorities. Their heads are bloody, but unbowed.

BURSTING INTO LAUGHTER BUT NOT MERRY

It seems to me that we already succeeded in discovering two characteristic features that differentiate Jewish witticisms from those of other people: namely the intimacy and the thinking in antitheses. It is, of course, not that these features form a unique character of Jewish wit; they are certainly also found in the humor of other people. It is thus a matter of quantity rather than of quality, or better a matter of density. Jewish jokes almost always show these peculiarities; they are impregnated with these two peculiar features. If I am allowed to use a comparison, I would remind the reader of the essential differences between French and British comedies. In British comedies you will sometimes find some risqué lines or frivolous and flippant remarks, but they are not, in general, characteristics of these plays while they are regularly met at the comedies of the Paris stage.

Since wit belongs to literature—witticisms are also works of art—the reaction of the listener or of the audience is as important as its objective character. Here I arrived at another significant feature of Jewish jokes, a feature so distinctive that it can be demonstrated and defined in isolation, and can be justifiably called pervasive. The next Jewish joke occurring to you or me might serve as a pattern or model to test my view. Here is one: a Jew consults a rabbi and complains that he, his wife and three children live in a very small room. The rabbi broods over the problem and asks after mature consideration: "Have you a goat?" "Yes," says the man "And have you a cow too?" "Yes," is the answer. "Then take the goat and the cow into your room!" "But, Rabbi, we can't even turn around in the room now!" But the rabbi is adamant and the Jew has to obey him. After a week the man returns and asks, "Please, rabbi, let me take the animals back to the stable!" and the rabbi permits it. Some time later the rabbi asks the Jew how he feels at home now and the man replies happily: "It is as if we live in a hall."

The joke certainly has a moral. It tells us that all happiness is relative. How little is necessary to make that miserable man happy! He begins to appreciate the little he has got only after even that was reduced and feels relieved after he can return to the status quo, to his previous condition which was poor enough. But we are more concerned with the comic effect of this little story that shows the characteristic features of the ghetto joke. Thus here is a third peculiarity of Jewish wit: *you laugh at it, but it is not merry.* This special feature, which is determined by the misery from which it arises, and which remains invisibly, but perceptibly its background. It is not mirth in misery, that expresses itself, not hilarity nor frolic, but making a joke out of suffering. It is such stuff that Jewish jokes are made of. The edge of sadness is not taken off, but lingers on. Jewish stories might be sad, but they are never desperate.

One is tempted to compare this attitude in Jewish jokes with another one that expresses itself in a grieved or sorry humor often called gallows-humor. Take an example: a murderer is led to execution on Monday and remarks: "This week has a fine beginning already!" Quite apart from other differences, there is here a sudden freeing breakthrough from a tragic situation. In Jewish jokes there is nothing comparable: no escape, no deliverance from a momentary emergency, but rather a moment of truth in a permanent emergency. The social situation of Jewry makes misery the normal and commonplace condition; the Jew only makes a joke out of it, a joke that can awaken laughter, but is not merry. That is the humor of it.

We discovered, I think, a triad of essential characteristics of Jewish witticisms, marks of distinction that differentiate them from the humor of other people. They show a kind of human intimacy, their trains of thoughts move in antitheses and one laughs at them, but they are not merry. The last characteristic is even recognized by a well-known proverb of Eastern Jews: "Suffering makes you laugh too."

MOMENT OF EXPLOSIVE TRUTH

Each Jewish story reveals a moment of truth in the individual or in the collective life of the people. Take the anecdote of the Schadchen whose young assistant has the function of confirming the qualities of the girl suggested as a future wife. The Schadchen says to a young man: "The girl to whom I shall introduce you is from one of the best families." The assistant: "The élite of the town." Schadchen: "Her father is a rich man." Assistant: "Rich as Rothschild." Schadchen: "The girl is very beautiful." Assistant: "As beautiful as Sulamith in the Song of Songs." Schadchen: "She has only a small drawback; a little slooped gait." Assistant: "And what a hump!"

This sounds like an automatism, but behind it is the truth that victoriously breaks through. The burden of lies is shaken off and the emotional result is a feeling of great relief or release. The satisfaction is comparable to the physical gratification experienced when one had to wear too narrow shoes the whole day and can finally pull them off. Jewish wit walks *"en pantoufles."*

We find this drive for veracity in all kinds of Jewish jokes, in those of the Schnorrer facing his benefactor, of the Jew in conversation with the rabbi, and in confrontation with the Catholic priest who wants to convert him, and even in the stories that show him rebellious against his own god.

But is not also the wit of other people characterized by such a sudden breakthrough of surprising truth? Yes, the point of witticisms of all people shows this dénouement, such a surprising relief from the burden of hypocrisy and conventional lies. Here are two examples: an old French anecdote and a recent story from Soviet Russia. The writer, La Fontaine (1621-1695) was in his old age once asked if he never wanted to marry and answered: "Sometimes, in the morning." (*"Quelquefois, le matin."*) This cynical sentence, alluding to the erection of the penis in the morning, debunks the social institution of marriage reducing it to a convenient means of sexual gratification.

In the anecdote from modern Russia an Ukrainian asks an Armenian how he could make a living since he has only a very small salary. The Armenian answers: "I don't know. I never tried." The meaning is, of course, that he always had black market dealings and was earning money by all kind of larcenies. There is, it seems no difference between the truth and truthfulness breaking through in these two stories and in Jewish jokes. There is perhaps some scarcely perceptible variance in tone: the sexual French story is cynical, the anecdote of the Armenian shows a casual indifference. In most Jewish jokes the moment of truth is, it seems to me, at the same time a moment of triumph, of inner satisfaction that at last the end of make-belief and lies has come and one can tell the truth against overwhelming odds.

The story of the Armenian, asked about making a living, leads us back to the most delicate point of the psychology or rather psychopathology of Jewish wit. This is the area of merciless self-caricature and self-criticism in the jokes demonstrating the fraud, deceit and dishonesty of the Jews of the Polish and Russian ghetto. Some commentators have pointed out that those faults and bad habits could be attributed to only a few individuals and could not be ascribed to the greater part of that minority-group. I think this apologetic explanation is inappropriate. Louis XIV said of the Duke of Savoy that his geographical position made it impossible for him to be an honest man. Similarly the social position of the Eastern ghetto-Jew made it at least very difficult for him to be an honest man in his business-dealings with the Gentiles and occasionally even with other Jews. In a life, that was permanently insecure and uncertain, he had to devise tricks and to commit fraud if he wanted to survive.

Let us return to the fact that the point in jokes marks a moment of truth also in the witticisms of other people. We feel we must search in his area for the distinctive feature of Jewish wit. The peculiar, precarious situation of the Jews makes it necessary to surpress the truth under the stresses of the circumstances, from sheer necessity. Yet sometimes the denied truth breaks through, nevertheless.

There is another factor we neglected until now, namely the

subjective one. In the Jew himself are resistances against telling what he knows as truth. It is easy enough in those cases in which the truth spills over, so to speak, to take him by surprise as in the Schadchen stories we quoted.

In those jokes in which the Jew at last comes out with the truth against his own advantage the burden of lie and deceit is felt and relief is experienced when it is cast off. But the situation is psychologically more complicated when there are inner resistances that have to be overcome.

We are reminded here of the numerous jokes in which doubts and rebellious feelings against Jewish religion and tradition are expressed. This revolt was first denied and brushed aside. The emergency of a tendency to voice rebellion or arguments against one's religion was anxiety-producing. It needed some moral courage to master this inner anxiety.

We guess that this is a valuable clue: the dark urge to truth, which means truth first denied, but deeply felt in spite of oneself, is the distinctive mark for which we searched. This subjective truthfulness "malgré soi-même"—not only against one's own external interests, but also against one's own anxiousness is, it seems to me, a special characteritics of Jewish wit which we must add to the three previously described. Subjective truth first denied and then acknowledged in spite of all external and inner resistances denotes the dividing line separating Jewish wit from that of other people. The free admission of one's own physical and material needs, the frank confession of one's own faults, foibles and failings, the casting off of all kinds of make-belief and superstitions, even within one's own religion, belong to the area of those emotional and intellectual conquests of oneself. It is this successful working through to the truth, this victory over oneself which gives the triumphant and explosive note to Jewish wit. Jewish jokes unmask not only the futilities of conventional societies and the ironies of life, but create their own truth in the spirit of an "immoralism bienveillant" when they tell with delight the complete and unvarnished truth. They surprise by the moral courage and the nonchalance with which they brush aside the preconceived ideas and lies of a hypocritical society.

They mark only a moment of explosive truth, do not shed an enduring light upon conditions and people, but a flashlight that suddenly glares and glimmers. But that dark urge to reveal the reality behind the facade is radiantly triumphant and proclaims: "And ye shall know the truth and the truth shall make you free." (St. John VIII.52.)

CHAPTER IV

Psychology and Psychopathology of Jewish Wit

LITERATURE ON THE SUBJECT

Quite a few books have been written on the philosophy and sociology of Jewish jokes, but so far as I know, none on their psychology. This is strange and the more surprising since the psychological aspect of the problem is clearly the most important. Historical and sociological factors must be taken into account, but the character and the properties of Jewish jokes remain unintelligible as long as they are not seen from psycho logical viewpoints.

Here is the area of the comparative psychology of a people. What does this relatively young branch of psychologic research have to say about Jewish wit? There are scarcely any thorough investigations of this kind of humor. The best and most penetrating insights are still in Freud's book *Wit and Its Relation to the Unconscious*. His remarks on Jewish jokes form the central jewel in the small necklace of psychological contributions to the subject.

In a recent article(1) on Freud, Ernst Simon aptly summarized the insights which that book offers on Jewish jokes. They show the following characteristic features: (1) sharp self-criticism of one's own people, (2) a democratic mode of thought, (3) emphasis on the social principles of the Jewish religion, (4)

the revolt against Jewish religion, (5) reflections on the miserable lot of Jewish masses, their grinding and hopeless poverty,
(6) the general spiritual atmosphere that permeates Jewish wit
is one of all-pervading scepticism.

Simon contends that Freud's observations on the jokes of
this people present "a theory of the Jewish soul in miniature." It
is not by chance that he linked it with the element of wit whose
origin and dynamics are so close to the unconscious.

Since Freud's book few contributions on the psychology of
Jewish wit have been published. A paper by Eduard Hitsch-
man(2) is primarily critical and does not present any original
theory on Jewish wit. There are also two essays by this
writer(3) contained in books on humor, not yet translated into
English. Since some insights contained in my two essays are
used in this book, a discussion of them here is not indicated.

Freud's remarks on Jewish jokes, whose most significant
features are distilled, recorded and analyzed in his book, blazed
a trail in virgin territory. Very few analysts have made further
progress in the same direction. Dr. Edmund Bergler was the
first who emphasized the tendency of "psychic masochism" in
the exposition of one's shortcomings in Jewish witticism(4). He
believes that certain external situations (seclusion, poverty, absence of opportunity and bitterness of life in the ghetto) favored
psychic masochism. The same circumstances explain, however, a
high degree of resiliency of the Jews. A recent, still unpublished
paper by Dr. Martin Grotjahn (used here with the kind permission of the author) is entitled *Psychoanalysis and the Jewish
Joke*. It is a lecture given in 1960 and is the only psychoanalytic
paper on this subject in many years. Its author announces that it
is a contribution to the understanding of masochism. It well deserves our attention and we shall deal with its results in the
following pages.

In the books and papers discussing the historical, sociological
or philosophical aspect of Jewish jokes quite a few good psychological insights are to be found. We occasionally commented on
one or the other of these works in the preceding sections of this
study. The puzzle of the Jewish joke remains unsolved and is

unsolvable so long as we don't know more and more significant facts about the psychology of the Jewish people.

This pilot study will, I fear, not reach all its aims, but I hope that out of a great deal of irrelevancies some significant psychological facts will be established. I wanted to write a thought-provoking and argument-inviting book, rather than a convincing or persuasive one. As far as possible, the conscious determinant factors are here neglected in favor of the unconscious, repressed and disavowed powers that reveal themselves to the psychoanalytic researcher. The devotion to the obvious, so often met with in the exploration of Jewish psychological problems, worked as a strong deterrent upon this writer. Consideration and psychological exploration of those unconscious factors will, I hope, cast a new light upon some unnoticed or unrecognized aspects of Jewish wit.

Before we enter the region of the emotional netherworld, it is only fair to warn the reader who has enjoyed many examples of Jewish humor. We would like to tell him with Goethe's Torquato Tasso:

Und lass dir sagen: habe die Sonne nicht zu lieb und nicht die Sterne Komm, folge mir ins dunkle Reich hinab.

And let me say to you, don't love the sun too much, nor the stars! Come, follow me down into the darkness.

THE ASPECT OF SELF-DEGRADATION

The paper *Psychoanalysis and the Jewish Joke,* by Martin Grotjahn, to whom we are indebted for other valuable psychoanalytic contributions, is remarkable for its courageous penetration into the core of the problem. Whatever one says about Jewish jokes—and much has been said about them—it remains obvious that they make merciless fun of the weaknesses and misconduct of their own people. As Freud has already remarked in his book on wit, the character of this self-exhibition and self-mockery is different from that of the jokes which Gentiles make up about Jewish properties. The spirit of the sharpest self-criticism and self-sarcasm is not restricted to the jokes of this people. It is there in the speeches of the prophets who cruelly castigate their contemporaries. Israel Zangwill even went so far as to call the Bible an anti-Semitic book. The distinctive mark compared with anti-semitic jokes which Freud called brutal farces must be a special kind of self-aggression or its mixture with other emotional trends.

It is on this point where the most recent attempt of Martin Grotjahn's recent attempt at interpretation of Jewish witticism sets in. His point of departure is the theory that witticisms start with an aggressive tendency, an insult or a shocking thought which appears in a disguised form. This release of aggression must be sudden. In the Jewish jokes the hostility or aggressiveness is in a masochistic manner turned against the Jew himself. The persecuted and derided Jew who makes himself the butt of every joke deflects his dangerous hostility away from his persecutors and turns it unto himself. The result is, says Grotjahn, not defeat, but "victory through defeat" (which is the formula at which I derived in my inquiry into the psychology of masochism(5). The Jew sharpens, so to speak, the dagger which he takes out of his enemy's hand, stabs himself, "then returns it gallantly to the Antisemite with the silent reproach 'Now see whether you can do it half as well.'"

The essential feature of the truly Jewish joke is, in Grotjahn's view, aggression turned against himself. It is as if the joke says "You do not need to attack us. We can do that ourselves and even better. We can take it, we know our weaknesses, and in a way, are proud of it." The Jewish jokes, Grotjahn adds, contain a kind of melancholy resignation and occasionally a stubborn pride. They seem to say "This is the way we are and will be as long as we are Jews."

The psychoanalytic explanation of Grotjahn is so serious and perceptive that one can, with good conscience, freely express one's criticisms. In contrast with other psychologists who only scratch the surface, Grotjahn's theory reaches for its depth, but it still remains at the surface of the problem. He acknowledges that the masochism of the Jewish witticisms is only "a mask," but he does not show the face behind the mask. He does not attempt to demask the joking Jew. Although it has to be agreed that aggression is perhaps the main tendency of Jewish witticisms, one has to emphasize that it is not confined to persons, not even to Antisemites, but is often directed against social institutions as religion and law that deprive people of so many valuable goods and prevent them from enjoying life.

Even within Grotjahn's theory of the masochistic character of Jewish wit some significant psychological factors are neglected. For example, the self pity inherent in this attitude. More important even than this aspect is the final aim of masochistic display, namely, the unconscious wish to win the approval or even the admiration of the audience, in the last analysis the subterranean desire to gain, or better, to regain love. In this sense, the exhibitionistic self-degradation and humiliation is equivalent to a confession: (6) "See how full of weaknesses and failings, how despicable and worthless I am. Therefore, you must forgive me and love me again."

Nor does Grotjahn's theory consider the fact that the masochistic element in Jewish jokes is founded on an unconscious guilt feeling. Psychoanalytic exploration of that unconscious guilt-feeling, manifested in the self-degradation and expressed in the jokes, would trace its origin to crimes committed in thoughts, especially to a rebellious attitude toward God and His laws(7). If I previously stated that the masochistic, self-humiliating side of Jewish jokes corresponds to a confession, it might now be added that it has the character of a substitute confession, since the true nature of that thought-crime remains unconscious, and the confession necessarily concerns only descendants of that primal atrocious rebellion against God.

At this point we begin to doubt whether the character of Jewish jokes is correctly defined if one describes them as masochistic. We think of the masochists we treated in clinical practice, and we miss certain distinctive marks of the masochistic character. Where, for instance, is the instinctual gratification of the social masochist? Should it really be restricted to the satisfaction that "he prefers making fun of himself to having others make fun of him?"(8). The Jew makes fun of himself, but he does not come out dirty and greasy, humiliated or humble. He is not delighted with social rebuffs, but feels miserable and in despair about them. His self-degradation and self-humiliation are perhaps a measure of defense protecting him against greater dangers, a kind of sacrifice made in order to survive, which is of the greatest importance for him.

The question here is whether the Jewish jokes are truly masochistic, which would amount to complete gratification in one's self-degradation, or whether they have only a pseudo-masochistic character.

It is true that the Jews show in their witticisms a high degree of self-degradation, and that they seem compelled to display themselves in this way. But is it not ultimately the meaning of that exhibition that if they do not sink they will not rise, and that survival is well worth the price of temporary self-humiliation?

While reading Grotjahn's paper, I was surprised to find no reference to certain Christian teachings which must certainly be known to the Gentile author. Did not Jesus speak to the multitude and to his people: "And whosoever shall exalt himself, shall be abased; and he that shall humble himself, shall be exalted." (St. Matthew, XXIII,12)?

It seems to me that Jewish wit is permeated with this very spirit. That implied conviction and hope is one of the many things the Jews have in common with the teachings of that Rabbi from Nazareth, later called the Savior.

Before probing the problem of Jewish wit in depth, we remind ourselves that the exploration will have the relativity and subjectivity, and with them the uncertainties of all such attempts. Einstein once remarked, "Everyone sits in the prison of his own ideas."

In the birth of a Jewish joke we will deal separately with the situation from which it emerges, the person who produces it, and the person or persons to whom it is conveyed. The situations in which these witticisms are born, are, of course, of various kinds, but some of them will be easily recognized as typical. One of these is inside the Jewish milieu, so that the joke is called forth from the conditions in which the Jews live among themselves and from the consequences of their special kind of existence.

The other typical situation results from the contact with Gentiles and from the contrast in which the Jewish minority group stands to the social and religious views of the people in whose midst they are living.

This is the setting of the stage and the dramatis personae. Turning now to the leading part, the teller of the story, we ask "What kind of person is he? How is he characterized?"

An easy thought association leads from this point to the differences existing between the old and the new drama. There is no monologue in the plays after Ibsen, and there are no aside remarks when the person is alone on the stage, nothing of that *"parler a part,"* as the French say. The main difference, aptly pointed out by the eminent German critic, Alfred Kerr(9), is that modern drama avoids direct characterization. This means that the new playwright shows a decided disinclination to use the technique of letting others explain the nature of his characters. The dramatists of our time prefer to let the audience see for themselves what kind of people his characters are through their actions or by their talk.

Yes, also by their words do they reveal themselves, but not in the same sense that they did in the drama of the past centuries. Even in Shakespeare's plays, a figure often explains himself, says what he thinks, how he feels, what makes him tick. But that belongs also to the method of direct characterization. The listeners are supposed to take such self-characterizations seriously, to believe in it. Alfred Kerr calls this kind of primitive self-characterization in drama a "that's the way I am"-technique, because he remembers an old French governess who used to say *"Voilà comme je suis."* Shakespearean characters reveal themselves through dialogue, others, Richard III, for instance, through monologue. We take what they say at face value. Thus the greatest playwright does not reject direct characterization, though he frequently and most efficiently uses the other technique of indirect characterization.

It has often been said that modern drama tries to be realistic and that it happens very rarely in real life that people explain their character to others. But it does happen, and it may even happen that we believe what these people say, namely a small part of it. Sometimes people talk a lot about themselves in this way, even as you and I. If we were questioned about it, we would say that one must differentiate between the character we pretend to have, the character we believe we have, and the character we really have.

Our dramatists also use such self-revelations, but they put them into the service of indirect characterizations. This means, we listen to them, smile at them or are touched by them, and almost always recognize in them self-deceptions or successful or futile attempts at giving other persons a certain image of oneself. We rarely accept them as objectively correct. Such psychological misconstruction is mostly used in modern plays to allow us listeners to draw our own psychological conclusions, to guess what the character conceals, often about himself, or herself. For instance, Hjalmar Ekdal in Ibsen's *Wild Duck* speaks of his strength of character, but we know what the purpose of the writer was in the self-commandation of this character.

We observed the story-telling Jew as though he were a character in a play. We looked attentively at him, at his gestures and facial expressions, and we listened to his jokes "with the third ear."

What are the conclusions we may draw about the character f the teller of the jokes and about the jokes themselves? In the preceding sections we arrived at several psychological insights about the properties of Jewish witticisms, recognized quite a few characteristic features of which the story-teller is unaware, for instance, that they move in antitheses of thought and that they are permeated by an intimacy of feelings. There were other characteristic features, until now unnoticed or unrecognized in their psychological significance, which we discovered in Jewish jokes.

Most observers have stated that these anecdotes and jokes make cruel fun of Jewish peculiarities and weaknesses. We have heard that this strange attitude was attributed to the masochistic character of Jewish wit. Some, for instance, Dr., Grotjahn sees in this feature the main unconscious nature of Jewish jokes. The name given to this peculiar factor is not as important as its significance for the psychology of the Jewish people, which is the only thing which interests us in this context.

We have already remarked that there are several reasons for doubting that the masochistic feature can be called an all-pervading character of Jewish wit. Quite apart from the fact that there are numerous jokes in which the self-mocking and self-degrading trend does not appear, there remains the important fact that this is frequently replaced by the opposite quality of overconfidence and even impudence. Here is an example of this kind. A poor Jew insists that he must speak personally with Rothschild, and asserts that he can not discuss his business with his secretary. Finally he is admitted to the Baron, to whom he eloquently describes his poverty, and whom he implores to give him money. "Therefore" says Rothschild, "you had to importune me? Could you not have told this to my secretary?"

"Herr Baron," replies the Jew, "you know more about bank business, but how one schnorrs best, that I know better than you." How does such an impudence jibe with the view of a pervasic masochistic character?

There is perhaps the possibility of the coexistence of masochistic humility and provocative insolence if these opposite trends are directed towards different powers. Poor ill Heinrich Heine assumed, rightly or wrongly, that there was such a division in his case. The invalid poet writes from his Paris mattress-grave to his brother Max: "Our forefathers were brave people, they humbled themselves before God and were therefore stubborn and unmanageable towards the worldly powers; I, on the contrary, impudently challenged Heaven and was humble and servile towards man—and therefore, I now lie on the ground like a worm crushed under foot."

Yet the assumption of an intensive self-humiliating and self-degrading tendency in Jewish wit is correct. It is not important whether we call it masochistic or pseudo-masochistic. We shall try again to "listen with the third ear" to those jokes—not only to their punch line, but also to what is said between the lines, and more, to what is left unsaid between the lines.

THE INSIDE STORY OF THE JEWISH STORIES

So far as I know, no one has pointed out that the same mixture of self-irony and elegy is to be found in the writings of Jewish authors, that is, outside the area of jokes. Let us take, as a random example, the manner in which Heinrich Heine, already very ill, describes his rare walks in the streets of Paris. He depicts such a pathetic walk in a letter to Madame Caroline Jaubert, dated April 3, 1847. He describes that pretty women turn around when they see him, eyes half closed, with hollowed cheeks, strange beard and abnormal gait. All this gives him a tormented look that is wonderfully becoming to him. He adds: "As a moribund, I am at present a great success"(10).

This description has all the earmarks of self-pity and cruel self-irony as well as the demonstrative or exhibitionist characteristic to be found in Jewish jokes. But there is another impression that barely reaches the level of registration, and this derives from another almost inaudible tune of vanity or pride. Is there anything similar in Jewish witticisms? It is easy enough to recognize the masochistic factor in them, but it becomes clear that it is not the only determining agent in them.

Let us for a moment concentrate our attention on that cruel display of the faults and foibles of one's own people. To remind you of an obvious case of such a masochistic attitude, you need only think of the anecdote of the Jew who comes to a party and says upon entering, "Please, slap me already!"

We now turn to the other still unrecognized or under-evaluated aspect of Jewish jokes. In the following paragraphs I refer not only to my own research and clinical experience, but I also make use of an unpublished lecture given by one of my gifted students, Jule Nydes, in the National Psychological Association for Psychoanalysis in 1960. Nydes, who graciously acknowledged that he is greatly indebted to my psychoanalytic study of social masochism, describes a certain type which he characterized by a feeling of suspiciousness, the impression of being critically watched or of being persecuted, and by a sense of superiority sometimes in the pathological exaggeration of ideas of grandeur. The paranoid character reacts to real or imagined attacks with great force, is very critical of others and makes them feel that they are inferior to him.

The masochistic character is overcritical of himself, sees his own person as weak, insignificant, despicable and dependent. He degrades and humiliates himself or servilely ingratiates himself with others, while the paranoid character behaves haughtily and sees mostly negative features in others. The masochistic character often punishes himself or provokes punishment by another, while the paranoid character, assuming that he will be the subject of hostility, forestalls the attack of his real or imagined enemies and degrades and offends them.

It is obvious from this comparison that paranoid and masochistic characters are opposite and complementary types. Not only do certain common features connect the two, but our clinical experience teaches us that behind the masochistic attitude there is often concealed a paranoid attitude. Lack of power is the common source for both attitudes. The paranoid type does not know how to get along with people and has to fight them. The masochistic character can get along with people only by ingratiating and surrendering himself. Great stubbornness is common to both characters. While the masochist insists that he is inadequate and inferior, his counterpart asserts and reasserts his own superiority.

Nydes, who is in his lecture not concerned with the problem of Jewish wit, arrived at the conclusion that one of the most significant characteristics of the two types is to be found in their relation to love. The masochist renounces power and dignity for the sake of being loved or forgiven. The paranoid character on the other hand will sacrifice love and affection in order to be acknowledged, to feel power, and to carry his will through.

Let me illustrate this contrasting attitude by two examples from my own experience. A two and a half year old boy who was repeatedly admonished not to tear pages from books was finally slapped by his father, who had lost patience with him. The crying boy followed the excited father, who walked the room, and shouted: "Daddy, kiss me, give me a kiss!" Compare the attitude of this boy with the behavior of a paranoid character type. A lawyer is accustomed to get ahead of any car that is in front of his own on the highway, often with considerable risk. Once he drove past a car whose fender he scraped without damaging it. When both cars had to stop, the other man, perhaps some years older than the lawyer, remonstrated with him about his high-handed behavior. The lawyer pretending that he did not understand what the gentleman said, asked, "What did you say, sonny?"

It is difficult to put the Jewish jokes into one of the pigeon holes which comparative psychology has established. The great number of jokes we quoted and their survey will be sufficient to justify the statement that the Jewish jokes oscillate between an ingratiating and a provocative attitude and that they move back and forth between a masochistic and a paranoid behavior-pattern. The paranoid attitude is certainly, in most cases, latent or hidden. Yet it reveals itself not only in the claim implied in many jokes that the Jews are the favorites of God, but also in their unconscious sense of superiority.

The melancholy feeling expressed in that proverbial ejaculation "It's hard to be a Jew" is occasionally replaced by the feeling that it is a privilege to belong to this people because of an enjoyment of the sense of common identity. The Jew in those jokes is never pompous nor pretentious. There is nothing decorative nor anything make-believe in his attitude. In social intercourse with other Jews, informality and familiarity form a kind of inner security, a "we-feeling." They know each other and there are not many things which need to be explained. Meeting and speaking with other Jews is accompanied by the feeling that they are "my kind of people." It is what Freud calls "the clear awareness of an inner identity, the secret of the same inner construction."

Even the characteristic of being self-centered is rarely absent in them. You remember the story of the Jewish father whose boy tells him that the Yankees were defeated and who asks, "Is that good or bad for the Jews?" This attitude approaches the symptomatic manifestation that is called idea of reference by psychiatrists. In oscillating between a masochistic and a paranoid attitude and in their occasional combination Jewish jokes form a complex of contradictions. In this conglomeration are reflected the contradictions that characterize the Jewish situation in our civilization.

Unconscious Claims

In the preceding chapter I presented the example of the little boy who tried to regain the love of his father as representative of a certain kind of masochistic behavior. Whoever has read the Bible and has followed the course of Jewish history with acute perception will realize that the attitude of the Jews toward their God presents a perfect analogy to the behavior of the little boy. By accusing themselves, by repentance and passionate submission they tried to regain His love and forgiveness whenever He had punished them. When the people were defeated and felt miserable, when famine or pestilence threatened them, they showed a self-degrading attitude towards God before Whom they humbled themselves. Whenever they felt powerful and secure, they showed a paranoid, haughty and rebellious attitude towards Him Whom they denied and disavowed. In this mood they imagined that they could get away with everything, even with the murder of God. This oscillation between those two extremes casts a new light on the psychology and the history of the Jewish people. Here is a highly interesting assignment for psychologists and historians of the future. But that is a far country, and I must restrict myself here to a much narrower and nearer area.

While, as mentioned before, that masochistic trend in the Jewish people was recognized by psychoanalysts, none, so far as I know, evaluated the opposite and complementary paranoid attitude that is implied in them. Freud pointed out that Jewish jokes show a hidden price, and Grotjahn applied my formula "victory through defeat" for the psychology of those witticisms. This was as far as psychoanalysis went, but it was not far enough.

Not a psychoanalyst, but a contemporary writer, Arthur Schnitzler, clearly recognized the paranoid character trend of the majority of Jews. In the novel *The Way to The Open,* one of the figures, Mrs. Ehrenberg, complains about her husband. "It's a fixed idea of his. He sees Antisemites everywhere, even in his own family." Schnitzler even uses the very term persecution mania. In the same novel, George von Wergenthin tells his Jewish friend: "It is a mania of yours that you have quite lost the capacity for seeing anything in the world except the Jewish question." Adding some apologetic words for being discourteous, he asserts that his friend is suffering from "persecution-mania." This word is clearly meant as another name for the persecutory form of paranoic delusions.

Some decades after Schnitzler, I tried to clarify that peculiarity of the oscillation between a masochistic and a paranoid attitude of the Jews in my book *Myth and Guilt.* This is, of course, not meant as a fixed group-characteristic, but as a mental trend, determined by the destiny of the Jewish people.

Schnitzler speaks, of course, of the modern Jews. Was the attitude he characterizes always there? A French writer of the XVIII century once remarked that the word "Roman" applied to a native of modern Rome is misleading. One should call the person an Italian from Rome, thus differentiating the mentality of ancient Rome from that of our time.

The masochistic attitude of ancient Israel was recognized at least in their relationship with God, whose punishment they took as deserved without complaint. They considered also the cruelty with which they were treated by their powerful neighbors as punishment for their sins, especially for deserting their

God. The paranoid attitude in the form of an idea of grandeur is obvious in the Jewish claim of being the "chosen people." There is even a subterranean tie between the masochistic and the paranoid attitude in the idea that God chastises those whom He loves. Such an exceptional position has been claimed by the Jewish people since ancient time. On what could they base this claim to exclusiveness?

The deepest psychological reason for it is concealed. Only an inconspicuous remark by Freud, until now unnoticed and certainly not recognized in its significance, discloses this secret. This secret, comparable to a side glance, or to an aside, is to be found in an essay(11) in which Freud discusses certain character types to be met with in psychoanalytic work. A person of this type acts as though he were an exception who is exempt from the necessities of life and for whom the common regulations do not hold. Freud puts Shakespeare's Richard III, whose monologue he analyzes into this category, which he calls "the exceptions." The unconscious base on which these men establish their claim is that they had a traumatic experience or a handicap in earliest childhood, of which they feel innocent. They expect compensation for the wrong or injury life has inflicted on them, for instance in the form of a congenital illness, or as in the case of Gloster, in the form of a physical handicap.

At this point of his psychoanalytic interpretation of those neurotic cases Freud inserts the meaningful remark to which I previously referred: "I shall not enter here into a discussion of the obvious analogy with character-deformation after long-lasting sickliness and with the behavior of a whole people with a past fraught with suffering." It is clear that Freud's side glance rests on the Jewish people. This is not the place to point out the meaningfulness of this passage nor the occasion to make use of Freud's allusion as a guidepost for future research.

In connection with the psychoanalytic explanation of these character types Freud points out that the claims which they derive from early injustices and from the rebelliousness resulting from them contribute much to the aggravation of the conflicts that resulted later in their neurosis.

We find a similar attitude reflected in the history of the ancient Hebrews. Their defiant paranoid attitude manifested itself not only toward their God, Who called them a "stiffnecked people," but also toward the nations amongst whom they lived and toward whom they maintained a concealed moral superiority and insubordination. Do we need to search for analogies of that twin-attitude in the literature of the Jews? Rabbi Levi Yitzhak of Berditchev asked(12) "And am I not your son, Lord of the world? I do not beg you to reveal to me the secrets of your way . . . I suffer, but only if it is for your sake that I am to suffer." That two and a half year old boy must have experienced similar feelings towards his punishing father. The paranoid attitude is clearly shown in the proclamation of Israel's election by God. The prayerbook says "Who has chosen us from all the nations and gave us the Torah."

Even the renegade Paul asks in his Epistle to the Corinthians, "What advantage then hath the Jew?" and answers: "Much, chiefly that to the Jews were committed the holy oracles of God." In the book of *Esther,* Haman complains about this people who lived dispersed among others: "Their laws are diverse from those of every people, neither keep they the king's laws." Without much success God Himself tried to educate His people and teach them obedience. So did the worldly authorities of diverse states and countries. The Jews remained self-willed and stubborn, the problem-children in the family of man.

We now return from these reflections on the psychopathology of the Jews to the area of their humor, by whose saving grave they were so often relinquished from their miseries. Do we also find in Jewish witticisms manifestations of those two essential responses we described? We anticipate that we will not often see pure types of them, but frequently mixed forms of that twin-attitude, for instance, mock-humbleness or impudence as a desperate break-through from intimidation and submission. The polarity of the masochistic and paranoid attitudes appears often and clearly in many Jewish jokes. Their claims are also heard, for instance, in that pathetic and comic complaint of the Jew directed to his God, "You take pity on utter strangers, why not on me?"

Our point of departure was that the masochistic attitude is not, as Grotjahn and other psychoanalysts asserted, the only and dominant agent in the psychology of Jewish wit. The truth seems at once simpler and more complex. There is an oscillation between masochistic self-humiliation and paranoid superiority-feeling. When we set aside individual characteristics and consider only the emotional soil in which these Jewish jokes are rooted, this is the main result that our psychoanalytic investigation has brought to light: Jewish jokes alternate between a subservient and a haughty attitude.

What is the summary of the new psychological insights we could add to the results of Freud's research? There are two sides to every Jewish story.

MOTIVES FOR TELLING JEWISH JOKES

This part of our exploration would be incomplete if we neglected the motives for telling Jewish jokes and the effect of laughter they create. This is, of course, a segment of a more general problem, namely of the psychological significance of telling jokes at all. The conscious motives are so obvious that they do not need to be discussed.

We know that one of the basic factors in the psychology of wit is that the teller of a joke finds in his audience a person who approves of the forbidden impulses expressed in the joke. Freud, in his book on wit, already referred to the relieving function of sharing "the underlying guilt in the offensive impulses concealed in the joke"(13).

In a book published in 1933(14) and not yet translated into English, I tried to continue Freud's research in this area. I described there the emotional process taking place in the listener of an aggressive or obscene joke as operating in the region "between fright and laughter." The first reaction to hearing such a joke is unconscious alarm. This emotion is

aroused by an unexpected attack on highly esteemed persons
or institutions, for instance religion, marriage, etc., which we
conceived of as sacred or at least very precious and inviolable.
In a sense, one could speak of the initial shock effect of jokes
of this kind. There must be in all of us an unconscious wish to
attack those respected persons or highly regarded social institutions. The latent anxiety connected with this temptation is
for a moment increased when we hear a cynical or obscene
witticism assailing them. For a split second all inhibitions seem
to be removed, but then the intensified fear reaction is recognized as overdue or superfluous and the alarm is suddenly
stopped. The effect is laughter; in cases where the anxiety was
not intensive, it is smiling.

Applying this theory to the producer of the joke, we must
assume that a similar process must have taken place in him,
but in reverse, when the joke occurred to him. He overcame
that latent anxiety, and telling the joke to others, weakened it
by sharing the social anxiety (= guilt feeling) with the listener.
When he succeeds, then, in making his audience laugh, he has
attained not only approval, but acknowledgment and momentary
admiration.

Returning now from these general psychological theories to
our subject, Jewish wit, we would assume that the initial
anxiety in the producer and listener was strong because the
effect is the explosive laughter of the listener. We would explain
the intensity of this response by the severity of Jewish moral
notions, by the strict inhibitions and suppressions induced by
religious education.

In the preceding parts of this book we quoted so many
Jewish witticisms attacking religious subjects that we would like
to test our thesis on Jewish jokes dealing with sexuality. Preferring Jewish personalities of our time to figures from the
ghetto, let me remind you of the anecdote of old Max Liebermann, who told the young woman, "Let's hope that's not true,"
when she assured him that looking at his pictures was "the
most beautiful hour" of her life.

Let me add to this relatively harmless sexual allusion a

quotation from the writings of Alfred Kerr(15), the most prominent critic of pre-Hitler Germany, a Jewish contemporary of
Liebermann. That sentence has certainly an obscene character
and its witty effect is strengthened because it parodies the last
line from Goethe's *Faust*, words that are, so to speak, sacrosanct
to everyone grown up in German culture. In this final scene
Gretchen, now transfigured, leads Faust into the highest spheres,
and the mystical choir of ghosts sings the words:

> Das Ewig-Weibliche
> Zieht uns hinan . . .

> The Eternal Feminine
> Draws us above . . .

Alfred Kerr once outlined the plays of Bernard Shaw in
whom he also recognized the ability to see the funny reverse
side of the sublime. Shaw, who often unmasks the lofty, appears
only rarely as a weakling, for instance when he idealizes Mrs.
Candida Morrell (in his play *Candida*). Kerr asks himself, "Why
just her? Is it worship of the Virgin Mary?" and continues:
"The memory of his phallus, now about fifty years old, influences here a moral evaluation. He whispers with Wolfgang
Goethe: "It draws us above," instead of boldly saying "It draws
it above." Here is a clear allusion to the erection of the penis.

This is clearly a crass, obscene joke (Alfred Kerr's writing
contains much wittier sentences.) More important to me than
the aesthetic value is the question of the psychological nature of
the joke. There was a preconscious thought, born of a tendency
to protest and contradict in thinking of the idealization of Shaw's
Candida. This preconscious thought was for a split second
submitted to an unconscious recasting. This means that the
thought sank into the recesses of the repressed for a moment,
and returned from there in the form of a witticism. In the
sacrilegious elaboration of that sublime sentence from *Faust*, the
writer reveals the crass, sexual attraction at the core of the
adoration of a female figure. The erection of the penis as the

expression of sexual arousal replaces then the lofty meaning of Goethe's lines. What is important to us, is the antithesis in thinking which we consider as one of the characteristic features of Jewish wit.

I am bold enough to assert that not all the important motives for telling Jewish jokes have been made transparent by the psychologists. One of those motives, hardly noticed and certainly not sufficiently appreciated, is the fact that humor presupposes a certain emotional solidarity. All people cry about the same things, but not all people laugh at the same things. American humor is often not understood by the French and Parisian humor not by the New Yorkers. "What's funny about that?" some foreigners might ask when they read a joke in the magazine *Le Rire* or look at a picture in the *New Yorker*. It is not the local or geographical difference which is the decisive factor here, but a common cultural background, more accurately, the evaluation of certain qualities, what a certain group of people, religious or other social community respects and what it despises. A change in the cultural pattern must thus inevitably lead to a change in the jokes at which this group laughs.

A very pious Jew will not be amused, but repelled by jokes that attack beliefs sacred to him, while another unbelieving or even skeptical Jew would enjoy the witticisms making fun of religious ceremonies or beliefs.

What I am driving at is that the enjoyment of the same jokes has the premise of a far-reaching emotional conformity or basic harmony. From these premises one must conclude that the telling of Jewish jokes also has the unconscious aim of cementing the bond that was originally founded on certain common values, and on the awareness of the Jewish isolation within the nations in which they live. Telling these jokes to each other has, so to speak, the significance of reaching out one's arms to the other fellow. In this sense, telling Jewish jokes to other Jews is not only a token of emotional brotherhood and fellow feeling, but also of affection. In the same sense it can only be considered progress that more and more Jewish jokes are appreciated and enjoyed by wide circles of American

Gentiles. "Laugh and the world laughs with you" was not true some decades ago when Jewish jokes were told to a Gentile audience. It is so today.

With regard to the ghetto Jews continuing to live in isolation and poverty, one must add another psychological motive for telling these jokes. Misery loves company, they say, and we may add, also company in joking about it.

FEATURES OF THE FUTURE

Jewish jokes have more than the function to amuse; they belong to the category of spoken literature. They often predict the future, or at least they announce the direction in which the people move, the line of action which they are inclined to follow. To remain in the field of literature: did not the mockery of the aristocrats who have taken the trouble of being born in Beaumarchai's *Le Marriage of Figaro* foreshadow the great social change in France? One has justifiably called Beaumarchais (1735-1799) the stormy petrel of Revolution.

We believe, with T. S. Eliot, in "time future contained in time past." The situation of a Hebrew tribesman coming from the desert fringes to a Babylonian city or from Goshen seeing for the first time an Egyptian metropolis, is essentially the same as that of a Polish or Russian Jew who has come from his ghetto to New York. The new immigrant is not less overwhelmed by the skyscrapers of the great city than the Hebrew shepherd by the grandiose monuments of Thebes. He is overwhelmed, but not taken, overcome, but not taken in. The situation did not change when the Jews went into the Diaspora. They took with them a tradition that derives from other climates and cultures. They were deeply affected by various societies, but never determined by them. Is it possible to draw from this past certain legitimate conclusions concerning the future?

Returning to the narrow domain of Jewish jokes, we may speak only of prevalent tendencies they reflect. Freud demonstrated that there are many psychological similarities between jokes and dreams. We know that dreams were once conceived as prophetic, as announcing the future. We learned that this notion is a superstitious distortion of their function. Psychoanalysis has shown us that dreams are disguised and distorted expressions of our repressed or disavowed wishes. But the wish fulfillment in dreams certainly shows what kind of drives and impulses operate subterraneously in us and have as such great psychological significance. Also, our wishes determine to a certain extent the current of our future.

A Jewish proverb proclaims that the heart is "half a prophet." Whether the future will realize these hidden wishes or frustrate them, we do not know. The solution of the Jewish question, or rather of the many questions with which Jewish survival and Judaism confront our society, is not only a problem of the Jews, but one of all mankind.

C. K. Chesterton once said that the center of every man's existence is a dream. We would like to add that this is also the center of every people's existence. What is the latent content of that dream as far as we can interpet it from its remnants in Jewish jokes?

The truly democratic spirit that breathes in Jewish jokes goes far beyond the goals defined up to now. It aims, of course, on the first level at social justice, at a better distribution of the goods of the world and at equality for all.

Jewish jokes inevitably proclaim that our kingdom is of this world. More than four hundred years ago a leader of the oppressed German peasants, Florian Geyer, engaged in a revolutionary movement which demanded the abolition of the power of throne and church, of kings and priests. They hunted him and killed him. On his sword, which I saw in Nürnberg, are engraved the words "*Nulla crux, nulla corona.*" These words stand as the motto for the Weltanschauung of Jewish wit, perhaps with the addition, "*Nulla stella Davidi.*" This means not only an end to the authority of kings and priests, but also an end to the principle of nationalities and states which divide mankind. As these jokes prove, the liberation from religion and religious laws takes place to an increasing extent and at a quickened speed. We live not only in a post-Christian, but in a post-religious age(16). Judaism as a religion will also slowly disappear, though its basic ethical commandments will survive the demise of God. Jewish jokes started with heresies and allusions of timid aggression against the exaggerated demands made in the name of religion and will end with the abolishment of the illusion of religion.

Jewish wit functions as avant-garde literature in other directions. The rapid shrinking of distances over the earth must lead to the abandonment of national frontiers and finally to the notion that the home of man is the earth.

The banning of violence will, says the Jewish joke, bring closer to realization those predictions of the Jewish prophets, the transformation of swords and spears into ploughshares. In the end, the brotherhood of men must be realized. Equality, not only before the law, but also in the evaluation of people, will some day reign over the earth.

What will remain of divisions, will be similar to those that determine families and will finally result in the one united family of man. (Do you remember the story of the Jew who shouts at the soldier who threatens to shoot: "Are you meschugge? Don't you see, here is a Mensch?")

George Eliot let one of her Jewish figures in *Daniel Deronda* say: "Our people wandered before they were driven out." They wandered for four thousand years and are still going or, rather, wandering strong. They wandered back to Palestine: they will not stop there. They are forerunners of the citizens of the world, not of a state.

The future as it announces itself in Jewish jokes is beyond the realm of slogans like isolation and assimilation. The writer Heinrich Berman in Schnitzler's *The Way Into the Open*, discusses these problems with his Gentile friend. He concludes that assimilation will come all right in a very long time, and adds: "It won't come at all in the way many want it to—it won't come either in the way many are afraid it will . . . Furthermore, it won't be exactly assimilation . . . but perhaps something that beats in the heart of that particular word, so to speak. Do you know what it will probably look like in the end?

That we, we Jews I mean, have been a kind of ferment in the brewing of humanity—yes, perhaps that'll come out in anything from one to two thousand years from now." Jewish wit is certainly one of the expedients of that fermentation.

What about the masochistic-paranoid attitude which we discovered at the root of Jewish wit, that concealed desire to suffer and the claim of being the chosen people? (By the way, the Hebrew expression has the connotation "a peculiar people.") Both trends meet in the common aim of being acknowledged and approved. At a time, not too far away, the name of Jew will not be "mud," but will be honored and appreciated as that of a people who formed the cake of yeast in the big, heavy dough of humanity. Like the power of Egypt and the glory that was Greece, Israel too will be acknowledged as the guiding light that led mankind on its march upwards.

Then, but only then, I am bold to assert, will the Jews renounce the masochistic as well as the paranoid attitudes that manifest themselves in their jokes. Then, but only then, will they take to heart Goethe's admonition:

> Wie viel bist du von andern unterschieden?
> Erkenne dich—leb mit der Welt in Frieden!

> How much are you distinguished from the others?
> Go, know yourself, call all men your brothers.

Until then, Jews will fight a lonely battle. Until then, when acknowledgment of their function will replace the open hatred and the unadmitted envy of the world, they have no choice and must walk along on their lonely street, encouraged by pride in their spiritual past and by unbroken faith in their future.

Then, but only then, those labels Jew and Gentile, slapped on people by a sick society, will disappear, and individuals will be judged as people, not as members of a group. Also high walls will crumble. But all these possibilities and potentialities will fade if mankind is threatened with annihilation in nuclear war. What the future will bring is not predictable, certainly not by means of Jewish wit. It is only implied there as a hope. Only time will tell, and the jokes of time.

In Retrospect

Now, as this book reaches its demarcation lines, we look back at its beginnings. I have tried to offer a contribution to comparative psychology, especially to the understanding of the Jewish people through a psychoanalytic investigation of their jokes. There is enough written about Jewish humor and its peculiarities, but almost all of it was written from the viewpoint of conscious psychology. My contribution approached the subject from a different perspective, which searches for the origin of Jewish witticisms in the regions of repressed and unconscious processes.

Here we stand again on the spot from which we departed. In retrospect, we think of the comparison that occurred to us at the selection of Jewish jokes. We said we had to look at them first as at the many compartments of a fan. Only after we attentively studied and reflected on the witty and wise inscriptions of those compartments—the main objects of Jewish jokes—could we venture to form a psychological theory of Jewish witticisms and their functions. Those fans of our mothers and grandmothers were used for several purposes: they provided refreshing coolness in the heat of the summer and in the ballroom; they were used to flirt with; to demonstrate certain feelings; and finally, to hide those feelings and oneself.

Similarly, Jewish jokes serve various purposes: To bring relaxation in the ardour of battle with the seen and with the invisible enemy; to attract him as well as to repel him; and last, but certainly not least, to conceal oneself behind them. Jewish wit hides as much as it discloses. Like the seraph in the Temple of the Lord it covers its face with two of its wings.

We also remember that we started with the supposition that a study of Jewish jokes must cast a new light on the psychology of these strange people, on their character and temperament, as it evolved from their heritage and destiny. In my Biblical tetralogy(17), I attempted to penetrate the deep darkness of the unknown prehistory of the Jews and of their formative centuries. In the present contribution I approached the Jewish question from another, different social viewpoint, from the psychology of Jewish jokes.

At this point we are confronted with the last and decisive question: How far did we succeed in our task? Did we accomplish our purpose? Scientific truthfulness compels us to admit that we did not reach our goal. We have, it is true, learned a little about the psychology of the Jewish people from the exploration of their jokes. We have learned, in particular, that we still do not know much about them.

The exploration resulted, it is true, in the discovery of certain characteristic features, marks of distinction peculiar to Jewish witticisms which had gone unnoticed until now, or whose significance has not yet been psychologically understood. Above all, those attributes or properties of Jewish jokes funnel into one essential insight: the acknowledgment of a singular ability of self-assertion and self-preservation in spite of an overwhelming world of enemies. In defiance of destructive and hostile powers surrounding them, the Jews maintained their mysterious identity. As long as the Jews live an authentic life and do not disavow their heritage, that identity will be maintained.

Some lines of Goethe were quoted earlier as a kind of psychological motto for this research. Other lines of the same poet lead us to its conclusion. They seem to proclaim the enduring power of the inner identity, so often demonstrated in the history of the Jew:

> Jedes Leben sei zu führen
> Wenn man sich nicht selbst vermisst,
> Alles könne man verlieren
> Wenn man bleibe, was man ist.

> There's not a life he need refuse
> If his true self he does not miss,
> There's not a thing he cannot lose,
> If he remains the man he is.

Notes

Notes to Chapter I

1. *Gesammelte Schriften*, Vol. XII, p. 385.
2. English translation in *Commentary*, March 1946, pp. 23ff.
3. Vienna Psychoanalytic Press, 1919.
4. *Carnegie Corporation of New York Quarterly*, July 1961, p. 7.
5. English translation, New York, 1916.
6. For history of fans, see S. Blondel, *L'Histoire des Eventails*, 1875, C. W. Rhead, *History of the Fan*, 1910, and M. E. Percival, *The Fan Book*, 1920.
7. In a review in *The New York Times*, September 4, 1961.
8. *L'Esprit*, Paris, 1958, p. 11.
9. *Faces of the Truth*, New York, 1961.
10. *Commentary*, April 1961.
11. *Collected Papers*, Vol. IV, p. 271.

Notes to Chapter II

1. In the pamphlet, *Eine Krone für Zion*.
2. Hugo Bieber, *Heinrich Heine*, Philadelphia, 1956, p. 49.
3. Quoted by permission of the publisher, Farrar, Straus and Cudahy, from my book *The Search Within*, New York, 1956, p. 637.
4. London, 1881. Soon to be republished by Gamut Press, New York.

5. Translated by Frederich Henry Hedge. Boston, 1899.
6. Herschel Revel in *Universal Jewish Encyclopedia*, Vol. IX, p. 511.
7. In my book *Masochism in Modern Man*, New York, 1941, pp. 427ff.
8. May 1959.
9. Given at the National Council of Jewish Women at San Gabriel Valley, California in February 1960. The lecture is an expanded edition of a chapter in Grotjahn's book, *Beyond Laughter*, New York, 1957.
10. In *Six Stories Written in the First Person Singular*, New York, 1923.
11. S. Landman, *Der Jüdische Witz*, Breisgau, 1960, p. 9.
12. Frederic Morton, "The House of Rotschild," *Holiday*, December 1961.
13. Quoted by Herman Adler in the magazine *The Nineteenth Century*, March 1893.
14. M. Froude, *A History of Thomas Carlyle*, Vol. II, New York, 1884, p. 480.
15. *As You Like It*, II/5.
16. Alma Mahler, *Gustav Mahler*, Amsterdam, 1940. Vol. I.
17. Ernest Jones, *The Life and Work of Sigmund Freud*, New York, 1957, p. 184.
18. S. Landman, *op. cit.*, p. 34.
19. *Heine und Sein Witz*, Berlin, 1908.
20. "And what were they going to do with the Grail when they found it, Mr. Rosetti?" (Jowett to Rosetti, quoted from Andre Maurois, *Disraeli*, New York, 1928, p. 166.)
21. I developed this hypothesis fifty years later in *Mystery on the Mountain*, New York, 1958.
22. Cf. my observations on Shakespeare's *Merchant of Venice* in *The Secret Self*, New York, 1952.
23. Quoted from a still unpublished translation by the late Ludwig Lewison.
24. *Jessel Anyone?* Englewood, N.J., 1960, p. 56.
25. S. Landman, *op. cit.*, p. 111.
26. Borrowed from Robert Gessner, *Some of My Best Friends Are Jews*, New York, 1936, p. 280.

27. Other examples in Paul Steiner's *Israel Laughs*, New York, 1960.
28. One of my first psychoanalytic books, not yet translated into English, was *Arthur Schnitzler als Psychologe*, Minden, 1913.
29. C. Lloyd Morgan in *Encyclopedia of Religion and Ethics*, Vol. VII, p. 803.
30. See Andre Maurois, *Disraeli*, New York, 1928, pp. 178ff.
31. I dealt with this motif in *The Secret Self*, New York, 1952.
32. In the *Jewish Encyclopedia* (article on cursing).
33. *A Walker in the City*, New York 1951, p. 32.
34. Translated by Karl Darmstadter.
35. Antonina Vallentin, *The Drama of Albert Einstein*, London, 1957.
36. *The Rise of David Levinsky*, New York, 1900.
37. *Deutschland, ein Wintermärchen*. English translation by Herman Salinger, New York, 1944.
38. *Der Überraschte Psychologe*, Leiden, 1935.
39. *Molly and Me*, New York, 1961, pp. 44f.
40. *Rejoice in Thy Festival*, New York, 1956.
41. Translated by my daughter Miriam.
42. Jean Piaget, *The Child's Conception of the World*, New York, 1929, p. 88.
43. English translation in *The Compulsion to Confess*, New York, 1959.
44. *Letters of Sigmund Freud*, New York, 1960, p. 404.
45. *Ibid.*, p. 905.

NOTES TO CHAPTER III

1. Internationaler Psychoanalytischer Verlag, Vienna.
2. Published in *The Search Within*, New York, 1956, p. 651.
3. *Zum Problem des Jüdischen Witzes*, Berlin, 1929.
4. See Freud's paper, "*Uber den Gegensinn der Urworte,*" *Gesammelte Schriften*, Vol. X.
5. *Ibid.*
6. *Im Lauf der Zeit*, Hamburg, 1954, p. 13.

7. *Ibid.,* p. 130.
8. David Polish, *The Eternal Dissenter,* New York, 1961, p. 5.
9. Isaiah XLVIII:4.

NOTES TO CHAPTER IV

1. *Sigmund Freud, the Jew,* in Publications of the Leo Baeck Institute Yearbook, Vol. II, 1957, p. 282.
2. "*Zur Psychologie des Jüdischen Witzes,*" Vienna, 1937.
3. "*Lust und Leid im Witz,*" Vienna, 1929, and "*Nachdenkliche Heiterkeit,*" Vienna, 1933.
4. *Laughter and the Sense of Humor,* New York, 1956, p. 112.
5. *Masochism in Modern Man,* New York, 1941.
6. I showed the psychic dynamics operating here in my interpretation of the Hebrew prayer Kol Nidre in *Das Ritual,* Vienna, 1919, English translation, London, 1931.
7. See my *Myth and Guilt,* New York, 1957.
8. M. Grotjahn, *op. cit.*
9. *Das Neue Drama,* Berlin, 1917, p. 433.
10. From *Juden und Judentum in deutschen Briefen aus drei Jahrhunderten,* Vienna, 1935, p. 230.
11. "Some Character Types Met With in Psychoanalytic Work," *Collected Papers,* Vol. IV.
12. Quoted from Martin Buber, *Israel and the World,* New York, 1948.
13. See O. Fenichel, *The Psychoanalytic Theory of Neurosis,* New York, 1945, p. 65.
14. *Nachdenkliche Heiterkeit,* Vienna, 1933.
15. *Das Neue Drama, op. cit.,* p. 354.
16. See G. Vahanian, *The Death of God,* New York, 1961.
17. *Myth and Guilt,* New York, 1958; *The Creation of Woman,* New York, 1959; *The Temptation,* New York, 1961; *Mystery on the Mountain,* New York, 1960.